*To Joanne and my family.*

# Preface

Alternative Dispute Resolution is in a period of dynamic growth and change. This book explores ADR principles and practices drawn from decades of experience in the trenches, primarily as counsel. In addition, my involvement in projects abroad to introduce ADR methods led me to revisit ADR concepts and ideas.

Thirty years in dispute resolution have raised my concern about certain legal processes becoming potentially unmanageable. Most disputes should be effectively resolved even though the litigation process will often be intertwined with ADR. Clients today are extremely sensitive to the cost (financial and personal) of conflict. Hence, I have increasingly supported effective negotiation, mediation and arbitration techniques, albeit within and under the shadow and guidance of the Courts and the law. Lawyers must master these techniques or be left behind.

Writing this book has strengthened my conviction that a desire for effective settlement of disputes is an ancient wish which has been recently rediscovered. The energy and success of dispute resolution processes today is a testament to their historic roots.

Notwithstanding the stresses and strains of modern dispute resolution, I remain extremely proud of my chosen profession, the legal profession, which will continue to be the torchbearer for better and more effective dispute resolution.

# Acknowledgements

This book would not have been possible without the help and support of many people. In the first place, I wish to thank Louis Benoit, a summer student at Gowlings (summer 2001), who helped me research and analyse material necessary to the final compilation of this book. I also benefited from the expertise of lawyers at Gowlings who have always impressed me with their detailed and careful work. In that regard, I wish to thank Laura Stewart for her work on privilege and confidentiality; Guy David for his insights into the negotiating process (Guy wrote the negotiation scenario between father and son in Chapter 3); André Ducasse for his work on the section on "Enforcement of Arbitral Awards" and Anne Mundy-Markell for her guidance on the section "Writing the Mediation Brief".

As a former Executive Director of ADR Canada, I wish to acknowledge the leadership and insights of its recent Presidents, Roman Evancic, Gervin Greaseley, Allan Stitt, and Barry Effler.

The Superior Court in Ottawa is a leader in Ontario, and, indeed in Canada and abroad, in the effective resolution of disputes, particularly in the interaction between mandatory mediation and court processes. In this regard, two individuals must be mentioned, namely the Honourable Mr. Justice James Chadwick (formerly Senior Judge) and Regional Master Robert Beaudoin. The invitations to Justice Chadwick and Master Beaudoin to speak in Canada and abroad about the effective resolution of disputes in the Ottawa region are a clear indication of the insight, care and professionalism which they have brought to these processes.

In 1999 and 2002, Gowlings won World Bank projects to introduce Alternative Dispute Methods into Russia and Albania, respectively. As Project Director, I was able to assemble an extremely gifted team to assist in this work. In particular, I would like to thank Rick Weiler, one of Canada's foremost mediators, who worked with me on the Russian and Albanian projects. Rick reviewed the mediation concepts and ideas in this book. Andrew Berkeley of England, an expert in international arbitration, assisted me in the synthesis of common law and civil law arbitral concepts. Further, Andrew provided me with insight into "pathological dispute resolution clauses". Professor David Cruickshank of New York built the pedagogical framework. David is a pioneer in creating teaching techniques for practising lawyers.

I also wish to acknowledge the Russian officials, Dr. Elena Vinogradova and Elga Sukianinen-Mikhalevskaya, who had the vision and courage to insist that Russia must follow a path of effective dispute resolution.

For the Albania project, in addition to the Russian team, Professor Julie Macfarlane assisted us ably in our endeavours. Professor Macfarlane has been prescient in the cultural shift that mandatory mediation will effect in our legal profession.

I would also thank my assistants Michelle Canning-Choi and Maureen Morden for their work on the manuscript.

To my daughter, Meredith Nelson (M.St, M. Litt (Oxon)) thanks for her contributions to style and language.

In conclusion, I wish to acknowledge the warm support and advice of my late partner, The Right Honourable Ramon J. Hnatyshyn, who passed away before the publication of this book.

Ottawa, Canada
January 2003

# Table of Contents

# Table of Cases

# 1

# Introduction

The Dispute Resolution Revolution and the resulting explosion in dispute resolution methods demand that lawyers master new skills, techniques and attitudes. Lawyers must be gladiators in the court room, when required, but also experts in negotiation, mediation and arbitration. Can the profession meet these challenges? Yes it can.

Disputes form an integral and inevitable part of human nature. However, as long as disputes have existed, so have means of dispute resolution. While some of these methods are fairly serene, such as negotiation or even litigation, others are arbitrary, like a coin toss, while others still are utterly destructive, such as war.

The term "ADR" has been used for at least 30 years in North America; its etymology is unknown. Originally the acronym "ADR" meant, "Alternative Dispute Resolution" — referring to a range of dispute resolution processes, including mediation and arbitration, which were alternatives to traditional litigation in the public court system. Over time, however, the initials "ADR" have also come to mean "Appropriate Dispute Resolution" — referring not only to the range of processes but also the selection of the most appropriate process in particular circumstances. One of the principal goals of ADR is to provide parties with choices for the effective and efficient resolution of disputes.

Although debate continues as to the real purpose and justification of ADR, there is consensus among practitioners that a key intent of ADR is to provide parties with choices for effective and efficient resolution of disputes.

After 30 years practising in litigation, mediation and arbitration, I am convinced that lawyers must master the basic principles of ADR. It is a field that has grown exponentially in the past years and will undoubtedly continue to expand in the future. The varied complexities of dispute resolution make this process similar to playing four-dimensional chess. This growth has resulted in the development or resurgence of diverse procedures to resolve conflict, an expansion in size and scope of the issues addressed by these means and an increase in the number of practitioners who are involved in this discipline.

The desire to resolve disputes using mediation and arbitration is very old.[1] Yet, for too long our adversarial court system offered only trial as a means of resolving disputes. However, in the last decade, an increasing number of individuals have voiced their dissatisfaction with the traditional court model of dispute resolution and have demanded that other mechanisms exist as a means of resolving conflict. Given the formal nature of the litigation process and the considerable costs related to it, there has been a growing need in our society to create a less expensive and more timely apparatus to resolve legal conflicts, which would be accessible to everyone.

Mediation is a sophisticated form of negotiation. The growing sophistication of negotiation techniques means that litigators — who have always conceived themselves as warriors — must now wear the hat of a peacemaker during such sessions. Whereas traditional litigators are at ease, and used to, litigating their clients' cases in the court room, they will now have to acquire a new skill-set to accommodate their clients' interests in settling disputes by these more expedient and economical means.

The introduction of ADR concepts and procedures into the litigation process — primarily mandatory mediation — is accelerating and, I believe, will be the world norm. In certain jurisdictions, mandatory mediation is incorporated directly into the court process. Mediation has the potential to unlock factors and issues that could otherwise never have been resolved through the litigation process. Hence, in the future world of dispute resolution, a lawyer's practice will move from the psychological components of mediation to the technicalities of arbitration to the skills of litigation.

A key theme of this book is the inter-relationship of dispute resolution methods and the legal skills required to master them. This complex inter-relation of dispute settlement methods will demand wise counsel. The high settlement rates of mandatory mediation may dictate that early settlement is often more beneficial to the client than a courtroom battle; nevertheless, some disputes can only be resolved after the litigation has commenced while others must be fought in court. Other disputes will settle only after delay, as the poet Ovid says:

> Delay gives strength, and ripens tender grapes,
> And what was grass it turns to healthy crops.[2]

---

[1] See chapter 2: History of ADR.

[2] Roebuck, D., *Ancient Greek Arbitration*, Holo Books - The Arbitration Press, Oxford, 2001, p. xii.

In the face of profound inter-relationships that have developed between a wide variety of choices in dispute resolution, counsel have to be competent enough to assess and recognize the approach that will be most beneficial to each client's concerns. Remember that at all times ADR works in the shadow of the courts.

The advantages of private dispute resolution are clear:

- **Costs.** ADR methods often cost less than litigation.

- **Confidentiality.** ADR methods are private and confidential.

- **Speed.** ADR alternatives are typically faster than litigation. Quick resolution of a dispute can be an important objective, particularly when a business relationship continues while a dispute is being resolved.

- **Risk Reduction.** Court decisions are unpredictable as opposed to a mediated settlement. To be fair, arbitrated solutions are also unpredictable.

- **Expertise of Decision Maker.** A decision maker who has some expertise in a particular field may lower costs and increase the chances of a fair and reasonable resolution of a dispute.

- **Promotion of Continuing Business Relations.** It is often important for corporations to preserve long-term relationships and keep hostilities to a minimum. ADR proceedings tend to be less adversarial and hostile than litigation.

# 2

# History of ADR

Some of the more advanced ancient civilizations used arbitration and mediation to settle disputes. The ancient Egyptians used these methods, as did the ancient Greeks and Romans. Some of the first references to early dispute resolution methods are found in Homer's early epics, *Iliad* and *Odyssey,* works that date back to possibly 750-650 B.C. The *Iliad* mentions peaceful methods of dispute resolution such as handshakes and taking hold of a symbolic staff, and describes the intervention of a third party (King Priam of Troy) in the supervision of a treaty, much like the role of a modern mediator.[1] The *Odyssey* makes much more discernible references to arbitration in the story of Odysseus's wanderings: Homer refers to King Minos's role in deciding disputes between the dead, and to a woman arbitrator, Eriphyle, who is perhaps the earliest named arbitrator.[2] Roebuck describes dispute resolution methods in Ancient Greece as follows:

> The surviving works of Homer describe societies in which the people were quite familiar with a range of methods and processes for the resolution of their disputes. They included all those we know today, other than litigation. There were no courts or judges or lawyers. Some were regular and replicable, others *ad hoc.* Doing nothing, shaming, exchange of abuse in public, self-help, compromise and mediation were common. Arbitration took different forms. There was the casual reference to someone acceptable to both parties, who might or might not have had qualities or experience making him, or her, specially fitted for the task. There was the often-used individual arbitrator with a reputation for success and dependability, like Arete and presumably Minos. Except among the savage Cyclopes, and in Ithaca — sunk into law-

---

[1] Roebuck, D., *Ancient Greek Arbitration*, Holo Books - The Arbitration Press, Oxford, 2001, pp. 52, 56.

[2] *Ibid.*, pp. 53, 71.

lessness in the absence of its basileus Odysseus — everywhere there was an assembly, one of whose regular functions was to resolve disputes.[3]

By the 5th century, Greek states had widely accepted arbitration. Most disputes settled this way concerned matters of territorial boundaries, possession or use of land and breaches of treaty obligations. In "Arbitration in Ancient Greece", H.T. King and M. LeForestier maintain that by the 5th century, arbitration had developed considerably in Greek states, such that one could consider it to be an early form of international law.[4]

Legal studies on the Anglo-Saxon era suggest that lawsuits, even in those early times, followed a predetermined continuum of dispute resolution. Claimants could choose to refer their lawsuits to either arbitration or adjudication, depending on whether they preferred to have their disputes exposed to the whole community or resolve them through the privacy of an arbitral tribunal. Yet, before judgments were made final, parties were presented with an opportunity to resolve their dispute through a compromise settlement agreement. Judges or arbitrators then acted as mediators to help facilitate negotiations between the parties, and if an agreement was reached, it was legally binding.[5]

Variations of arbitration have been in use for quite some time in England. In the Anglo-Saxon era, the arbitral process was commonly referred to as "lovedays", a reference to the quiet and tranquillity that was supposed to follow the settlement of conflict.[6] In the 13th and 14th centuries, the courts started using voluntary submissions to arbitration in a number of pending cases as an extension to the judicial process by accepting an arbitral award as a court judgement. The *Statute of Staples, 1353* (which stated that "in disputes over the quality of or method of packing wool, the award of six assessors was to be final on the court")[7] recognized the use of arbitration in judicial procedures, enshrining it in legislation.

Institutional arbitration began with organizations regulating disputes in specific trades. These institutions first appeared in Italy, where commerce and related activities were advanced for their time. Special courts and tribunals which dealt with various areas of trade disputes then started de-

---

[3] *Ibid.*, p. 89.
[4] See *Dispute Resolution Journal*, September 1994, Vol. 49, No. 3, p. 40.
[5] See Sanchez, V.A., "Toward a History of ADR: The Dispute Processing Continuum in Anglo-Saxon England and Today", *Ohio State Journal on Dispute Resolution*, Winter 1996, Vol. 11, No. 1, pp. 1-39.
[6] Yarn, D.H., "Commercial Arbitration in Olde England (602 - 1698)", *Dispute Resolution Journal*, January 1995, Vol. 50, No. 1, p. 68.
[7] *Ibid.*, p. 70.

veloping. Once again these bodies were first introduced in Italy and then spread to Southern France.[8]

Arbitration began as a contractually based agreement between individuals, which made it a private and voluntary procedure. Today, there are various forms of non-consensual arbitration such as disputes arising under a collective agreement, which must be arbitrated.[9]

Most religious societies also have an established history of mediation. Western Christian churches often acted as sanctuaries for criminals, and the clergy frequently acted as mediators between the authorities and the accused. Clergymen also conducted mediation sessions in family matters and diplomatic conflicts. Likewise, rabbis (mainly through rabbinical interpretations of the Torah) played a role in resolving disputes between members of the Jewish faith. Similarly, in Chinese and other Asian cultures, Confucian and Buddhist traditions encourage dispute resolution through compromise rather than coercion. In such cultures, litigation is seen as a last resort which involves considerable loss of face. Finally, in many native cultures, village elders and tribal councils play an important role in mediation and reconciliation.

In modern society, mediation resurfaced in response to an increasingly costly, time consuming and unpredictable adversarial system. Winning a lawsuit often meant losing. Mediation allowed the parties to address the real issues of their conflict and formulate their own settlement which could often end up being beneficial for both parties.

In 1999, Rules 24.1 and 75.1 of the Ontario *Rules of Civil Procedure* established a pilot mandatory mediation programme in two regions of the province for all civil, non-family related, case managed actions, including estates, trusts and substitute decisions matters. Ironically, these recent innovations were rooted in history.

---

[8] Mustill, M.J., "Arbitration: History and Background", *Journal of International Arbitration*, June 1989, Vol. 6, No. 2, p. 44.

[9] See *Weber v. Ontario Hydro* (1995), 125 D.L.R. (4th) 583 (S.C.C.), where the Supreme Court found that any dispute arising under a collective agreement must be arbitrated and cannot be litigated in the courts.

# 3

# Negotiation Theories

## 1. INTRODUCTION

Negotiation, the most common method of conflict resolution, is the foundation of mediation. Litigators must master the intricacies of negotiation. Modern litigation expertise demands a mastery of these principles. In fact, most people engage in some type of negotiation or other every day, whether it involves haggling over the price of a vehicle, discussing the terms and conditions of an employment contract, settling a dispute, or any number of other day to day occurrences. Individuals learn the value and techniques of negotiation early on in their lives. Essentially, negotiation is about understanding relatively predictable responses that occur in the negotiation process. One's ability to react to these responses is instrumental in determining the outcome of any negotiation. For example, most children quickly master effective techniques to negotiate with their parents over their established bedtimes. Some even apply sophisticated techniques.

Consider the following scenario:

| | |
|---|---|
| Dad: | "Johnny! 10 o'clock; bedtime; school tomorrow." |
| Johnny: | "But you said I could watch the special two-part Simpsons today and tomorrow." (*Establishes Johnny's credibility; puts father on defensive.*) |
| Dad: | "I didn't know it was at 10." (*Admits lack of information — unprepared.*) |
| Johnny: | "You didn't ask me." (*Selective withholding of information until it's the right time to use it; implies Johnny would have told him — builds credibility.*) |
| Dad: | "OK, Johnny. Let's go. It's 10 o'clock." |

| | |
|---|---|
| Johnny: | "What time did you go to bed at my age?" (*Distraction.*) |
| Dad: | "I don't remember. It doesn't matter." (*Creates uncertainty, defensiveness. Note that power balance begins to change in Johnny's favour without conflict.*) |
| Johnny: | "Hey, Dad. Come look at this. You'll think it's funny." (*i.e., new car technique: "go on, take it home"; "take it for a spin".*) |
| Dad: | "OK, Johnny. It's 10:15. Let's go." |
| Johnny: | "OK. Too bad. I don't think this special will be on again." (*Creating perception of scarcity to increase value: same as "this is the last one we have, we won't be getting any more".*) |
| Dad: | "Yeah. Too bad. It's really quite a good show, but I can't let you watch it. You know mom would never agree. You know how she is about bedtime." (*Dad catching on; pleads "higher authority".*) |
| Johnny: | "Why don't you ask her. Tell her you're watching it with me." (*Calls his bluff; neutralizes higher authority.*) |
| Dad: | "I can't. You know she has to finish that report for tomorrow and we can't disturb her." |
| Johnny: | "OK. I guess I better go then." [Gives Dad a big hug and a kiss.] (*Uses the power of a gift to create obligation; obtain something more valuable from the other side.*) |
| Dad: | "I love you too. Now good night. Get up there." |
| Johnny: | "This is a two-part series. Can I stay up to watch it tomorrow night?" |
| Dad: | "No. Now get to bed. It's 10:20." |
| Johnny: | "OK. I'll only watch tonight. I don't have to watch tomorrow because you didn't know it was on at 10:00." (*Scales back demands — compromise creates an obligation; note nothing is really given in by Johnny at this point.*) |
| Dad: | "This ends at 11:00. I *think* that's just too late." (*Dad has blinked. Johnny needs to clinch the negotiation.*) |

Johnny:     "All my friends are watching it. We talked about the Simpsons in social studies about nuclear plants. Mrs. James said she likes the Simpsons." (*Johnny invokes third party endorsement; short-circuits logic; uses vague quotation.*)

Dad:        "Did she really? OK. You can stay up until 10:30 but no later." (*Dad, ambushed, failed to pick up on defective logic — looking for ways out, makes first offer.*)

Johnny:     "Just 10:30! It's already 10:20. You're only letting me stay up another 10 minutes and I said I would give up all of tomorrow's episode. That's a whole hour. Come on, Dad." (*"Reluctant buyer". Another defective syllogism; rejects first offer.*)

Dad:        "Look. It's 10:20 and the show finishes at 11:00. That's 40 minutes and it's way beyond your bedtime. We can split the difference. I'll give you another 20 minutes. That's it." (*Dad makes mistake of being the first to offer to "split the difference". Dad has now made two offers, while Johnny has held firm.*)

Johnny:     "What about tomorrow night? Can I watch the first 40 minutes too?" (*Johnny accepts Dad's concession on splitting difference but keeps negotiation alive by having preserved another issue. Feels justified in withdrawing previous offer of not watching tomorrow because it wasn't accepted and it was conditional on watching whole episode tonight.*)

Dad:        "No." (*Hardline strengthens Johnny's position for tonight.*)

Johnny:     "Well, can I just ask you again tomorrow?" (*Maintains lines of communication on remaining issue.*)

Dad:        "OK. But I'm going to say no anyway."

Johnny:     "OK. I'll take the 20 minutes you've given me tonight and I won't ask you about tomorrow until tomorrow. I'll do what you say." (*Knows when to clinch the deal, but "nibbles" on open issue.*)

Dad:        "OK. We've got a deal."

*Five Minutes Later*

| | |
|---|---|
| Johnny: | "That commercial was so long. I'm sure you don't mind if we just add the five minutes to my time." (*Johnny starts to "nickel and dime", but only after main agreement is reached.*) |
| Dad: | "Only five more minutes. OK?" |
| Johnny: | "I like it when you watch the Simpsons with me. Can you do this again some time? Maybe tomorrow." (*Bonding with the other side.*) |
| Dad: | "Maybe. We'll see." |
| Johnny: | "You know how you said we'd split the difference and I could only watch half of the rest of the show." |
| Dad: | "Yeah. That's our agreement, plus another five minutes for the commercials." |
| Johnny: | "But that's not really splitting the difference perfectly fairly because I wanted to watch tonight and tomorrow night. So if we split the difference, I should be able to watch all of tonight." |
| Dad: | [Looks at watch.] "Johnny, we have an agreement. That's it. Our agreement is just for tonight, so it's only tonight's difference that we can split." |
| Johnny: | "OK. But there's only 20 minutes left, and you already said I could stay up for another five minutes. I'll go right to bed (*i.e., we have a deal*) if we just split the difference again Dad. I'm only asking for seven-and-a-half minutes, and you get the other seven-and-a-half minutes and you can watch till the end because I'll go straight to bed and you don't have to tuck me in. You got to split the difference so I should too." (*Note: Johnny uses splitting the difference to gain more time after deal is made, whereas Dad gave it as a concession.*) |
| Dad: | "OK. That's the deal." |
| Johnny: | "Can you tape the last seven-and-a-half minutes for me so that I can watch it tomorrow?" (*Seeking win/win solution.*) |
| Dad: | "OK. Do we have a blank tape?" |

| Johnny: | "I don't know. I can't look for one because my time is up. Dad, can you find a tape and tape the rest?" |
| Dad: | "Well, there's just seven-and-a-half minutes left. I guess . . . but promise me you'll go straight to bed when it's over." (*Accept win/win approach.*) |
| Johnny: | "I love you Dad." |

In legal disputes, the terms of the conflicts are more complex and the stakes are higher, but in a positional negotiation many of the techniques will be the same. The techniques employed in any negotiation must be refined to suit the situation. Negotiation is a key skill for lawyers. While intuitive to some (such as Johnny), for those to whom it does not come naturally it can be learned through practice, thoughtful preparation and experience.

## 2. OVERVIEW OF NEGOTIATION THEORIES

Most literature on negotiation theories refers to two main types of bargaining options: positional or competitive negotiations and principled or cooperative negotiations. The main difference between the two lies in the approach taken by the negotiator. In a positional negotiation, the negotiator tries to gain as large a share of the pie as possible, whereas in the latter, the negotiators work side by side to try to increase the size of the pie which then increases the benefits accrued by each party.

There is no single well-defined process of negotiation that functions in every type of dispute — the dynamics and issues of every conflict are unique. The skilled negotiator must adapt to the situation and employ negotiation methods appropriate to the specific circumstances. Two of the most fundamental facts underlying every negotiation are that:

- each side is trying to obtain something owned or controlled by the other; and
- there are predictable responses that you can count on in the negotiating process.

How you elicit and/or react to these responses will determine the course of the negotiation. However, an underlying principle of every successful negotiation is that both parties must "win". This holds true whether the negotiation was "positional" or started from a "win/win" approach.

## (a) Positional Negotiation

Positional negotiation is a more traditional method of settling agreements. The essence of this strategy involves trying to agree on who gets how much of the available resources. Critical elements of success in positional negotiation are: power, information and time. A serious imbalance in any one of these factors makes a win/win result unlikely.

Positional negotiation often involves adopting a definite position of demands from the outset. This position typically plays to the other side's weakness. Positional negotiators often make unreasonably high demands, so as to have room to make "concessions" — they give up things they do not care as deeply about while chipping away at what they want from the other side. A key to success in any negotiation, positional or principled, is to anticipate what the other side wants and, especially, to be aware of any hidden agenda.

In a purely positional negotiation, the negotiator often seeks to emphasize the inflexibility of his/her own position. Positional negotiators are often able to argue that they do not really need a settlement — the ability to "walk" on the part of one party or the other, or both, often keeps both parties at the table. In a positional negotiation, one attempts to change the other side's perceptions in order to convince them to make concessions. Information in a positional negotiation is often used only when it is advantageous. Usually one party will not be aware of the other party's resistance point or their best alternative. The negotiator's goal, therefore, is to learn as much as possible about the other side's resistance point and then to influence the other party's perceptions in order to reach an agreement as close to the other party's resistance point as possible.

Positional negotiators generally perceive the problem as a division of pre-determined resources — the negotiation is a contest to obtain the bigger piece of the pie. Tactics employed in positional negotiations include:

- Choosing a setting the negotiator is comfortable in, such as his office, where the other party might not be as comfortable and therefore is at a disadvantage.
- Outnumbering the opposing side. If the negotiator is aware of the number of people that the other party is bringing along at the negotiation

meeting, he may try to have at least an equal number on his side, so as to maintain the appearance of an equal balance of power.
- Making the first demand unreasonably high. This strategy makes subsequent demands, although still quite high, seem more like a compromise.

Although this strategy of negotiation seems rigorous and contentious, it is sometimes the best available method of bargaining. For example, positional bargaining is often effective when there is virtually no trust between the parties.

Several techniques exist for increasing one's effectiveness in a positional negotiation. Consider the three crucial elements: power, information and time. Consider them from both your point of view and that of your opponent's. Adopt a negotiating strategy that will accentuate your strengths, neutralize your weaknesses and exploit your opponent's weaknesses.

## Consider these rules:

- Never say yes to the first offer.
- Always maintain "walk away" power, or the illusion of having an alternative.
- Make a big deal of any concession you make and never make a concession without receiving a counter-concession.
- Don't be the first to name a price.
- Hold the pen.
- Make offers low but flexible.
- Never offer to "split the difference"; get the other side to make that offer to you.
- Remember that 80% of concessions are made in the last 20% of the time of any negotiation — don't leave details till later. The time will never be better than now to resolve those points.
- Never reveal you have a deadline — the person under the greatest pressure typically pays a price for meeting a deadline.
- Don't negotiate anything important on the phone — body language often tells you more about the other side than words.
- Watch for sudden changes in body language, not just body language itself.

## Consider these principles:

- Gain as much information about the other party as possible, both before and during negotiations; ask open-ended questions; ask for responses; repeat answers to "nail them down".

- Know where to sit: make sure you can watch everyone on the other side; don't let the opponent sit on your side of the table.
- If you have the larger group, keep it together for more power; but if you have the smaller group, try to mix with the larger group to "diffuse" the power of its greater numbers.
- Never narrow negotiations down to just one issue.
- Recognize that different people may want different things: know what your opponent wants. Never assume.

(i)  *Using Ploys and Gambits*

Little Johnny used ploys and gambits skilfully to negotiate his bedtime extension and obtain a win/win result. When used properly, these techniques can help achieve good bargains:

- **Pleading higher authority.** This helps to separate the negotiator from an unpopular position, to allow for sober second thought, or to obtain additional concessions before agreeing to an important point while the negotiation proceeds pending the decision of the "higher authority".

- **Good cop/bad cop.** This technique is most useful in preserving the lead negotiator's rapport with the opponent.

- **Dumb is smart/smart is dumb.** Let the other side educate you — in doing so, they will undoubtedly provide information, lay out the logical consequences of their position, perhaps eventually negotiate against themselves.

- **Parking.** Know when to set aside or "park" an issue, especially when it seems that you are unlikely to prevail. The other side may come up with compromises on the parked issue when it is brought back that would not be likely in a direct discussion and resolution. This is most effective when you lack the information to negotiate the issue fully.

- **Flinching.** Body language can be an effective way of communicating your position without overtly extracting, and having to acknowledge, a concession. A properly timed facial flinch can effectively and subtly communicate "that's just not enough" without a word being said.

- **The Printed Word.** Nothing communicates a position's validity more effectively than a credible written example (e.g., a previous agreement, an article written by an expert, or any other documentation that confirms the validity of a position).

(ii) *Shifting the Power Balance in Your Favour*

It is more challenging to negotiate with personality types that are different from yours than with a like-minded opponent.

The analytical introvert will have the hardest time with an assertive and emotional extrovert and vice versa. The non-emotional assertive pragmatist and the amiable type (emotional and non-assertive) are unlikely to get along. Generally, negotiators with similar degrees (whether high or low) of assertiveness and emotionalism are most likely to negotiate successfully together. Armed with this knowledge, the successful negotiating team will appoint a leader who is compatible with his/her opponent.

It is important to understand "power" since there are different types of it. The following should be considered when assessing the other side's power:

- Authority Power    power of title
                      power to reward
                      power to punish

- Natural Power       right to "reverence"
                      charisma

- Situational Power   expertise
                      information
                      experience

Consider the facts of the situation and then determine what type of negotiation power you and your opponent have, and how best to shift the power balance to your advantage. Regardless of the approach and ploys or gambits used in a negotiation, maintaining (or establishing) trust should be a key objective. Never intentionally deceive or mislead your opponent, and remember that a "win/win" outcome is only likely to be sustainable if the parties are to have an on-going relationship.

## (b)  Principled Negotiation

Roger Fisher and William Ury introduced and popularized principled negotiation in their book entitled *Getting to Yes*.[1] This type of negotiation concentrates on solving a problem rather than on winning. It aims at reaching a result referred to as a structured settlement. Such settlements strive to recognize and satisfy the mutual interests of both parties and involve identifying the underlying concerns, needs, desires and fears that motivate each party's position. The key concept underlying the negotiation is *why*. The parties discuss *why* they are seeking a certain position rather than defending *what* they are seeking.

There are two particular methods of attaining a win/win outcome, and both require explicit information exchange. One method is based on similar interests, while the other relies on dissimilar interests, as long as they are not in direct opposition.

There are five basic elements to undertaking a principled negotiation approach. First, the negotiators have to learn to separate the people from the problem at hand. Second, they must focus on their interests rather than taking on a set position. Third, to attain a structured settlement that is mutually beneficial, the parties must invent and generate options for mutual gain. Fourth, the negotiation should be based on objective criteria, and finally, each party should be aware of their best alternative to a negotiated agreement (BATNA).

### (i)  *Separate the People from the Problem*

Parties in a principled negotiation should perceive themselves as working together towards solving a common problem rather than rivals in a competition or dispute. One way to do this is to understand the other party's thinking. A principled negotiator would put himself in the other side's position and try to perceive the problem from their point of view.

In a principled negotiation, the parties also discuss each other's perceptions. According to Fisher and Ury, this is an excellent way to have the other party take what you say seriously and vice versa. However, one must do this honestly without putting blame on either side. While discussing their interests, the parties should listen actively to what the other side is saying. This enables the negotiator to grasp and better understand the other party's

---

[1]  *Getting to Yes: Negotiating Agreements Without Giving In*, New York, Penguin Books, 1983.

emotions and perceptions. A principled negotiator will sometimes ask the other side to clarify or repeat what they have said. When doing so, the negotiator will phrase his question in a way that makes it positive to the other side, thus making it clear that he has understood what is being said. The parties will also define the problem together, in a way that is mutually acceptable to both sides. Statements such as "We're both out for the same thing" can keep negotiations on course. "I'm not suggesting . . . " similarly underscores that you continue to be aware of the other side's interest. "I'm not offended" separates the people from the problem.

### (ii)  *Focus on Interests, Not Positions*

A major assumption of principled negotiation theorists is that compatible interests exist behind opposed positions. To uncover these interests one might consider why the other party is taking on a certain position. When the adverse side voices a position, the principled negotiator should ask "Why is it that this position is being taken?" He should also ask the other side, "Why would you do that?"

Negotiators should not hesitate to communicate and explain their party's interests. While doing so, the negotiator should ensure that the other side understands exactly how important and real these interests are. However, one must be careful not to imply that the other side's interests are not as important. Again, statements such as "We're both out for the same thing" and "I'm not suggesting . . . " underscore that you continue to be aware of the other side's interest. Likewise, negotiators should acknowledge the other party while they are explaining their interest. Fisher and Ury emphasize that in a principled negotiation one must be "hard" on the problem and "soft" on the people. Essentially, a party should be hard in discussing his interests rather than his position and should attack the problem without putting blame on the other side. Each party should be personally supportive of the other and listen to each other with respect, dignity and courtesy.

### (iii)  *Invent Options for Mutual Gain*

Principled negotiators do not see negotiation as a competition that involves dividing pre-determined resources. "Split the difference" and "nickel and dime" techniques only result in a loss of credibility. Rather, bargaining options may exist that can advance the interests of both parties. Principled negotiation therefore involves brainstorming with the other party on possible options. However, it is important to separate this creative act from the evaluation stage. The parties should be encouraged to suggest any possible ideas without anyone evaluating or even commenting on them. Negotiators should explicitly identify the shared interests and formulate them as goals. Brainstorming might generate a number of ideas that would not have come up without such a session.

(iv) *Use of Objective Criteria*

Not all issues in disputes are susceptible to a principled approach. In such situations, the parties should focus on objective criteria to govern the outcome of their bargaining. Nevertheless, they should not lose sight of the need for a win/win situation. For example, some negotiations are based on distributive issues such as determining the price of an item. In these situations, the parties should agree on the standards to apply to the bargaining before setting the terms. For example, in setting the price of a vehicle, the buyer might refer to the blue book value or the current market value of similar vehicles.

The benefit of finding objective criteria on which to base the negotiations is that it may narrow the range of disagreements.

(v) *Know Your BATNA*

The main reason people negotiate is to find a result that will leave them better off than if they had not negotiated. If one accepts this premise, in order to evaluate the results of a negotiation, the parties must be aware of their best alternative if they do not reach an agreement. Without an understanding of their best alternative, the parties risk agreeing to a settlement they would be better off declining, or rejecting a solution that they should have accepted. Where one party perceives that they are in a much weaker position than the other, they may conclude that a positional negotiation approach may be the most effective way of levelling the negotiation playing field. However, one should never discount the fact that they have something the other side wants. The art of negotiation is to obtain as much of what you want as possible while giving away as little as possible.

### (c)  Creating Value in Negotiations

Robert Mnookin, Director of the Harvard Negotiation Research Project, has recently published a book in which he adopts the Principled Negotiation theory but focuses more in-depth on creating value in a negotiation.[2] His view is that negotiation is the use of problem-solving skills to create value in the agreement.

Creating value for this author means reaching a deal that, when compared to other possible negotiated outcomes, either makes both parties better off or makes one party better off without making the other worse off. In his view, differences are quite often more useful in making a deal than are similarities. In any negotiation, whether positional or principled, extracting value from asymmetry can yield results that exceed the cost. Differences set the stage for possible gains from trade, through which the best deals are most often created. Mnookin realizes that in most, if not all, negotiations each party has at least some information that the other party does not have. In order to create value in a negotiation, parties have to disclose this information and discuss their interests and preferences. The goal of the negotiator is to uncover what drives the other side and what their concerns and interests are. Only when this is uncovered and discussed openly can the parties contemplate value creating options. A typical example is where one party can make a payment that is tax deductible to him but can be sheltered from tax by the recipient. The tax savings represent the "value" created and shared by the parties.

Mnookin, however, realizes that value creating is much easier to achieve in deals than in disputes — the possibility and threat of litigation always lurks over the parties during negotiations. The author also realizes that a one-sided disclosure can lead to that party being exploited. Therefore, this book introduces ways to establish a relationship with the other side that permits value creation without exploitation.

Mnookin suggests that a negotiator explain to the other lawyer from the beginning how he would like to work. Parties should discuss various approaches available and their respective benefits and create an agenda together. He also suggests that if one party points out the drawbacks of the traditional hard-bargaining game, then the other side will often be more inclined to some alternative method.

Another thing to watch is not to let the other side's rigid tactics inhibit you from using your problem-solving approach. Mnookin believes that progress is still possible if a negotiator remains focussed on interests and generating creative options while the other side adheres to the hard-bargaining approach. One way around this scenario is to reformulate what the other side says as an interest, an option, or a suggestion. In a divorce case,

---

[2] *Beyond Winning: Negotiating to Create Value in Deals and Disputes*, Cambridge, The Belknap Press of Harvard University Press, 2000.

for example, if the other party's lawyer states a final and non-negotiable demand for $4,000 a month alimony, the problem-solving negotiator could reply by saying, "I see that financial security is obviously important for your client. Let's discuss her other interests."[3]

Another way around rigid tactics is to try to change the players. For example, at one time or another, most of us have probably asked to speak to a manager or supervisor when an employee was unwilling to give us a discount. This can be tricky in legal negotiations. However, the problem-solving negotiator can generally arrange to have a meeting with both the other party and his lawyer and direct the appeal to the client, thus trying to bypass the hard-bargaining lawyer. Another method Mnookin recommends involves making a written proposal containing your reasoning and stating why your course of action makes sense, and communicating this offer directly to the client.

## 3. NEGOTIATION THEORIES REDUX

Most of the theories on negotiation described above make assumptions that are not always true in the real world of legal disputes. For example, the principled negotiation theory seems to depend on a balance of power between the parties in a negotiation. However, in reality there is seldom a balance of power between the parties. One side is always advantaged in one way in the negotiation. Either one party will have access to information that the other side does not, or that its BATNA is a lot better than the other party's, or simply that it has more resources and time, and the outcome of the negotiation is not as important for it as it is for the other party. Deals are often based on desperation and need rather than desire. For example, one might be selling the family company because one does not have the funds or time needed to keep operating it.

Also, not every party is trustworthy, frank and open. A party who freely discloses information during a negotiation may not be met with the same openness from the other side. There is a risk that in such a one-sided disclosure, the non-disclosing party will take advantage of the disclosing party. Brainstorming and discussing interests to create value are not always as easy as some theories seem to suggest.

---

[3] *Ibid.*, pp. 216-217.

## 4.  CONDUCTING NEGOTIATIONS TO SUCCESS

Lawyers and other negotiators use a variety of techniques while negotiating. In fact, a good negotiator will draw on many of these tactics during any one negotiation. Each technique can prove helpful in different situations. The appropriateness of a specific method will depend on the mood at the bargaining table, the other negotiator's style, the willingness of the other party to cooperate and the issues in dispute, as well as many other factors.

Some tactics, however, are unprofessional and utterly unacceptable. Yet, the Superior Court of Justice in Ontario recently decided that there is no obligation in law to negotiate in good faith.[4] Therefore, one has to be careful when negotiating. Lawyers and negotiators have no obligation to negotiate in good faith and may be using objectionable tactics to exploit the other party or to manipulate the procedure. Nonetheless, lawyers should still act with respect and professionalism towards each other while following the basic rules of civility. Why bother negotiating if it is not done in good faith and without any intention of settling the dispute?

Below is a description of some of the most useful techniques to successfully conduct a negotiation.

### (a)  Building Relationships

In a negotiation the parties have to be careful not to compromise their relationship. For example, when a dispute arises between two organisations, the negotiators have to be careful to keep the existing relationship between the companies on good terms so as not to compromise future endeavours together.

Where there is no prior relationship between the parties, the negotiator should work towards building a working relationship between them. If the parties in a negotiation can establish mutual trust and understanding, it might prove a lot easier to discuss possible agreements. Lawyers sometimes tend to forget this. Many think their role is to settle or negotiate for the highest or least amount they can, whatever it takes. However, building a relationship with the other side can prove to facilitate negotiation talks and can even help reduce the possibility of future disagreements.

---

[4] *EdperBrascan Corp. v. 177373 Canada Ltd.* (2001), 53 O.R. (3d) 331 (S.C.J.) at 333.

## (b)  Sincerity and Honesty

A negotiator should always be honest. This does not mean that it is always beneficial to reveal all your interests and needs to the other party. A negotiator may conceal certain information if he judges that it is to his advantage to do so. However, if the negotiator wishes to disclose information to the other party, he should always be forthright and share genuine information. Negotiators are sometimes tempted to lie about their true interests in order to trade off a somewhat unimportant issue for a crucial one. One must keep in mind that a negotiator or a lawyer's reputation is critical. If the other side becomes aware that you are crooked and conniving, your ability to negotiate an agreement can be greatly reduced.

## (c)  Watch Positional Obsessions

The more a negotiator explains a position and defends this position against the other side's attacks, the more committed he becomes to it. When negotiators try to convince the other party that they will not budge from their position, their egos become associated with that position. At this point the negotiator becomes more interested in "saving face" and tends to pay less attention to bridging the underlying interests and concerns of the parties.

Lawyers and negotiators must be careful not to commit to specific positions on incidental issues. A negotiator will often stipulate a certain position on such an issue and once it is defended, it becomes very difficult to back out because the negotiator's ego comes into play.

# 4

# Privilege and Confidentiality in ADR[1]

## 1. INTRODUCTION

Confidentiality is a fundamental element of any ADR process. Simply put, people are more likely to be honest and forthright in their discussions about disputes when they are assured that their comments will be confidential. As Section 2 of the *Uniform Mediation Act* in the United States sets out, in mediation it is important to "promote candour of the parties through confidentiality of the mediation process, subject only to the need for disclosure to accommodate specific and compelling societal evidence".[2]

There are several ways to ensure confidentiality in ADR. However, an emerging question in ADR is whether privilege applies to mediation proceedings. Privilege, which is a subset of confidentiality, is the most powerful protection accorded to communications. A privileged communication renders the communication inadmissible in court, even if it is relevant and probative.

Whether or not mediation communications are privileged is the source of some debate. Some jurisdictions have enacted statutes creating a "mediation privilege". Various common law tests also suggest that ADR communications enjoy privilege.

A hallmark of ADR is its flexibility. Yet it is this flexibility that poses challenges in summarizing the issue of privilege in ADR. Given the number of ADR processes available, the variety of legal disputes that lend themselves to ADR and the different contexts and settings (domestic, interna-

---

[1] Section written by Laura Stewart, Gowling Lafleur Henderson LLP.
[2] See the draft of this Act online at www.pon.harvard.edu/guests/uma. The Act was approved and recommended for enactment in all the States in August of 2001.

tional, court-annexed, non-court related, etc.) within which ADR takes place, it is impossible to make general statements about privilege and when it applies.

This chapter defines privilege, explores the sources of privilege (both generally and specifically as it applies to ADR) and discusses exceptions to the privilege rule. In cases where privilege will not attach to ADR communications, the sources of confidentiality are discussed.

## 2. DEFINITION OF PRIVILEGE

The law of privilege is a complex and evolving subject in and of itself. There is a significant body of case law, legislation and academic commentary on the subject. This chapter briefly defines privilege and emphasizes its impact on ADR.

At its most basic level, a privilege is a particular advantage or benefit enjoyed by a person, company or class, beyond the common advantages of other citizens.[3] In the legal context, a privilege is "an advantage conferred over and above ordinary law".[4]

When disputes arise that are tried and judged by the courts, the "ordinary law" is that all evidence that is relevant, trustworthy and probative is admissible. It is in the public interest that a tribunal have available all the necessary evidence in order to make a fair and informed ruling. In the 1991 case of *Gruenke*, the Supreme Court of Canada described this public interest (that all relevant evidence is admissible until proven otherwise) as a "fundamental first principle".[5] The dissent sets out the basis for this principle:

> One of the primary aims of the adversarial trial process is to find the truth. To assist in that search, all persons must, if requested, appear before the courts to testify about facts and events in their realm of knowledge or expertise. This requirement — some would call it a duty — can be traced far back into the history of the common law, and can now be found in statutory form in the federal and provincial Evidence Acts. If the aim of the trial process is the search for truth, the public and the judicial system, must have the right to any and all relevant information in order that justice be rendered. Accordingly, relevant information is presumptively admissible.[6]

---

[3] Definition from *Canadian Law Dictionary*, John A. Yogis, Q.C., 2nd ed., pp. 175-176.

[4] *Ibid.*

[5] *R. v. Gruenke*, [1991] 3 S.C.R. 263 at 288, per Lamer, C.J.

[6] *Ibid.*, at 295, per L'Heureux-Dubé J.

The "advantage over and above ordinary law" of privileged communications is that these communications are *inadmissible*, regardless of the fact that the information may be relevant to the legal proceedings and of use to the tribunal.

In attaching privilege, there must be a public interest in maintaining the secrecy of the communication that overrides the public interest of having all relevant evidence available to the tribunal. When privileged communications exist it is necessary to balance these competing interests.

For instance, the best recognized privilege is that between a solicitor and client. Full and frank discussions between a solicitor and client are a cornerstone of the effective operation of the legal system. Therefore, the courts have attached privilege to the communications between solicitor and client. These communications are inadmissible; neither the solicitor nor the client can be compelled to testify about the information and advice exchanged. Just as privilege can be recognized and granted, there can also be exceptions, which are discussed below. Granting exceptions also involves a balancing of competing public policies and interests.

## (a) Confidentiality vs. Privilege

Privilege and confidentiality are not the same. Although the two terms give rise to different legal obligations and consequences, they are often used interchangeably, and improperly so. It is essential that all parties involved in an ADR process understand this distinction. A number of confidential communications are not privileged, although all privileged communications are confidential. Privilege is a subset of confidentiality.

The parties often expect privacy when they impart information (a parishioner to a clergy member, a patient to a physician, a client to a banker, etc.). In other circumstance, parties will agree that the information they exchange is to be kept confidential (for example, due diligence during a business transaction). Such confidentiality agreements can be legally binding and remedies are available in the event that confidentiality is breached (as discussed in Section 6 of this chapter). However, not *all* confidential communications are privileged. Despite the fact that information was exchanged in confidence, the parties may still find themselves compelled to testify about that information before a tribunal.

## 3.  THE SOURCES AND TYPES OF PRIVILEGE

### (a)  Sources of Privilege

Privilege can be granted by legislation or common law.

### (i)  *Legislation: Statutes and Treaties*

Privilege can be granted in the domestic sphere by statute. Privilege can also be granted in the international sphere by treaties. Any privilege created by statute must be interpreted and applied by tribunals. It is therefore possible that the scope of the privilege will be broadened or restricted in the course of interpreting the intentions of the legislation.

### (ii)  *Common Law*

Privilege can be recognized by the common law. For instance, the common law recognizes solicitor-client privilege as well as a privilege attached to settlement negotiations. In the absence of a "class" of privilege at common law, the courts use a four-part test to determine whether privilege should be attached to a communication and therefore render it inadmissible. The four criteria require the tribunal to weigh the competing social and policy interests at stake. In order to be privileged, each condition must be satisfied:

- **Expectation of Confidentiality**. The communications must originate in a confidence that they will not be disclosed.

- **Maintenance of Relationship**. The element of confidentiality must be essential to the full and satisfactory maintenance of the relation between the parties.

- **Fostering Relationship**. The relation must be one which in the opinion of the community ought to be sedulously fostered.

- **Balancing**. The injury that would inure to the relation by the disclosure of the communications must be greater than the benefit thereby gained for the correct disposal of litigation.

The courts have adopted this test on numerous occasions. It was cited once again with approval by the Supreme Court of Canada in the *Slavutych*[7] and *Gruenke*[8] cases.

## (b)  Types of Privilege

In *Gruenke*, the Supreme Court of Canada observed that there are two categories of privilege. The first is a "class or blanket" privilege and the second is a "case by case" privilege.[9] The type of privilege has an impact on the rebuttable presumptions a tribunal can make, impacting the strength of the privilege.

### (i)  *Class Privilege*

The class privilege is more desirable than case privilege. It is also known as "blanket", *prima facie*, or common law privilege. If a relationship falls within a recognized class, there is a presumption of inadmissibility. This presumption can be rebutted if the party seeking to admit the evidence can show that the evidence falls within an exception to the rule of inadmissibility.

The solicitor-client communication is the most recognized class of privilege. Other classes include litigation privilege and settlement discussions privilege. Legislatures have the power to create further classes of privilege. As discussed in Section 5 below, the Saskatchewan legislature appears to have created a class of privilege for mediation communications.

While further classes may be created by statute, it is unlikely that the courts will recognize further classes in the absence of legislation. Privilege is an extraordinary exception to the rule that a tribunal must hear all relevant evidence.

In *Gruenke*, the Court addressed whether there was a class privilege for religious communications (the accused had made statements to her church pastor and a lay church counsellor concerning the murder). Chief Justice Lamer found that in order to recognize a class privilege for religious communications, there must be public policy reasons for the privilege which are as compelling as those in support of solicitor-client privilege.[10] While

---

[7] *Slavutych v. Baker* (1975), [1976] 1 S.C.R. 254 at 260.
[8] *Supra*, note 5, at 284.
[9] *Ibid.*, at 286.
[10] *Ibid.*, at 283.

the Court acknowledged that religious communications are important, a new class of privilege was not conferred on them.

## (ii)  *Case by Case Privilege*

Communications which do not fall within a privileged class are presumed to be admissible. However, privilege may be extended on a *case by case* basis if the four-part test is satisfied in each specific circumstance.

## 4.  CONFIDENTIALITY AND PRIVILEGE IN ADR: A FUNDAMENTAL ELEMENT

A fundamental element of any ADR process is confidentiality. The ADR process often requires the parties to "bare their souls". As J. Hamilton notes in her article "Protecting Confidentiality in Mandatory Mediations" about mediation (but is also applicable to any ADR process):

> The collaborative, integrative, problem-solving focus of mediation depends upon the participants disclosing their underlying interests and needs, rather than just their bargaining positions or demands. It is the identification of the substantive, procedural and psychological interests of the parties, and the education of each party about the other's interests that is the key to this process. It is only after the parties' interests have been revealed and explored that the parties can begin a mutual search for solutions that will meet their needs.[11]

Confidentiality of mediation proceedings contributes to the resolution of disputes for some basic reasons. First, confidentiality promotes candour. As was noted by the Second Circuit Court in *Lake Utopia Paper Ltd. v. Connelly Containers, Inc.*, without confidentiality the parties to ADR will most likely adopt a less productive approach:

> If participants cannot rely on the confidential treatment of everything that transpires during these sessions then of necessity [they] will feel constrained to conduct themselves in a cautious, tight-lipped, non-committal manner more suitable to a poker game than to adversaries attempting to arrive at a just resolution of a civil dispute.[12]

---

[11]  (1999), 24 *Queen's L.J.* 561 at 569.
[12]  608 F.2d 928 (U.S. N.Y. Ct. App., 1979) at 929.

Second, confidentiality promotes the integrity of the ADR process: the mediator/arbitrator must appear neutral and impartial. This can only be accomplished if the parties have some degree of assurance that the mediator will not discuss the ADR process outside the ADR process:

> If mediators are witnesses in legal proceedings, and if production of their notes and records is compelled, then the evidence that they give is likely to favour one side over another. Then, no matter how impartial and neutral the mediator might have been in fact, he or she will be perceived or suspected of favouritism.[13]

The importance of the mediator remaining neutral (and therefore credible) is underscored by the family law mediation experience in Ontario. The Ontario *Family Law Act*[14] has provided for mediation for many years. Section 3 of the Act provides that the parties must decide whether the mediation will be open or closed. In open mediation, no privilege attaches to any of the communications or conversations between the parties and/or the mediator, and all communications are admissible. In a closed mediation, none of the communications are admissible without the consent of all the parties, including the mediator. At a 1992 conference on Dispute Resolution, Ken Naftel (an Ottawa lawyer/mediator) commented that he did not know any Ottawa mediator who would consent to an open mediation (although Toronto mediators were willing to conduct open or closed meditations).[15] Further, most mediators now insist upon confidentiality agreements being signed. Some agreements even provide that the mediator is not a compellable witness. While the decision as to whether the mediator could be compelled to testify is one which is ultimately made by the court (not by an agreement between the parties), Naftel notes that the courts generally respect these agreements.[16] The provisions even provide that the mediator is not a compellable witness.

Finally, although confidentiality is important for any ADR process, it is particularly important where the ADR process (usually mediation) is court-annexed, meaning that parties to a civil action are required, as part of the civil litigation process, to engage in mediation. Likewise, parties to a labour dispute may also be required to attend an ADR session prior to a labour board hearing. Having an ADR process in tandem with adversarial

---

[13] *Supra*, note 11, p. 573.
[14] R.S.O. 1990, c. F.3.
[15] Naftel, K., "Preparing Yourself and Your Client for Mediation", presented at Dispute Resolution Program, Law Society of Upper Canada, May 15, 1992.
[16] *Ibid.*

proceedings creates a direct clash of goals and strategies; the adversarial process discourages the disclosure of information except where required and the ADR process hinges upon open and frank discussion. When parties are expected to attend an ADR session within an adversarial proceeding, the parties will naturally fear that anything they say in an ADR session may be reported back to the tribunal.[17]

For all of these reasons, confidentiality is essential to mediation. Indeed, a review of the literature in the United States reveals near universal agreement that confidentiality is necessary to the survival of mediation.[18] Since confidentiality is such a cornerstone of ADR, many advocate the creation and enforcement of a strong mediation privilege. As noted previously, confidentiality and privilege are not one and the same. While confidentiality provisions in ADR attempt to ensure that the ADR discussions are not disclosed, an ADR privilege goes further and provides that these confidential communications are privileged and therefore inadmissible.

## 5. THE SOURCES OF CONFIDENTIALITY AND PRIVILEGE SPECIFIC TO ADR

The different types of ADR processes can occur in a variety of contexts – ADR is not always connected to litigation. Most ADR processes are confidential. Confidentiality is ensured by way of agreement, common law and/or statute. In addition to confidentiality, some ADR processes are also privileged. This section will explore the sources and scope of confidentiality and privilege specific to ADR processes.

### (a) Statute

For instance, in the case of the blanket mediation privilege created by Saskatchewan legislature, there has been at least one narrow interpretation of the provision by the courts. Given the well intentioned, but very wide scope of a blanket mediation privilege, academic commentators query whether such legislation will be truly effective in protecting mediation communications from disclosure in court.[19]

---

[17] *Supra*, note 11, p. 566.
[18] *Ibid.*, p. 569.
[19] *Ibid.*, p. 569.

### (b) Model Statutory Privilege

Hamilton's article that reviewed the Saskatchewan and Ontario legislation regarding mediation privilege concludes that the legal protection for mediation confidentiality in these statutes is "neither certain nor comprehensive",[20] and suggests that only a "uniform statutory provision" can address the current deficiencies in mediation privilege.[21]

In the spring of 2001, after three years of effort, the American Bar Association Section of Dispute Resolution, National Conference of Commissioners on Uniform State Law to Collaborate on Mediation Law[22] proposed a model statutory provision. The *Uniform Mediation Act* was approved and recommended for enactment in all the States in August 2001.

Below are transcripts of Sections 4, 5, 7 and 9 of the *Uniform Mediation Act*.

#### SECTION 4. PRIVILEGE AGAINST DISCLOSURE; ADMISSIBILITY; DISCOVERY.

(a)   Except as otherwise provided in Section 6, a mediation communication is privileged as provided in subsection (b) and is not subject to discovery or admissible in evidence in a proceeding unless waived or precluded as provided by Section 5.

(b)   In a proceeding, the following privileges apply:

   (1)   A mediation party may refuse to disclose, and may prevent any other person from disclosing, a mediation communication.

   (2)   A mediator may refuse to disclose a mediation communication, and may prevent any other person from disclosing a mediation communication of the mediator.

   (3)   A nonparty participant may refuse to disclose, and may prevent any other person from disclosing, a mediation communication of the nonparty participant.

(c)   Evidence or information that is otherwise admissible or subject to discovery does not become inadmissible or protected from discovery solely by reason of its disclosure or use in a mediation.

---

[20] *Ibid.*, p. 604.
[21] *Ibid.*, pp. 605-613.
[22] All information about the National Conference of Commissioners on Uniform State Laws Mediation Project can be accessed at www.pon.harvard.edu/guests/uma.

## SECTION 5. WAIVER AND PRECLUSION OF PRIVILEGE.

(a)    A privilege under Section 4 may be waived in a record or orally during a proceeding if it is expressly waived by all parties to the mediation and:

    (1)    in the case of the privilege of a mediator, it is expressly waived by the mediator; and

    (2)    in the case of the privilege of a nonparty participant, it is expressly waived by the nonparty participant.

(b)    A person that discloses or makes a representation about a mediation communication which prejudices another person in a proceeding is precluded from asserting a privilege under Section 4, but only to the extent necessary for the person prejudiced to respond to the representation or disclosure.

(c)    A person that intentionally uses a mediation to plan, attempt to commit or commit a crime, or to conceal an ongoing crime or ongoing criminal activity may not assert a privilege under Section 4.

## SECTION 7. PROHIBITED MEDIATOR REPORTS.

(a)    Except as required in subsection (b), a mediator may not make a report, assessment, evaluation, recommendation, finding, or other communication regarding a mediation to a court, administrative agency, or other authority that may make a ruling on the dispute that is the subject of the mediation.

(b)    A mediator may disclose:

    (1)    whether the mediation occurred or has terminated, whether a settlement was reached, and attendance;

    (2)    a mediation communication as permitted under Section 6; or

    (3)    a mediation communication evidencing abuse, neglect, abandonment, or exploitation of an individual to a public agency responsible for protecting individuals against such mistreatment.

(c)    A communication made in violation of subsection (a) may not be considered by a court, administrative agency or arbitrator.

## SECTION 9. MEDIATOR'S DISCLOSURE OF CONFLICTS OF INTEREST; BACKGROUND.

(a)    Before accepting a mediation an individual who is requested to serve as a mediator shall:

    (1)    make an inquiry that is reasonable under the circumstances to

determine whether there are any known facts that a reasonable individual would consider likely to affect the impartiality of the mediator, including a financial or personal interest in the outcome of the mediation and an existing or past relationship with a party or foreseeable participant in the mediation; and

(2)   disclose any such known fact to the mediation parties as soon as is practical before accepting a mediation.

(b)   If a mediator learns any fact described in subsection (a)(1) after accepting a mediation, the mediator shall disclose as soon as is practicable.

(c)   At the request of a mediation party, an individual who is requested to serve as a mediator shall disclose the mediator's qualifications to mediate a dispute.

(d)   A person that violates subsection [(a) or (b)][(a), (b), or (g)] is precluded by the violation from asserting a privilege under Section 4.

(e)   Subsections (a), (b), [and] (c), [and] [(g)] do not apply to an individual acting as a judge.

(f)   This [Act] does not require that a mediator have a special qualification by background or profession.

[(g)   A mediator must be impartial, unless after disclosure of the facts required in subsections (a) and (b) to be disclosed, the parties agree otherwise.]

### (c) Common Law

To date, there is no class of "mediation privilege" recognized by the common law in Canada. However, Canadian common law does recognize the class of settlement negotiation privilege, which is similar and can be expanded to include ADR communications. In the absence of a statute conferring a mediation privilege, the common law may be an alternative source for a claim of privilege.

In their book on solicitor-client privilege, Manes and Silver define settlement negotiations privilege as follows:

Where there is a dispute in existence, the common law generally protects confidential communications made in the contact of settlement negotiations conducted to resolve that dispute and accords privilege to them.[23]

---

[23] *Solicitor-Client Privilege in Canadian Law*, Butterworths, 1993, p. 115.

Communications that arise from settlement negotiations are often referred to as "without prejudice communications". While labelling a document "without prejudice" is an indication that it is intended to be used in settlement negotiations, the heading does not, in and of itself, guarantee that the communication will fall within the class of settlement negotiation privilege. The content and intention of the communication must be assessed to determine whether privilege will attach.[24]

The underlying rationale for privilege attaching to settlement negotiations is to encourage parties to settle, rather than litigate their disputes. The courts consider attaching privilege to these communications a sufficiently worthy objective, rendering them inadmissible. The concern is that there would be fewer settlement efforts in the absence of this privilege.

Settlement negotiation privilege applies to communications made during a litigious dispute or within contemplation, or for the purpose of attempting to effect a settlement, with the express or implied intention that such communications would not be disclosed to the court if the attempt failed. In most cases, the privilege is used to prevent the admission of evidence regarding settlement negotiations between two litigating parties. However, situations exist when settlement negotiation privilege operates against strangers to the settlement discussions. In *Waxman v. Texaco*, the Ontario Court of Appeal found:

> Communications written "without prejudice" and with a view to settlement of issues between A and C are privileged from production at the instance of C in subsequent litigation between A and B on the same subject-matter or subject-matter closely related to that with which the correspondence in question was concerned.[25]

Like settlement negotiations, the purpose of ADR is to resolve a dispute. In fact, ADR is often described as assisted negotiation. Since the two processes share a common goal, it can be argued that mediation communications fall within the ambit of settlement negotiation privilege.

Some commentators have queried whether settlement negotiation privilege is of sufficient scope to protect ADR communications.[26] One concern is that settlement negotiation privilege applies to the parties to the dispute. Will it be extended to include the communications between the parties and the mediator/arbitrator? The few cases in this area clearly extend the priv-

---

[24] *Supra*, note 23, p. 117.
[25] *I. Waxman & Sons Ltd. v. Texaco Canada Ltd.*, [1968] 2 O.R. 452 (C.A.) at 453.
[26] Hamilton, *supra*, note 11.

ilege to the mediator. There is a series of English cases that establish that settlement negotiation privilege extends to those who functioned as mediators during reconciliation discussions. The privilege extends to communications between the mediator and one party (in the absence of the other) as well as communications between the parties.

In the *Porter* case, the Unified Family Court in Ontario also found that settlement negotiation privilege extends to a "mediator".[27] *Porter* is significant because the privilege was extended to a neutral third party who was attempting to assist the parties, although the parties were not formally mediating. The parties had separated and retained a psychologist to mediate custody and access issues. The parties reconciled and separated again several years later. Litigation ensued and one of the parties sought to introduce the psychologist's report. The Court ruled that the report was inadmissible as the parties were engaged in settlement discussions. Further, the Court found that the four-part test (for application of privilege on a case by case basis) was met.

The *Porter* decision was recently cited with approval in the non-family law case of *Marchand*,[28] although it should be noted that the issue was the disclosure of a draft settlement agreement, drafted and agreed to by counsel. There was no attempt to introduce communications from the mediator.

In *Marchand*, the parties were litigating a medical negligence claim. During the trial, all counsel attended upon a retired judge in an attempt to reach a settlement. At the end of the session, all counsel executed a settlement agreement which would have resolved the litigation subject to the receipt of client instructions. It was agreed that the three legal counsel would take the agreement to their clients and seek their instructions.

The two defence counsel later advised that the settlement terms were acceptable to their clients. The plaintiffs' counsel advised that his clients declined the agreement. The litigation therefore continued and a decision was rendered on the merits. The parties were asked to present argument on costs.

The plaintiffs' argued that neither defendant had ever made an offer of settlement during the course of the litigation. The defendants attempted to introduce the draft settlement agreement. The plaintiffs' counsel argued that this agreement arose from a mediation session and, relying on *Porter*, submitted that the agreement was therefore privileged and inadmissible.

---

[27] *Porter v. Porter* (1983), 40 O.R. (2d) 417 (U.F.C.).

[28] *Marchand (Litigation Guardian of) v. Public General Hospital of Chatham*, [1997] O.J. No. 1805 (Ont. Gen. Div.), Granger, J.

The trial judge accepted the reasoning of *Porter* in its entirety and found that the draft settlement agreement and its terms would not be admissible in the evidentiary phase of the trial. However, the Court found that the draft agreement was essentially an offer of settlement. In an important distinction, the trial judge commented:

> The [draft settlement] agreement does not contravene the statements of Carthy J.A. in *Bell Canada v. O & Y Dev. Ltd.* as the [draft settlement] *agreement does not in any way set out or ask me to take into account what occurred at the mediation.* The fact that the plaintiffs did not instruct Mr. Wunder to settle this matter as set out in the agreement is not relevant to the issue of costs, but the agreement is admissible as previously stated to evidence the settlement position of the defendants at that time.[29] [emphasis added]

In *Marchand*, the trial judge clearly respected the privilege arising from a mediation session, while admitting evidence of settlement positions. At the conclusion of the decision, the judge noted that this result was only fair, particularly given that the plaintiffs had submitted to the Court that the defendants had not made any efforts to settle the litigation when this clearly was not the case.

Another concern about extending settlement negotiation privilege to ADR processes is whether the privilege should be extended to *all* ADR communications or just those communications relating strictly to settlement. The "independent fact doctrine" provides that there can be information exchanged during settlement negotiations which is severable from the negotiations and relevant on other matters. Essentially, the independent fact doctrine encourages a strict interpretation of settlement negotiation privilege: those communications which are "offers of settlement and discussions which are conducive to arriving at settlement" are covered by the privilege and other communications are not.

As noted above, the ultimate goal of any ADR process is resolution or settlement, but the parties may have to canvass a huge number and variety of facts, issues and interests before arriving at a settlement. There is one case which gives credence to Hamilton's concerns. In *Springridge Farms Ltd., Re*,[30] a bank trying to petition a farming operation into bankruptcy sought to introduce evidence that it had demanded payment from a debtor during an unsuccessful mediation session. The bank's petition would fail unless this evidence was admitted. The Court of Queen's Bench applied

---

[29] *Ibid.*, at para 17.
[30] (1991), 79 D.L.R. (4th) 88 (Sask. C.A.).

settlement negotiation privilege and found that the demand was inadmissible. The Saskatchewan Court of Appeal overturned this decision and seems to have applied the independent fact doctrine:

> . . . it is not every statement made at such a meeting which is protected. Clearly, offers of settlement and discussion which are conducive to arriving at settlement are protected. However, a repetition of the original demand does not fall within this definition. Just as portions of a document headed "Without Prejudice" may be admissible if they are severable from the negotiations and relevant on other matters, portions of a discussion, even if a settlement discussion, may contain other matters which are the legitimate subject of testimony. It is difficult to see how the bare repetition of a demand for payment is in any way in need of protection to foster the process of voluntary settlement of disputes.[31]

Although this decision is worrisome for proponents of ADR, it should be noted that the decision has been criticized for its failure to understand the nature of mediation.[32]

The case of *Rodic v. Centre for Addiction & Mental Health* seems to reject the use of the independent fact doctrine to undermine the privilege extended to mediation. On a motion, one party filed an affidavit which referred to various communications at the mediation session. Master MacLeod took a very common sense approach to this issue and it is worthwhile to quote his entire analysis:

> Mr. Samac asked me to strike certain paragraphs of the affidavit in support of motion. Specifically he objected to paragraphs 10-16 of the affidavit of Jasmine Ghosn. I reserved on the preliminary objection and, because in my view the evidence does not establish prejudice, it is strictly speaking not necessary to rule on the point. Nevertheless, *it is worth comment so that parties may be guided on the point in future.*
>
> *Paragraph 10 and 16 are unobjectionable. They detail that the mediation took place, who the mediator was and the fact that the mediation was not successful in resolving the dispute.* Paragraphs 11 & 12 identify the persons who were present at the mediation and who will be examined for discovery . . . *I do not consider deposing who was present at a mediation session to be improper if it is relevant to a procedural issue.* Paragraphs 13 & 14 detail some pre-mediation discussion between counsel. The point of the paragraphs was to demonstrate that Mr. Samac encouraged the representatives of the defendants to fully participate and to speak during the mediation. Paragraph 15 states that

---

[31] *Ibid.*, at 92.
[32] *Supra*, note 11, at footnote 28.

the defendants representatives did fully participate and took an active role in discussing certain issues. The issues are then itemized but not the content of the discussion.

Communication in mediation is privileged. Settlement offers are privileged. The question is whether the negotiations about how to conduct mediation are privileged? *While Rule 24.1 speaks of the "mediation session", the common law privilege may well be broader.* In my view, discussions between counsel or between counsel and the mediator about how to make the mediation most effective are part of the mediation and should be privileged. Similarly, what was discussed in mediation, whether or not the contents of the discussion are revealed should be regarded as communications in the mediation session. Accordingly, information such as that set out in paragraphs 13, 14 & 15 should not ordinarily be disclosed and I would strike those paragraphs.[33] [emphasis added]

It would seem that Master MacLeod distinguished between procedure and substance in assessing the scope of privilege conferred on mediation. While procedural information may be disclosed, he applied a wide privilege over all substantive mediation discussions. Essentially, he used the common law to expand the privilege conferred by statute.

In cases where mediation is court-annexed, the parties will continue to litigate if the ADR initiative fails. It is important that the settlement negotiation privilege not be extended too broadly, which would prevent the disclosure of legitimately discoverable information on the basis that the issue or document had been raised during a mediation session. Otherwise discoverable documents should not be precluded from proof in subsequent proceedings merely because they are disclosed during mediation, otherwise, mediation becomes a "black hole" in which to bury damaging evidence.

Another concern about applying settlement negotiation privilege to mediation is potential restrictions as to the "time and place" of the privilege. Privilege means that a communication is inadmissible in court hearings between the disputants. However, common law privilege does not necessarily prevent the disclosure of such communications to third parties. While privilege may not address this concern, the parties and their counsel must adhere to the deemed undertaking rule in many Canadian jurisdictions.

Finally, although there is a dearth of case law about the scope of settlement negotiation privilege as applied to ADR processes, and potential concerns have been addressed about the application of the privilege to ADR, it is worth noting that no cases have been identified where a court has

---

[33] 2001 CarswellOnt 1755, (May 11, 2001), Doc. 99-CV-180194CM (Master) at paras 13 to 15.

interfered in an ADR process and compelled a mediator or parties to testify about the substance of an ADR session. Canadian courts clearly recognize the value of ADR and the early indication is that the courts will attempt to preserve the integrity of the ADR process, unless the communication falls within one of the exceptions to the privilege and these exceptions are discussed in the next section.

### (d) ADR Confidentiality Agreement

Parties to an ADR process usually sign an ADR agreement. The mediator/arbitrator is also a signatory, as well as any legal counsel representing the parties. These agreements deal with housekeeping issues (fees, division of responsibility for payment of fees, length of ADR session, etc.) as well as more substantive issues, such as the structure and style of the ADR session.

These ADR agreements frequently impose confidentiality obligations upon the parties, their counsel and the mediator/arbitrator. Some agreements go so far as to provide that the mediator will not be a compellable witness in litigation in the absence of the consent of all parties.[34]

It is important to understand that these ADR agreements *do not and cannot create privilege.* That said, these agreements may be useful in support of a privilege argument. In applying any of the common law tests for privilege, the court must have regard for the intentions of the parties, and the intention and expectation of confidentiality may be evidenced in these agreements.

As a practical matter, many mediators and arbitrators have standard form agreements which they present to parties at the outset of an ADR session. In cases where confidentiality is a concern for one or more parties to the ADR process, legal counsel should review these draft agreements carefully and ensure that there are adequately drafted clauses which clearly establish the confidentiality duties and expectations.

### (e) Codes of Conduct

Even in the absence of an agreement which provides for confidentiality, ADR confidentiality may still arise from the ethical obligations imposed upon a mediator or arbitrator. Many ADR associations now have Codes of

---

[34] Ken Naftel, "Preparing Yourself and Your Client for Mediation", presented at Dispute Resolution Program, Law Society of Upper Canada, May 15, 1992.

Ethics or Codes of Conduct. These codes recognize that confidentiality is essential to successful ADR. This is succinctly captured in the AMIC Code of Ethics (AMIC being a founding member of the ADR Institute of Canada):

> A member shall be faithful to the relationship of trust and confidentiality inherent in the office of arbitrator or mediator.[35]

Despite the fact that confidentiality is a fundamental component to ADR processes, these Codes of Conduct also acknowledge that the participating parties may want varying degrees of confidentiality to attach to the mediation. For instance, the Family Mediation Canada Code of Conduct mandates confidentiality for family law ADR,[36] whereas the American Arbitration Association, which focuses on commercial disputes, mandates that the mediator must meet the confidentiality expectations set out by the parties, as confidentiality may not be as important to commercial disputants.[37] The ADR Institute of Canada Code of Conduct summarizes this duty in Article Five, in requiring mediators to "maintain the reasonable expectations of the parties with regard to confidentiality".[38]

Like ADR agreements, these Codes of Conduct *do not and cannot create privilege*. The Codes merely impose duties upon arbitrators and mediators to uphold the confidentiality inherent in the ADR process and expected by the parties. Some Codes of Conduct (such as that of Family Mediation Canada) require mediators to specifically advise the parties of the lack of privilege which may exist.[39]

## 6. EXCEPTIONS TO CONFIDENTIALITY AND PRIVILEGE

ADR processes should be designed to foster productive discussion which, ideally, leads to the resolution of a dispute. As a general rule, ADR proceedings are confidential (and sometimes privileged). There are exceptions to this rule. Some of these exceptions are contemplated by statute. Others must be argued at common law. In order to assess whether there is an exception to the confidentiality or privilege, the underlying basis for the confidentiality or privilege must be assessed.

---

[35] Available at www.amic.org.
[36] See Article 7, available at www.fmc.ca.
[37] Commercial Dispute Resolution Procedures, available at www.adr.org.
[38] *Supra*, note 35.
[39] Article 7, *supra*, note 36.

### (a) Statutory Provisions

Participating in ADR does not exempt the parties from complying with existing statutory obligations. For instance, professionals subject to the Ontario *Child and Family Services Act* have a statutory duty to make a report to the Children's Aid Society if they have a reasonable belief that a child is in danger or potential danger.[40] This duty exists regardless of whether the information regarding the danger to the child is disclosed during an ADR session.

Parties must also have regard for conflict within various statutory provisions. For instance, if a public body is party to ADR, the public body will sign on to the usual confidentiality provisions. However, are those provisions (or any privilege) overridden by other legislation which provides for freedom of information? To date, there are no cases on point.

### (b) Malpractice by Mediator or Lawyer during Mediation

If a party wishes to bring an action against the mediator or its counsel for negligence during the mediation session, it appears that an exception to the privilege exists which would permit the party to rely on mediation communications to prove its allegations. Likewise, the mediator or legal counsel should be able to rely on otherwise privileged mediation communications in order to defend himself.[41] In at least two Ontario cases, this exception seems to be assumed to exist by the courts. In *Harper*[42] and *Dos Santos*,[43] there were issues about the scope of settlement agreements. In both cases, the parties raised issues about the advice given by their lawyers. The Court commented that if there was any misconduct by legal counsel, that was a matter between solicitor and client. In both decisions, the Court assumed that the parties could rely upon privileged communications in order to bring an action against their counsel.

---

[40] R.S.O. 1990, c. C.11, s. 72.

[41] *Supra*, note 11, at footnotes 82-85.

[42] *Harper v. Kami's Eating & Meeting Place* (1996), 16 O.T.C. 153 (Gen. Div.).

[43] *Dos Santos v. Waite* (1995), [1995] O.J. No. 1803, 1995 CarswellOnt 3384 (Gen. Div.), affirmed (1996), 1996 CarswellOnt 3554 (C.A.).

## (c)  Model Statute

As noted above, the National Conference of Commissioners on Uniform State Laws recently released the *Uniform Mediation Act*. Section 6 of the legislation codifies exceptions to mediation privilege as follows:

### SECTION 6. EXCEPTIONS TO PRIVILEGE.

(a)    There is no privilege under Section 4 for a mediation communication that is:

    (1)    in an agreement evidenced by a record signed by all parties to the agreement;

    (2)    available to the public under [insert statutory reference to open records act] or made during a session of a mediation which is open, or is required by law to be open, to the public;

    (3)    a threat or statement of a plan to inflict bodily injury or commit a crime of violence;

    (4)    intentionally used to plan a crime, attempt to commit or commit a crime, or to conceal an ongoing crime or ongoing criminal activity;

    (5)    sought or offered to prove or disprove a claim or complaint of professional misconduct or malpractice filed against a mediator;

    (6)    except as otherwise provided in subsection (c), sought or offered to prove or disprove a claim or complaint of professional misconduct or malpractice filed against a mediation party, nonparty participant, or representative of a party based on conduct occurring during a mediation; or

    (7)    sought or offered to prove or disprove abuse, neglect, abandonment, or exploitation in a proceeding in which a child or adult protective services agency is a party, unless the [Alternative A: [State to insert, for example, child or adult protection] case is referred by a court to mediation and a public agency participates.] [Alternative B: public agency participates in the [State to insert, for example, child or adult protection] mediation].

(b)    There is no privilege under Section 4 if a court, administrative agency, or arbitrator finds, after a hearing in camera, that the party seeking discovery or the proponent of the evidence has shown that the evidence is not otherwise available, that there is a need for the evidence that substantially outweighs the interest in protecting confidentiality, and that the mediation communication is sought or offered in:

    (1)    a court proceeding involving a felony [or misdemeanor]; or

(2)    except as otherwise provided in subsection (c), a proceeding to prove a claim to rescind or reform or a defense to avoid liability on a contract arising out of the mediation.

(c)    A mediator may not be compelled to provide evidence of a mediation communication referred to in subsection (a)(6) or (b)(2).

(d)    If a mediation communication is not privileged under subsection (a) or (b), only the portion of the communication necessary for the application of the exception from nondisclosure may be admitted. Admission of evidence under subsection (a) or (b) does not render the evidence, or any other mediation communication, discoverable or admissible for any other purpose.

# 5

# Conflict Analysis

The introduction of mediation into formalized dispute resolution requires that counsel master conflict analysis. Further, as ADR provides alternatives to traditional litigation, counsel will be constantly tested by clients to ensure that disputes are resolved in the most efficient way possible.

Formerly, our judicial system only offered a formal trial as the means to resolve a dispute. Now, advanced dispute resolution expertise on the part of counsel and clients will dictate a sophisticated knowledge of these techniques so that minimizing the cost of conflict is the standard by which excellent counsel will be judged.

**Tip**: To repeat, some conflicts, however, can only be resolved in a court battle!

## 1. CONFLICT VS. DISPUTE

Conflict is part of life! It is neither good nor bad — it simply is. "Conflict" may be defined as a situation in which seemingly incompatible elements exert force in opposing or divergent directions. These divergent forces evoke tension, but not necessarily hostility or fighting. The word "conflict" does not necessarily connote argument or battle. Conflicts may be silent and unexpressed. Individuals who avoid speaking to one another, or who refrain from discussion of sensitive issues, may be manifesting signs of conflict. The term "conflict" denotes only that elements appear to be in opposition.

The usual definition of "dispute" is "to engage in discussion or argument; to quarrel angrily".

Using these definitions, we can see that "conflict" describes the natural state of things: the natural competitiveness that is common to all living things. A "dispute", on the other hand, may be seen as a symptom of an unresolved or poorly managed conflict. There has been an escalation. Heat has been added. Disputants are upset or angry.

It is helpful to distinguish between "conflict" and "dispute". When conflict is well managed it is a positive, dynamic catalyst for change, growth, improvement and learning. When conflict is poorly managed it escalates into a dispute that can be costly for all involved.

### (a)  The "Cost" of Poorly Managed Conflict

Everyone has experienced a situation in which conflict has been poorly managed. When we start to think of the "costs" experienced by the disputants some of the following types of costs come to mind:

- **Relationships.** When conflict is poorly managed, relationships are strained, weakened and sometimes destroyed.

- **Dignity and Respect.** Often, people's dignity is left in tatters and there is a general lessening of respect when conflict is poorly managed. It is difficult to save face in such situations.

- **Productivity.** We are less effective and less efficient when conflict is poorly managed.

- **Stress.** Conflict is often stressful for everyone involved. This stress can have an impact on people's health.

- **Time.** Poorly managed conflict usually takes a long time to resolve.

- **Money.** It can be very expensive for everyone when conflict is poorly managed.

- **Certainty.** When conflict remains unresolved everyone involved lacks certainty about the outcome, making it difficult to plan for the future.

- **Recurrence.** When not well managed, the same type of conflicts keep coming up again and again. The same people may also become involved in other types of conflicts.

Individuals and organizations are often oblivious to the costs of poorly managed conflict or believe that the costs simply have to be incurred —

that there is no alternative. However, if they think about it, disputants will generally have a mutual interest in reducing the cost of conflict.

This mutual interest in reducing the cost of conflict management is often a key inducement to encourage disputants to explore different process approaches for the resolution of their dispute.

## (b) Process Approaches to Resolving Dispute

There are three basic process approaches to resolving disputes: Power, Rights and Interests.

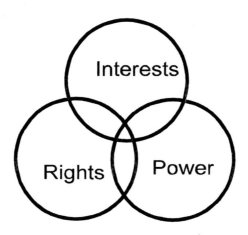

## (i) *Power Based Approaches*

Power has to do with the ability to make another party do what they would not do if the power were not exercised. In a power based approach to resolving conflict, one or both of the parties will use or threaten to use their own power to achieve their desired outcome.

There are many sources of power such as manpower, money, time, information, technology, etc. Power based approaches to resolving disputes are well known and commonly understood. Examples of power based dispute resolution processes include war, violence, civil disobedience, strikes, lockouts, embargoes, votes and referenda.

(ii) *Rights Based Approaches*

Rights based approaches resolve disputes by focussing on the "rights" of the disputants. These processes seek to determine who is right and who is wrong. Rights arise from law, statute, regulation, by-law, common law, contract, tradition and convention. Generally, rights based approaches to conflict resolution are adversarial in nature in the sense that one side is opposed to another.

Rights based dispute resolution processes include determinative processes such as hearings before courts, administrative tribunals or arbitral panels as well as investigative processes such as those performed by a traditional ombudsman.

Arbitration is a rights based dispute resolution process.

(iii) *Interest Based Approaches*

Interest based approaches to dispute resolution seek to resolve disputes in a way that acceptably addresses the interests of the disputants. "Interests" refer to the wants, needs and concerns of the disputants.

Generally, negotiation is the predominant interest based dispute resolution process. Indeed, arguably, negotiation is the predominant dispute resolution process used by individuals and organizations in the world today.

Reduced to its basics, negotiation is a process by which one party expresses his or her needs, wants and concerns to another party with the expectation that the other party will do likewise and with the objective that a mutually acceptable outcome will be achieved which meets the interests of both sides.

Mediation, which is basically facilitated or assisted negotiation, is, likewise, generally considered an interest based dispute resolution process.

## (c)  Linkage between the Approaches

Lawyers are trained to think of their clients' rights and the means by which those rights may be adjudicated. Until recently, most lawyers were focussed on "rights" and were not sensitive to the interplay amongst power, rights and interests. For example, negotiation, an interest based process takes place "in the shadow of the law". Rights have relevance in an interest based process. Similarly, the relative apparent power of the disputants will also be a factor in any negotiation.

Whenever ADR processes become part of the litigation process, clever counsel will learn quickly to use a mix of interest and rights based approaches to obtain the best result for their client. It is naive to believe that one approach alone will work. Often, mediation or negotiation is successful after discovery or cross-examination on an affidavit. Success in interim court processes can grant the successful party "leverage", that is power in subsequent negotiations. Powerless parties often fail at mediation while parties with legal rights will succeed in negotiations.

### (d)  Sequencing of Approaches

At the core of ADR theory is the idea that rational parties, given the choice, would prefer to resolve their disputes at a lower cost. A growing body of experience and research (and, perhaps, common sense) suggests that generally interest based approaches to conflict resolution will be less costly than rights based approaches that, in turn, generally will be less costly than power based approaches.

It therefore follows that the choice of dispute resolution processes should generally be sequenced to begin with interest based approaches followed by rights based approaches, with power based approaches as a last resort.

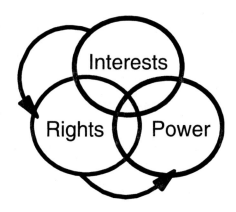

### (e)  The Sequenced Approach to Dispute Resolution

For example, if a dispute arises between A and B with respect to the interpretation of a contract and if A and B are interested in resolving the dispute in the least costly manner to both of them, they should first attempt to negotiate a resolution directly. If that fails they could seek the assistance of a mediator to assist them in their negotiations. If they were still unable to resolve the dispute then they would sequence to a rights based approach such as the state courts or private arbitration for a final determination. The use of power is seen as a last resort to be avoided as much as possible.

There are at least two reasons why power based approaches should be avoided (or at least only used when all else has failed): first, the costs associated with power based approaches are commonly understood to be high; second, power based approaches are notoriously unpredictable. There are countless examples in history of the apparently less powerful party prevailing. This is the problem with power. While apparently power can be observed, even measured, the impact of the application of power cannot be predicted with accuracy.

The basic principle of sequencing the three approaches to dispute resolution can be applied in practice using the Dispute Resolution Stairway. Generally, parties in conflict would prefer to resolve their conflicts lower on the stairway — where the costs, hostility and frustration are lowest and where the control of outcome and predictability is the highest.

## (f) The Stairway of Dispute Resolution

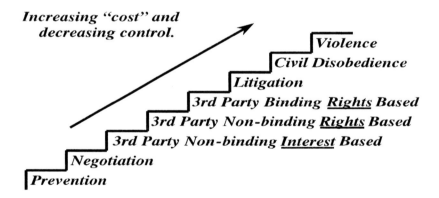

- **Prevention.** Processes which attempt to prevent disputes from occurring such as Partnering and Training.
- **Negotiation.** Unassisted discussions directly between the parties.
- **3rd Party Non-binding Interest Based.** Assistance from a mediator

who will facilitate an interest based negotiation rather than evaluate the relative strengths and weaknesses of parties' positions.

- **3rd Party Non-binding Rights Based.** Assistance from a mediator who will focus on and evaluate the relative legal strengths and weaknesses of the parties' positions. Non-binding arbitration works the same way as binding arbitration except that the neutral's decision is advisory only. The parties may agree in advance to use the advisory decision as a tool in resolving their disputes through negotiation or other means.

- **3rd Party Binding Rights Based.** Typically, binding arbitration. Binding arbitration is a private adversarial process in which the disputing parties choose a neutral person or panel to hear their dispute and to render a final binding decision or award. The process can be less formal than litigation; the parties can craft their own procedures and determine if any formal rules of evidence will apply. Unless there has been fraud or some other defect in the arbitration procedure, binding arbitration awards typically are enforceable by courts and not subject to appellate review.

- **Litigation.** Traditional state court based process.

- **Civil Disobedience.** Extra-judicial power based approach, but stops short of violence.

- **Violence.** Physical force exerted for the purpose of violating, damaging, or abusing.

## (g)  An ADR Process Approach

Disputants or their representatives sometimes seek advice on the most effective way to resolve a particular dispute. From an ADR perspective the following general principles can often guide disputants:

- Consider using interest based processes before rights based processes.

- Consider a "stepped" approach in which, for example, an interest based process such as mediation will be tried first. If that process does not result in resolution of the dispute within a pre-agreed time, then the parties will use a rights based approach like arbitration.

- Power based approaches should be avoided because of their high cost and uncertain outcome.

# 6

# Mediation — Philosophy and Practices

## 1. INTRODUCTION

Mediation has become a growing method of processing disputes in Canada. Ontario is moving to mandatory mediation in all non-family civil cases. Consequently, lawyers have been presented with the challenge of merging the "traditional" practice of law with the contrary principles of mediation. As E.F. Schumacher wrote:

> The philosophical map employed by most practicing lawyers and law teachers, and displayed to the law student — which I will call the lawyer's standard philosophical map — differs radically from that which a mediator must use. What appears on this map is determined largely by the power of two assumptions about matters that lawyers handle: (1) that disputants are adversaries . . . and (2) that disputes may be resolved through application, by a third party, of some general rule of law.[1]

These assumptions are in sharp contrast to the principles underlying mediation; namely that both parties create and agree to innovative solutions for their problem, and that each problem is unique and not governed by any general principle.[2]

---

[1] Leonard L. Riskin, *Dispute Resolution and Lawyers*, St. Paul, Minn.: West Publishing Co., 1987, p. 57.

[2] *Ibid.*

## In The Bleachers

**The batter is hit by a pitch, tempers flair and a mediator is summoned.**

## 2. WHAT IS MEDIATION?

Mediation is a process of intervention in a dispute or negotiation by an acceptable, neutral third party who is knowledgeable in effective negotiation procedures. This third party is called a mediator. The mediator has no authoritative decision making power. The mediator's purpose and objective is to act as a facilitator who assists the disputing parties in voluntarily reaching their own mutually acceptable settlement of some or all the issues in dispute.

Mediation is based upon the democratic principle of self-determination which recognizes the rights of persons to make their own voluntary non-coerced decisions. In a mediation, the parties themselves shape the outcome of the negotiation.

Mediation, negotiation and arbitration are often confused with one another. Mediation differs from negotiation in that negotiation consists of the parties meeting with one another in order to solve their dispute, whereas mediation consists of having a third party facilitate and control the discussions between the parties. Similarly, mediation and arbitration should not be confused with each another. Arbitration is a private hearing using one or more neutral decision makers called arbitrators who have the power to issue a binding award. On the other hand, a mediator's role is not to make decisions but to facilitate and assist the parties to communicate and reach their own mutually acceptable settlement. That is:

> The role of the mediator is to create and maintain an atmosphere that allows the parties to speak freely while addressing their views. He or she provides a harmonious environment for the mediation to take place. Anywhere that is quiet, comfortable, and without distraction. The mediator expresses confidence, compassion, and understanding toward each party. By doing so a sense of self-esteem is created in each and every individual. This has the double effect of alleviating any stress, fear, anger, or feelings of guilt induced by the problem, and secondly it minimizes any balance of power problems that may arise. This sets the stage for opening communication barriers.[3]

While the parties are encouraged to participate and speak freely, there are rules of conduct that must be followed. By getting the parties to agree to follow three fundamental rules while in mediation, the mediator sets the conditions for open communication. The rules are:

- to refrain from interrupting, in any way, another party while they are speaking,
- to avoid the use of any offensive, derogatory language, innuendo or implication, and

---

[3] Michael L. Smith, Ottawa Carleton Dispute Resolution Centre, quoted in Nelson, R. "Arbitration and Mediation of Business Disputes" (1987), *Gowling and Henderson Centennial Series* 1 at 16-17.

•    to show respect for the other party and the mediator.[4]

Once the parties agree to follow the ground rules, the mediator leads through the mediation process.


## 3.  MEDIATION: AN OVERVIEW

At a basic level, mediation is negotiation carried out with the assistance of a third party. The mediator, in contrast to an arbitrator or judge, has no power to impose an outcome on disputing parties.

Mediation is not a new process. We can find references to mediation and mediators throughout recorded history:

> Kings and Queens frequently mediated the disputes of neighbouring nations. Priest, shamans and wise men mediated disputes arising in their communities. Jesus Christ is referred to as the mediator between God and men.[5]

Although the word "mediator" does not appear in the Holy Koran, there are at least 46 references to a "helper" and, at a fundamental level, this is the role of the mediator.

A more formalized and ritualized form of mediation (the "Western Mediation Model") has grown rapidly in the United States and Canada in the last 20 years and is now adapting and spreading to other parts of the world.

In the Western Mediation Model, "mediation" is defined as "the intervention into a dispute or negotiation of an acceptable, impartial and neutral third party who has no decision making authority, but who will assist the parties in finding a solution which acceptably meets their interests".

The rapid growth has been fuelled by the benefits commonly associated with the mediation process. A list of these benefits includes the following:

•    **Cost Efficiency.** Mediation has proven to significantly reduce the monetary costs associated with dispute resolution when compared with arbitration or traditional litigation.

•    **Timeliness.** Mediation can significantly reduce the duration of the

---

[4] *Ibid.*
[5] Holy Bible, 1 Timothy, 2:5.

dispute as well as the amount of individuals' time actually required to bring the dispute to resolution.

- **Confidentiality.** Like arbitration, mediation is generally a confidential process making it preferable to the public dispute resolution of the court system.

- **Face Saving.** Related to confidentiality, it is simply true that an effective mediator can assist all parties in finding an acceptable solution and still save face — individual dignity remains intact.

- **Durability and Sustainability.** Resolutions crafted by the disputants in mediation appear to be more durable than outcomes imposed by a court or arbitrator.

- **Relationships.** Mediation can be less damaging to the relationship between disputants than traditional court processes — an important consideration where the future integration of the parties is a factor.

- **Control over Outcome.** In mediation, the disputants agree on their own resolution to the dispute. A court or arbitrator does not impose it.

- **Creativity.** Mediation encourages disputants to think "outside the box" and consider creative solutions to their dispute that go far beyond what a judge or arbitrator could order.

- **User Friendly.** People that have participated in mediations have reported that they find the process much more satisfying than the traditional court process.

- **Transformation.** It is suggested that mediation provides the opportunity for individuals to better understand the perspective of others and that this "acknowledgement" leads to personal empowerment that can be transformative for the parties involved.

At the same time, it is important to realize that the Western Mediation Model has had its detractors. Concerns raised about the process have included the following:

- **Justice.** Some are concerned about whether or not just results are being obtained in mediation. The confidential nature of the process makes it difficult to answer this question.

- **Verification of Benefits.** Although the Western Mediation Model has seen growing popularity, there remain few reliable, longitudinal studies of the benefits of mediation.

- **Qualifications and Standards.** At present there is no commonly accepted professional accreditation process for mediators. Various jurisdictions have established guidelines and a variety of mediator umbrella organizations exist. Still there is concern about the appropriate qualifications for mediators as well as controversy regarding standards of mediation practice.

- **Professionalization.** Related to qualifications and standards, there is a perceptible trend towards professionalization of mediation. Some are concerned that this will create unnecessary and undesirable barriers to accessing a proven helpful process.

- **Private or Public.** Should mediators be employed by the state as part of the justice system or should mediation service be provided by the private sector?

- **Mandatory or Voluntary.** In its early development, the Western Mediation Model was seen as a voluntary dispute resolution process. However, in recent years, a number of jurisdictions have made mediation a mandatory aspect of their court systems.

The discussion of benefits and concerns swirling around mediation was brought to a head by a controversial book in 1994 in which the authors[6] grappled with the question: what is the real purpose of mediation? In answering the question they identified four "stories" that people tell about the mediation process. These stories may be summarized as follows:

- **The Satisfaction Story.** The purpose of mediation is to provide a dispute resolution process that is faster, cheaper and more satisfying than litigation.

- **The Social Justice Story.** The purpose of mediation is to provide a forum in which the sub-dominant individuals and organizations in society can converse as equals with the dominant ones and create solutions to their problems.

- **The Oppression Story.** The purpose of mediation is to allow the dom-

[6] Robert A. Baruch Bush and Joseph P. Folger, *The Promise of Mediation: Responding to Conflict Through Empowerment and Recognition*, Jossey-Bass, San Francisco, 1994.

inant to maintain their hegemony. This is why it is so popular among the powerful institutions in the public and private sector.

- **The Transformation Story.** The mediation process provides an opportunity for people to talk with one another. This creates the opportunity for one person to acknowledge the perspective of the other person that, in turn, empowers the other person to similarly acknowledge the perspective of the first person. This leads to a transformation in which the parties see their dispute and themselves more clearly.

Folger and Bush also identified two distinct models of mediation:

- **The Problem Solving Model.** Focussing on a resolution of the presenting dispute; and

- **The Transformative Model.** Focussing on addressing the opportunity for transformation thereby dealing with the underlying root cause of the dispute.

It is clear that what has been referred to here as the Western Mediation Model and the Problem Solving Model are one and the same. The popularity of this model has been due to the telling of the "Satisfaction Story" identified by the authors of *The Promise of Mediation.*

Real life experience in mediation reveals that the choices about which Story to tell and which model to use are not so clear cut. In many mediations, echoes of all of the four stories can be discerned and there is room for a mediator to combine the best elements of the Problem Solving and the Transformative Models in assisting parties to find a mutually acceptable resolution to their dispute.

## 4. OVERVIEW OF THE STAGES OF MEDIATION

### (a) Pre-Mediation

- Involvement by the mediator at this stage will depend upon the framework in which mediation occurs. If there is an established mediation process in an organization or through a service provider, much of the pre-mediation may take place on an administrative level. Where the mediation must be custom designed, there will be greater pre-mediation involvement on the part of the mediator.

- Initial contact with the parties.
- Educating the parties about the process and establishing the ground rules for mediation.
- Mediation Agreement/Mediation Rules.
- Begin to set the tone for effective mediation.
- Identifying the time, venue and attendees.
- Identifying the information needs of the parties and the mediator.
- Obtaining mediation briefs from each party.
- Establishing credibility of the process and the mediator.
- Preparing the mediation site.
- Preparation for the mediation session.

### (b) Introduction

- Introduction of participants, establish rapport, set positive tone.
- Description of the process.
- Establishing "buy-in" to the ground rules, execution of mediation agreement, verification of time frame.
- Clarification of roles and behavioural guidelines.
- Verification of authority to settle.
- Obtaining commitment to explore options and demonstrate flexibility.
- Clarification of the use of caucus and confidentiality.
- Opportunity for questions.

### (c) Identifying Issues/Setting Agenda

- Opening statements from each party establishing the issues.
- Identification and agreement upon broad topic areas and key issues.
- Identification of areas of agreement.
- Expression and understanding of each party's point of view.
- Neutral organization and framing of the issues.
- Agreement on the topics for discussion and the sequence.

### (d) Discussion/Identifying Interests

- Exchanging of information and ensuring understanding.
- Probing for interests — substantive, procedural, psychological.
- Identification and exploration of assumptions.
- Breaking down issues into manageable components.

- Searching for objective criteria.
- Discourage "bottom lining".
- Backing up from positions to find common ground.
- Identification of points of agreement and overlapping interests.
- Maintaining pace and movement.
- Building empathy and managing emotional climate.

### (e) Negotiation/Considering Options for Settlement

- Generation of options.
- Offers and counter offers.
- Solidifying and building on points of agreement.
- Caucus.
- Building on overlapping interests (usually procedural and psychological).
- Evaluating BATNAs — risk analysis/cost-benefit analysis.
- Testing options using objective criteria developed by the parties.
- Reality and practicality checks.

### (f) Final Stage

- Probing and clarifying agreements reached to eliminate ambiguity.
- Documenting agreements.
- Agreeing on procedural and implementation steps.
- Developing agreement on alternative processes if a final agreement is not reached.

## 5. WHAT MEDIATORS DO: SKILLS, TASKS AND ATTRIBUTES

While many mediators argue that what they do is more of an "art" than a science, others have identified the following five types of activities:

- **Investigation.** Mediators engage in intensive investigation of the facts behind the dispute early during the case. For the most part, this takes the form of questioning spokespersons and other team members in a caucus. Under this heading, the mediator performs two functions at once: obtaining hard information, sometimes information the party did not want to give; and demonstrating to the same party some potential holes in its point of view.

- **Empathy.** Mediators take various steps to try to establish empathy with the disputants. This tends to occur at the same time as investigative attempts. Mediators are willing to hear and discuss matters of concern to the parties or individual team members, which were not necessarily "relevant" to the dispute.

- **Persuasion.** Mediators attempt to obtain concessions early in the mediation process, at a relatively low level, and typically these efforts rise in intensity during each case. Though one mediator may start out at a level of intensity that resembled another's last-ditch effort, it is the progression, not the general level, which is significant. The progression in intensity signifies to parties both the mediator's rising self-confidence in pressing for concessions (based on an increased understanding of the dispute) and the increasing need for action as the dispute draws to a head.

- **Invention.** Mediator attempts to create solutions to an issue, or more likely a series of potential solutions, are generally reserved until after the mediator has become intimately familiar with the parties' situation. An early attempt by the mediator to invent a solution may appear condescending to the parties, even when the mediator happens to find the "right" answer. Attempts by the mediator to come up with an invented solution early in the mediation generally fail.

- **Distraction.** Mediators distract the parties regularly. This could be described as a function of entertainment; some mediators describe it as the "vaudeville element" in mediation. Distraction, such as jokes or other conversation on "light" topics, is frequently necessary in order to keep the parties from assuming a "set" which sours the atmosphere and makes settlement more difficult.

Some have refined the foregoing list into two basic categories: Tasks and Attributes. The following is not an exhaustive list of mediator tasks and attributes, but it is a good starting point. Some commentators have pointed out that the terms used here arise predominantly in North American culture and that these lists may need to be revised extensively for use in other societies.

**(a) Tasks**

- **Gathering Background Information**

  - Read the case file to learn about the background and disputants.
  - Gather background information on a case from negotiators or other mediators (e.g., settlement patterns in similar cases).
  - Read legal or other technical materials to obtain background information.
  - Read and follow procedures, instructions, schedules and deadlines.

- **Facilitating Communication**

  - Meet disputants and make introductions.
  - Explain the mediation process to disputants.
  - Answer disputants' questions about mediation.
  - Listen to disputants describe problems and issues.
  - Ask neutral, open-ended questions to elicit information.
  - Summarize/paraphrase disputants' statements.
  - Establish atmosphere in which anger and tension are expressed constructively.
  - Focus the discussion on issues (i.e., not personalities or emotions).
  - Convey respect and neutrality to the parties.

- **Communicating Information to Others**

  - Refer disputants to specialists (e.g., accountants, engineers, subject matter experts) or other services, or bring such specialists into the mediation process.
  - Refer disputants to sources of information about their legal rights and recourses.

- **Analysing Information**

  - Help the parties define and clarify the issues in a case.
  - Help the parties distinguish between important issues and those of lesser importance.
  - Help the parties detect and address hidden issues.
  - Analyse the interpersonal dynamics of a dispute.

- **Facilitating Agreement**

  - Assist the parties to develop options.
  - Assist the parties to evaluate alternative solutions.
  - Assess parties' readiness to resolve issues.
  - Emphasize areas of agreement.
  - Clarify and frame specific agreement points.
  - Clearly convey to parties, and help parties understand, limitations to possible agreement.
  - Level with the parties about the consequences of non-agreement.

- **Managing Cases**

  - Estimate the scope, intensity and contentiousness of a case.
  - Ask questions to determine whether mediation service is justified or appropriate.
  - Ask questions to determine appropriate departures from usual practice for a given situation.
  - Terminate or defer mediation where appropriate.

- **Documenting Information**

  - Draft agreements between disputants.

## (b) Knowledge, Skills, Abilities, and Other Attributes

- **Reasoning.** To reason logically and analytically, effectively distinguishing issues and questioning assumptions.

- **Analysing.** To assimilate large quantities of varied information into logical ideas or concepts.

- **Problem Solving.** To generate, assess and prioritize alternative solutions to a problem, or help the parties do so.

- **Reading Comprehension.** To read and comprehend written materials.

- **Writing.** To write clearly and concisely, using neutral language.

- **Oral Communication.** To speak with clarity, and to listen carefully and empathetically.

- **Non-verbal Communication.** To use voice inflection, gestures, and eye contact appropriately.

- **Interviewing.** To obtain and process information from others, eliciting information, listening actively, and facilitating an exchange of information.

- **Emotional Stability/Maturity.** To remain calm and level-headed in stressful and emotional situations.

- **Sensitivity.** To recognize a variety of emotions and respond appropriately.

- **Integrity.** To be responsible, ethical and honest.

- **Impartiality.** To maintain an open mind about different points of view.

- **Organizing.** To manage effectively activities, records and other materials.

- **Following Procedure.** To follow agreed-upon procedures.

- **Commitment.** Interest in helping others to resolve conflict.

## 6. PREPARATION FOR MEDIATION

### (a) Is Mediation Appropriate?

The first thing that must be determined is whether mediation is the best form of dispute resolution for the client. The *Rules of Professional Conduct* state that "the lawyer should consider" ADR and "if instructed, take steps to pursue those options."[7] Arguably, this imposes a duty on lawyers to consult with clients concerning mediation in all cases. Practically speaking, this gives clients the right to choose whether or not to pursue mediation. The lawyer should help the client determine whether a particular dispute is appropriate for mediation, when mediation might be most effective, and what type of mediation is needed.

It is generally agreed that mediation works best where the parties wish to continue their relationship in some capacity. Factors to consider in determining whether mediation is appropriate include:

- the nature of the case and prior dealings between the parties;
- the relationship of the parties;
- the nature of relief sought by the plaintiff; and

---

[7] *Rules of Professional Conduct*, Province of Ontario, Rule 10 at Commentary 6A.

• the size and complexity of the claim.[8]

In addition, mediation may not be appropriate in disputes involving important matters of legal principle that ought to be decided by the courts in the interests of the parties and in the public interest.

Overall, the decision about whether or not to mediate cannot be made by adhering to strict rules. Mediation can be conducted in many ways with many goals, and the best rule for lawyers is to consider each case individually. Familiarity with the different processes and experience will assist lawyers in determining whether their client will be best served by mediation.

### (b)  Key Considerations of Mediator Training

Key considerations of mediator training include:

• **Much of mediation is common sense.** The training should help you recognize the mediation practices that you are already using, discover inherent abilities, and use mediation in all aspects of your life.

• **There is no prescribed or "right way" to conduct a mediation.** Mediators are craftspeople. They use the same essential processes, tools and skills, but apply them in unique ways as fits the individual mediator's talents, the needs of the disputants and the nature of the dispute.

• **This training will not make you a master mediator.** The processes and skills can be taught, but the ability to use these tools requires practice and experience in real life disputes. The purpose of the training is to equip you with the tools of mediation. Mastering mediation means developing your personal approach.

### (c)  Choosing a Mediator

The best way to choose a mediator who has training and experience in interest based mediation is to consult with other lawyers who have undergone mediation in similar circumstances, or select from the roster of court-connected mediators compiled by the office of the local ADR co-ordinator. In choosing a mediator, it is useful to ask the following questions:

---

[8] Stephen Goldberg, Nancy Rogers and Frank Sander, *Dispute Resolution*, Toronto: Little, Brown and Co., 1992, p. 436.

- How does the mediator typically conduct a mediation? Are there private caucuses?
- What is the mediator's knowledge about the court process? What is his or her background?
- Where will the mediation session be held?
- What is the mediator's hourly fee?[9]

The most important characteristic of any mediator is a commitment to impartiality and neutrality.[10] A skilled mediator committed to these fundamental principles will be able to tailor a particular mediation to suit the needs and interests of the parties.

## (d)  Roles at Mediation

Prior to the mediation, the roles of the client and the lawyer at mediation should be discussed. The lawyer should make sure that the client understands that the mediation is an opportunity for active participation of the client. Tentative decisions should be made about what areas the client or lawyer will lead in the discussion, depending on the client's comfort and expertise.[11]

## (e)  Initial Meeting

The initial meeting with the mediator allows the parties to voice their intentions and expectations. The initial meeting should not serve as a first meeting in the mediation process, but as a short general meeting to:

- complete the screening process;
- establish intentions (both the mediator's and the disputant's);
- determine the disputant's expectations as to preferred outcomes;
- enable the disputants to evaluate the mediator face to face (this could include a review of credentials and experience);
- apprise the disputants of the expected duration and probable costs;
- formalize the mediation engagement with the completion of an agreement to mediate, contract to mediate or an engagement letter;

---

[9] Brochure: Ottawa Court Connected Mediation.
[10] Riskin, *supra*, note 1, p. 210.
[11] *The Commercial Mediation Practice Handbook*, Arbitration and Mediation Institute of Canada Inc., February 1998, p. 2-11.

- determine if production of documents or written presentation should be made available to the disputants and the mediator in advance of the next meeting.[12]

The initial meeting allows the mediator to make a preliminary assessment of the dynamics of both the disputants and their counsel. In addition, it provides the mediator an opportunity to build trust and rapport with the disputants.

## (f) Parties

For a mediation to be successful it is important that the parties are well prepared. Knowledge of the file is an integral part of that preparation. In order to be fully prepared, the lawyer should work with the client to analyse and identify:

- the facts of the case;
- the strengths and weaknesses in the case;
- the outstanding issues;
- the client's interests;
- criteria to be used in calculations and valuations;
- the perceived interests of the other party;
- possible settlement options;
- the client's best and worst alternatives to a negotiated settlement.[13]

A client's best alternative to a negotiated agreement (BATNA) is the best result the client can hope to achieve if a settlement cannot be negotiated. It is important for each party to identify their BATNA since it enables them to determine whether a negotiated agreement is in the party's best interest.

A client's worst alternative to a negotiated agreement (WATNA) is the potentially unacceptable outcome if the parties are unable to come to a negotiated agreement. Considering one's WATNA helps to assess potential alternatives and may increase commitment towards more cooperative conflict resolution.[14]

Under the current court-connected program, each of the parties is required to provide a Statement of Issues to the other side and to the mediator. The lawyer should assist the client in preparing this statement. In

---

[12] *Ibid.*, p. 8-3.
[13] *Ibid.*, p. 2-10.
[14] *Ibid.*, p. 6-5.

terms of identifying the issues, it is important that the lawyer and client identify not only the obvious issues in dispute, but all the issues or underlying interests affecting the dispute.

### (g)  Authority to Settle

It is important that the parties engaged in the mediation have the authority to settle the dispute. The ADR Institute of Canada explains that "the 'authority to settle being at the table' enables the development of a true 'settlement synergy' which is not possible if authority has to be obtained from persons who are outside the process."[15] It is also important to the settlement process that those who make the decision have "hands on" knowledge of the issues, the interests and the process which developed the settlement.

## 7.  THE MEDIATION AGREEMENT

There are two keys to mediation: the first is the desire of the disputing parties to come to the "table", the second is finding the appropriate agreement. The essence of mediation is the dynamic negotiation which exists between the parties. The role of the mediator is to facilitate negotiation between the parties using the methods and skills of a trained mediator.

The mediation agreement is normally signed prior to the commencement of the mediation. The parties may engage a Private Mediator (Example A) or engage a Mediation Organization which has its own mediation rules (Example B). The essential purpose of the mediation agreement is to ensure that the mediation proceeds smoothly. It must be emphasized that mediation is a dynamic process.

## Example "A" – Sample Commercial Mediation Agreement

## AGREEMENT TO MEDIATE

Case Name:
Date of Mediation:

This **Agreement to Mediate** is made as of the date indicated on the signing

---

[15] *Ibid.*, p. 9-4.

page hereof between the Parties named on the signing page (the "Parties") and (the "Mediator").

The Parties are involved in a dispute and wish to attempt to resolve the dispute through mediation using the services of the Mediator.

The Parties agree as follows:

1. Mediation is a voluntary and informal settlement process by which the Parties try to reach a solution that is responsive to their interests. The signing of this document is evidence of the agreement of the Parties to conduct this mediation process in an honest and forthright manner and to make a serious attempt to resolve the outstanding matters.

2. The Mediator agrees to serve as mediator in connection with this matter.

3. The Mediator is a neutral facilitator who will assist the Parties to reach their own settlement. The Mediator does not offer legal advice and has no duty to assert or protect the legal rights of any Party, to raise any issue not raised by the Parties themselves or to determine who should participate in the mediation. The Mediator has no duty to ensure the enforceability or validity of any agreement reached.

4. It is understood that full disclosure of all relevant information is essential to the mediation process. Accordingly, there will be a complete and honest disclosure by each of the Parties to the other and to the Mediator of all relevant information and documents.

5. Each Party shall provide a written summary of no more than five (5) pages summarizing their perspective on the dispute. This summary shall be provided to the Mediator and the other Parties no later than one week prior to the scheduled commencement of the mediation event.

6. The mediation event shall be attended by the Parties and their legal counsel, and such other individuals as each of the Parties may believe would be helpful in resolving this matter; provided that notice of such additional parties shall be provided to the other Parties prior to the commencement of the mediation event. The mediation shall commence at a time, date and location mutually convenient to the Parties and to be arranged by the Parties or their Counsel.

7. The representatives of the Parties have full, unqualified authority to reach a settlement in this matter.

8. The Parties agree that they will not call the Mediator as a witness for any purpose whatsoever. No party will seek access to any documents

prepared for or delivered to the Mediator in connection with the mediation including any records or notes of the Mediator.

9. Statements made by any person and documents produced in the mediation and not otherwise discoverable shall not be subject to disclosure through discovery or any other process and shall not be admissible into evidence in any context for any purpose including impeaching credibility.

10. Other than what is stated above, the mediation is a confidential process and the Parties agree to keep all communications and information forming part of this mediation in confidence. The only exception to this is disclosure for purposes of enforcing any settlement agreement reached. The Mediator will not voluntarily disclose to anyone who is not a party to the mediation anything said or done or any materials submitted to the Mediator, except:

   10.1 to any person designated or retained by any party, as deemed appropriate or necessary by the Mediator;

   10.2 for research or educational purposes on an anonymous basis;

   10.3 where ordered to do so by judicial authority or where required to do so by law; or

   10.4 where the information suggests an actual or potential threat to human life or safety.

11. Mediation is a voluntary process and may be terminated by any Party to this Agreement at any time and for any reason.

12. The estimated fees and expenses for this mediation and the basis upon which they are calculated are set out in Schedule "A". The Parties agree that the fees and expenses of the mediation shall be paid by the Parties equally.

13. The Parties hereby jointly and severally covenant and agree to indemnify and save the Mediator harmless for any and all liability, cost, claims, demands, proceedings and causes of actions, howsoever arising under this Agreement or as a result of the conduct of the mediation and its consequences, provided that the Mediator has carried out his or her duties honestly.

14. This Agreement shall be made and construed in accordance with the laws of the _____.

15. This Agreement may be executed by the Parties and the Mediator in separate counterparts each of which when so executed and delivered shall be an original, but all such counterparts shall together constitute one and the same instrument. This Agreement shall enure to the benefit of and be binding upon the Parties and the Mediator, their heirs, executors, administrators, successors and assigns.

IN WITNESS WHEREOF the Parties have signed this Agreement as of this _____ day of _____, 200_____.

**Party**                                    **Party**

**Per:** _____      **Per:** _____
**Authorized signing officer**      **Authorized signing officer**

_____

**Mediator**

## Example "B" – Sample Mediation Agreement Adopting Organization's Rules

Date:

The parties hereby agree to private and confidential non-binding mediation of a dispute pursuant to the attached Rules of Procedure of the [Organization] and hereby adopt and incorporate by reference said Rules with the following modifications:

The parties have selected and _____ has agreed to serve as the Mediator of the dispute, and the parties agree to pay the Mediator an hourly fee of $_____, plus reasonable expenses and costs incurred within 30 days after the submission by the Mediator of a statement for said fees, expenses and costs.

The parties and their counsel agree that mediation shall constitute confidential settlement negotiations. Statements made in mediation shall not be admissible in any legal proceeding, and neither the Mediator nor the [Organization] shall be made a party to, or called as a witness in, any legal proceedings.

The parties have caused this Mediation Agreement to be duly executed as of the date first set forth above.

## 8.  THE ADVANTAGES OF MEDIATION

### (a)  Informal

The relatively informal nature of mediation, as compared to other forms of ADR and conventional litigation, allows the parties to feel more comfortable and be less intimidated by the dispute resolution process.

### (b)  Empowering

Mediation resolves disputes through a process that calls upon personal effort, creativity, and understanding of others' points of view and experience. While in litigation the parties are simply observers; in mediation the process is structured to value everyone's participation. The parties are empowered to, and do, make their own mutually agreeable decision to settle. This process of including the parties in the resolution process builds self-esteem, promotes self-reliance and leads to a positive dynamic culminating in a settlement in which the parties have an "ownership interest".

### (c)  Confidential

Normally, mediation sessions are held in private and all proceedings are confidential to the mediator and the parties. The "terms of mediation" that the participants agree to before entering mediation typically provide that the process is "without prejudice" and that the mediator cannot be called upon to give evidence, in any subsequent action, on any matters that took place during the mediation session. This encourages frank discussion and full disclosure.

### (d)  Final

Mediation can provide a cathartic effect, producing the opportunity for "closure". The terms of a Memorandum of Agreement reached through mediation are not subject to appeal, and are therefore final. *Thus, one should not forget to put a dispute resolution clause in the agreement reached at the mediation itself.*

### (e)  Preserves Ongoing Relationships

The mediation process tries to address all parties' interests and seeks to accommodate a "win, win solution". This helps to preserve and promote future relationships and provide a model for resolving future disputes.

### (f)  Encourages Tailored, Workable Solutions

Mediation is limited only by the creativity of the participants. Tailored solutions that fit their needs can be explored and created. Of course this is a sharp distinction to the imposition of statutorily defined penalties or remedies that the law offers. Some of the imaginative resolutions available through mediation include:

• providing an apology or acknowledging some degree of culpability; and
• gathering independent expert evaluation.

### (g)  Timely

Inconvenience to the parties is minimized because of the flexibility inherent in the process — place and time can be scheduled on consent of the parties with little or no delay. Mediation is not controlled by court dates and waiting periods for decisions to be handed down.

### (h)  Cost Efficient

Disputes handled through mediation are most often settled for a fraction of the cost of a formal hearing process.

## 9.  THE DISADVANTAGES OF MEDIATION

The greatest disadvantage of mediation is that it can make the dispute worse, or one party, in subtle bad faith, can use the process to dash the settlement hopes. The very freedom that permits the parties to deal directly with one another enables a more powerful party to seek to emotionally intimidate the weaker.

## (a) Voluntary

Mediation is only successful if the parties agree to "go to the table". Obviously this is a fundamental hurdle. This is not a problem if mediation is compulsory.

## (b) Not Always Appropriate

It is well recognized that mediation is not appropriate for all disputes. Legal process and legal rights safeguard individual and societal interests which can be circumvented and undermined by private settlement. The Task Force Report of the Canadian Bar Association stated:

> The Task Force recognizes, however, that it may not be appropriate in all cases to focus on dispute resolution in isolation from "victory". Many cases involve important matters of legal principle that ought to be decided by the courts in the interests of the parties and in the public interest . . . As well, litigation often brings to light issues that demonstrate a specific instance of a more generic problem requiring public attention and reform.[16]

Also in *Wilson v. Canada (Attorney General)*,[17] the Court held that mediation may not be appropriate in resolving Charter disputes. Constitutional cases which involve issues paramount to societal concern must have the ability to influence and shape future conduct and to prompt necessary behavioural changes. This requires adjudication within a public forum where the public interest is represented and binding decisions are rendered.

## (c) Success Not Guaranteed

Mediation cannot make the claim of being successful in every case. If an agreement is not reached by the parties, then arguably mediation has only served to delay litigation and add to the overall expense of resolving

---

[16] *Report of the Canadian Bar Association Task Force on Alternative Dispute Resolution: A Canadian Perspective,* Ottawa: Canadian Bar Foundation, 1989.

[17] [1998] O.J. No. 1780, 1998 CarswellOnt 1836 (Master).

the dispute. However, even if a settlement is not reached mediation can still be a worthwhile process. In *Rundle v. Kruspe*, Master Beaudoin points out:

> A settlement is not the only success outcome of a mediation. If the parties can narrow the issues in the dispute or, at the very least, can come away with a better understanding of the other sides' position, the mediation can still be considered a success.[18]

### (d)  Power Imbalances

Mediation may not be suitable if there is a substantial power imbalance between the parties. While power imbalances are inherent in every dispute, the presence of parties around a table in the presence of a mediator is a dynamic that may create a balance and symmetry amongst the parties.

### (e)  Inconsistent Outcomes

The outcomes generated though mediation are dependent on the parties and the mediator, possibly leading to inconsistent and unpredictable outcomes.

### (f)  Confidentiality

Mediation may be either open or closed by the decision of the parties. It is normally closed. In open mediation, anything that is discussed by the parties and the mediator can later be used at trial. Each party to the mediation is considered to be both a competent and compellable witness in any proceeding that may arise. Closed mediation, on the other hand, holds that anything said by any of the parties involved in the mediation is considered privileged, and therefore cannot be brought up in court. In closed mediation situations, the mediator, at the end of the mediation process, may only report whether the disputants have, in fact, reached a settlement. No other terms may be disclosed and none of the parties are considered competent or compellable witnesses with respect to anything that was discussed during the mediation process. The concepts of open and closed mediation are widely recognized both by academic and legislative authorities.

The next important concept to grasp in discussing confidentiality is that mediation currently remains a largely unregulated process. As a result,

---

[18]  [1998] O.J. No. 2078, 1998 CarswellOnt 2193 (Master) at para 17.

the mediation environment is contract based. The aforementioned concepts of open and closed mediation are by no means exhaustive. The parties are generally free to structure the terms of mediation as they wish, including those terms relating to confidentiality. However, as mediation becomes more accepted as a valid and sound form of dispute resolution, it will become increasingly more standardized and regulated. The current non-standardized and unregulated state of mediation is a double-edged sword. While some standardization is clearly required in order to control the quality of mediation and to make the rules more certain, the ability of the parties to freely design the terms of the mediation process serves as an important asset in making mediation more attractive to prospective users. In terms of confidentiality, then, as a general rule the parties are free to structure their confidentiality agreement any way they wish.

In understanding issues of confidentiality in mediation, there are several relationships which must be considered. Firstly, there is the relationship between the solicitor and client. Secondly, there is the relationship between each party and the mediator. Finally, one must consider the relationship between the parties themselves.

### (g)  The Solicitor-Client Relationship

The solicitor-client relationship is the least problematic of the three relationships described above. Solicitors have strict rules of professional conduct that regulate their relationships with their clients. These rules do not change in the case of mediation. In terms of confidentiality, the solicitor-client relationship can best be thought of in two ways. First, the laws of evidence hold that information passing between a solicitor and client is privileged from court proceedings. Second, a lawyer's professional responsibility to the client requires that the solicitor not reveal any information that passes between the solicitor and the client without the express permission of the client. The basis for these obligations is well documented, and it is not my intention to review them here.

### (h)  Consequences of a Breach of Confidentiality

It follows that if the mediation process is governed primarily by contract, should there be a breach of said contract, an action for damages will ensue. Should a party to the mediation, who is bound by a contractual term requiring confidentiality, reveal anything stated during the course of mediation to a third party, then the revealing party can be sued for resulting damages. While this is true enough in theory, breaches of confidentiality that result in lawsuits are extremely rare.

## 10. ABUSING THE PROCESS OF MEDIATION

### (a)  Using the Process in Bad Faith

Since the mediation process currently occurs without strict guidelines binding those who decide to use it, there exists a strong potential that a party may attempt to use the process in bad faith. This so called "bad faith" may arise as a result of many different motives. Most frequently, it is thought that parties abuse the process by getting opposing sides to reveal their cases without having any intention of settling or having the dispute properly mediated.

Another possible motive for using the mediation process in bad faith is where a party wishes to intimidate the opposing side. In this situation, a party may attempt to harass, intimidate, and verbally abuse the other party in an attempt to scare them away from pursuing their case. This difficulty is illusory because if the parties are on such unequal footing to begin with, they should not be in mediation. It is the responsibility of counsel to ensure that their client's situation is properly suited to mediation. Furthermore, a party who is being intimidated during the mediation process may simply walk away from the mediation at any time without any strings attached. Counsel must be sensitive to the progress made during the mediation and should be attentive to any discomfort that a client feels. There should not be any reluctance on the part of counsel to advise a client to walk away from mediation if it is proving to be detrimental.

Finally, using the process of mediation as a means of stalling the settlement of a dispute is another frequently cited criticism. Stalling occurs where one party participates in the mediation with the sole purpose of dragging it out. While it is true that mediation may take some time to initiate, the length of this time is limited. Furthermore, once commenced, mediation by its very nature is streamlined. Any use of the process to stonewall will become readily apparent, and the opposing party is free to simply stop the process at will. The time loss, given such a scenario, is minimal. Mediation is, therefore, not realistically worth pursuing as a method of stalling. Still, it is important for counsel to monitor the progress and to act if it feels that the process is being abused in this way.

As mentioned, the most frequently cited criticism of the mediation process is that it sets up the situation where one party may seek to expose the other side's case whereas they, in fact, may have no intention of settling or having the dispute mediated. Although in theory, this belief may seem intuitive, in practice it is more fiction than fact. While it is true that mediation does foster and require a fair degree of trust which may eventually lead to open discussions regarding the dispute, as discussed above, the courts will not allow these communications to be admitted as evidence. Provided the formalities regarding confidentiality are attended to (i.e., putting a confidentiality clause in your agreement), the court will attach a common law privilege to any communications made.

Furthermore, if mediation is commenced once there is a view to litigation, as is often the case, these negotiations may also be considered "without prejudice" as they are in furtherance of settlement in accordance with the *Rules of Civil Procedure*, as mentioned. Although the *Rules of Civil Procedure* discuss "offers to settle", it is quite likely that any discussions during mediation may be broadly construed by the courts as constituting parts of an eventual offer to settle.

## 11. LAWYERS' ROLE IN MEDIATION

In disputes which are already in litigation, or in cases which involve disputants' vital interest, the parties may wish to have their legal counsel involved in the mediation. Lawyers play a diverse role in the mediation process. They may: act as advisors of parties to mediation; be asked to review mediated agreements; refer clients to competent mediators; help prepare their clients for mediation; themselves act as mediators; or design, engineer or sponsor mediation programs.[19]

According to the ADR Canada:

Lawyers can make significant contributions to the mediation process and can greatly increase the possibility of a successful settlement being reached if they understand the dynamics of the mediation process and use the appropriate skills.[20]

The skills required by a lawyer at mediation are essentially:

---

[19] Riskin, *supra*, note 1, p. 205.
[20] *The Commercial Mediation Practice Handbook, supra*, note 11, p. 2-9.

... collaborative communication skills such as active listening and open-ended questioning. Lawyers should understand their own client's interests and the solutions that will satisfy those interests while also trying to understand the interests of the other party. A lawyer has to be prepared to help develop options that will satisfy the interests of both parties and encourage her/his client to walk in the other party's shoes.[21]

The traditional "adversarial" role will likely not be effective in a mediation which requires a "problem solving" approach. In order to fully respond to the needs of clients, lawyers must learn to see beyond the immediate dispute and consider the emotional, economic and community interests of their clients.

## 12. THE PSYCHOLOGY OF MEDIATION

### (a) Lighting the Way

It is critical that counsel appreciate that mediation can unleash strong psychological forces. This phenomenon, if creative and positive, accounts for the ability of mediation to arrive at solutions constructed outside the narrow confines of the actual dispute. In such a case, mediation is excitingly dynamic and satisfying as deep, and often hidden, concerns have been satisfied. Unfortunately, the reverse phenomenon is also true. If counsel are not careful, the hostility generated in the mediation will make the dispute worse. In such a case, unleashed factors will drive the parties further apart.

Mediation is a dynamic conflict resolution process in which people, personalities and defence mechanisms are at play. For this reason, the mediator and counsel must understand human psychology and the characteristics which are needed to allow the participants in conflict to communicate effectively with one another.

### (b) Mediation is Not Therapy

Although mediation does offer therapeutic release by permitting a venting of frustration and an expression of one's emotions and position, it is not to be confused with psychoanalysis. Although mediation permits the expression of feelings and involves skills on the part of the mediator which

---

[21] *Ibid.*, p. 2-11.

are employed by a therapist, mediation is not therapy. Mediation and therapy both deal with people who are often trying to resolve certain problems, but they do not share the same objective.

> Mediation is a form of problem solving, and the problem to be solved is usually concrete, specific, and wordly rather than internal, emotional, and general. Mediators must deal with the strong feelings and emotional tangles of the parties to the dispute but their focus in doing so is to foster agreement, not healing.[22]

Both mediation and psychology deal with human beings in conflicting situations who must try to find their own way through the darkened path with the help of a guiding third party who will try to shed light on the road lying ahead.

> The mediation process allows the parties to express and deal with some of the underlying feelings which may be fuelling their dispute and preventing settlement. The mediator validates and acknowledges such feelings and their effects upon the negotiation process but does not attempt to help the parties understand or necessarily change their behaviour.[23]

Nonetheless, both the mediator and the therapist adopt similar behaviours to frame their sessions. For example, although their language, style and objectives will differ, both mediators and therapists will strive to remain impartial throughout the process. The mediator is essentially trying to sail the parties through the stormy waters of negotiation and compromise in order for them to reach an agreement.

> Despite the differences, there is a great deal of overlap in how mediators and couples therapists work. Both will intervene to see that feelings do not become too explosive, to ensure certain levels of communication, and to focus clients back on the issues they say they want to work on. Both also tend to facilitate movement of a couple from past grievances to future plans; this focus is, in fact, at the very heart of mediation while it is a discretionary, tactical choice for the therapist.[24]

---

[22] Michael Meltsner, "The Jagged Line Between Mediation and Couples Therapy", *Negotiation Journal*, Vol. 9, No. 3, July 1993, p. 263.

[23] Judith P. Ryan, "ADR Practioner: Practice Tips for Lawyers Who Would Be Mediators", *The Canadian Journal of Dispute Resolution*, No. 1, August 1994, p. 8.

[24] *Supra*, note 22, p. 263.

## (c)  People must be Treated with Respect

Another reason mediation is so effective is that it answers people's needs to be heard, respected and empowered. In mediation it is important for the mediator to treat the parties equally in a respectful manner which will enable them to feel at ease in the process. While the court process is caught up in its formalities, mediation can easily be adapted to the parties sitting around the table. While mediation does not follow formal rules of procedure or presentation of evidence, it remains important that all of its participants treat one another with courtesy, dignity and respect.

> As the large body of research on the psychology of procedure has shown (see generally Lind & Tyler, 1989; Tyler, 1990), people all over the world value the law when it treats them with respect — when it offers them a voice in a context in which they are treated with politeness and dignity in a state of equality. The solemnity and majesty of the legal process match the seriousness of the concerns to which it responds and the values that it protects and pro-motes.[25]
>
> . . .
>
> In social science, research also has shown that, regardless of the adversariness of the prevailing legal process, people value procedures in which they are treated with respect and given a say in matters pertaining to them (Lind & Tyler, 1988).[26]

## (d)  Freedom to Decide

A mediator should be aware that people generally do not like to be caged by the will of others. For this reason, mediation answers the freedom sought by the individual when confronted with a conflictual situation — the freedom to choose the outcome. Therefore, mediation enables the parties to deal with their problems without becoming prisoners of the adversarial process which can leave them at the mercy of other players. If it is true that all the world is a stage and each must play his or her part, when the curtain rises in the mediation process the concerned parties are permitted to assume their role and personally deliver their lines.

---

[25] Gary B. Melton, "The Law Is a Good Thing (Psychology Is, Too): Human Rights in Psychological Jurisprudence", *Law and Human Behaviour*, Vol. 16, No. 4, 1992, p. 385.

[26] *Ibid.*, p. 387.

In mediation, an issue is important if the parties define it to be so. In court, an issue is important only if the judicial system deems it to be so.[27]

## (e) Active Participant

Mediation empowers the parties because it makes them active participants in the resolution of their conflict. It enables people to find creative solutions by better understanding their own emotions as well as comprehending the needs of the other parties. The mediator therefore acts as a facilitator between the individuals, while trying to maintain a certain degree of balance between them. The mediator often acts as a bridge between two islands.

> The core of mediation is reconnecting people to their own inner wisdom or common sense . . . The role of the mediator — insofar as any therapy takes place in mediation — is to put people back in touch with their own decision-making process and the common sense that has taken them through life so far.[28]

## (f) Power Imbalances

Poor self-esteem, poverty, race, gender and class can cause significant power imbalances in a mediation. Should mediators strive to maintain balance in the mediation? The danger of this lies in how the mediator views the power imbalance. Since everything is a question of perception, the mediator must be acutely aware of his or her own biases and prejudices. The mediator must struggle against a deep rooted human trait to side with the party he or she favours. Also, a mediator who would interfere too much could be seen as being biased. Nonetheless, "mediators make a clear distinction between managing the process and managing the content of the dispute — the former is considered empowering and the later, disempowering".[29] In the context of mediation control is therefore exercised over the process, but not in exercising influence in the discussion or decisions which are being taken by the parties.

---

[27] John M. Haynes, "Mediation and Therapy: an Alternative View", *Mediation Quarterly*, Vol. 10, No. 1, Fall 1992, p. 32.
[28] *Ibid.*, p. 26.
[29] Sara Cobb, "Empowerment and Mediation: A Narrative Perspective", *Negotiation Journal*, Vol. 9, No. 3, July 1993, p. 248.

## (g)  Dynamics of Conflict

When trying to resolve a problem, one must understand the underlying dynamics which have led to the conflict. For example, when a couple is having difficulties in their relationship, emotions such as anger, sorrow and confusion have to be expressed before the conflict can be resolved. That is why mediation helps people deal with their conflicts in a constructive manner — it does not impose or judge, it listens and answers its own questions.

> The rehabilitative/developmental model of empowerment reflects the stages of the mediation process itself (Swift and Levin, 1987). The first stage terminates with the awareness of self-interests and the development of a "position", that is, individuals become cognizant of their own needs (which are constructed or displayed in the public and private sessions of mediation). The second stage includes the acknowledgment of strong feelings with respect to this position (i.e., "venting"). And the third stage terminates in the purposive moves that persons undertake to meet those needs (i.e., the mediation agreement).[30]

The process of mediation is not always an easy one, but more parties are embarking upon what was once the road less travelled. To truly understand the dynamics of mediation, one must be familiar with the complexity of human personalities and the dynamics of conflict resolution. Mediation has taught us that people are not always looking to have their conflicts settled by others from a legal perspective. Sometimes what the parties need is a chance to tell their side of the story without being interrupted. Other times they are looking for an apology or even the opportunity to simply vent their frustrations. Although there are different types of personalties, people generally want the opportunity to be heard, to be respected and also to resolve their conflicts.

Mediation is about human conflict resolution and the psychological dynamics which surround the process. The mediator must therefore possess certain qualities which enable him to insightfully draw upon the experiences shared by the parties to lead them towards a better understanding of the options which are available to them. Since mediation involves people or groups in conflict, psychological skills are required to guide the parties through the journey towards compromise and understanding.

---

[30] *Ibid.*, p. 246.

As the practice of mediation becomes more widespread, and as more people come in contact with it, our inability to define standards of quality may well result in increasing numbers of people who are adversely affected by mediation and who consequently become opponents of the practice.[31]

Therefore, it is important that mediators are not only familiar with the conflict situation presented to them, but to also be aware of the participants seated around the table. For example, a different tone should be set if the mediation deals with a divorcing couple rather than two corporations who are arguing about the interpretation given to their contractual obligations.

The mediator must be a mirror of its participants — he should be a chameleon — not one who sets the tone but one who monitors it and blends with the different colours of each member's personality. Therefore, the mediator must make the participants feel at ease, while letting them truly express their views and their emotions at the opportune time.

The mediation process allows for the safe and productive expression of feelings. Suppressed or prematurely expressed feelings can kill — ourselves and others . . . If you are denied recovery from hurt, the next step is to deny the hurt, to deny the feelings. Of course, that doesn't work either. The price is to deny your intelligence, deny your spontaneity, deny your creativity, and often to wreak havoc on your body. As Anais Nin (1943) wrote, "When one is pretending, the body rebels."[32]

### (h)  Road to Reconciliation

The mediator is a neutral party who lets people express their feelings while keeping them on the road towards reconciliation. Although the success of the journey depends on the parties, one should not overlook the importance of the mediator. The mediator should obviously be someone who is at ease with people and gives the impression that he or she truly cares about the parties and their conflict. The mediator is someone who mirrors what the participants are saying by actively listening to their stories with an open mind and without judging their thoughts or their actions. When one mediates, one should not only be aware of what people are saying, but also what they are expressing without words. Being in touch with the feelings of the participants can be done by understanding body language, acknowledging

---

[31] Christopher Honeyman, "On Evaluating Mediators", *Negotiation Journal*, Vol. 6, No. 1, January 1990, p. 23.

[32] Albie M. Davis, "The Logic Behind the Magic of Mediation", *Negotiation Journal*, Vol. 5, No. 1, January 1989, p. 21.

the need for silence or by granting a pause in the process. It has been recognized that the mediator:

(1)   manages conflict by either intervening to block its excessive expression or stimulating disagreement when withdrawal or other cues suggest agreement is passive or superficial;

(2)   relentlessly insists that participants not get "position-bound" — in short, urges the parties to examine and possibly revise their positions in light of their larger interests, often the interdependence of those interests with the interests of others;

(3)   focuses the parties on the present interests (rather than past grievances) and the manner in which those interests might look in the future;

(4)   tells the parties the way the world outside of the consulting room (judges, lawyers, children, relatives) may view their arrangements;

(5)   gathers data and shares information so that options can be generated and serious negotiation can take place; and

(6)   helps to produce an articulated agreement.[33]

In order to achieve these objectives, the mediator must be able to recognize and acknowledge the needs and the concerns of the participants. The mediator must also be able to get the people sitting around the table to open up and lower their protective armour. When asked what skills were necessary to be a mediator, students at a Middle School in Massachusetts responded confidence, patience, active listening, caring about people, calmness, the ability to ask good questions, silence, open minded and not taking sides.[34]

As we develop in experience, we sometimes forget that the most effective solutions are often the most simple. We intellectualize, theorize, analyse, draw complex arguments and expect bureaucratic systems to effectively answer our needs and resolve our conflicts.

If the law is to confirm the importance of the individual, then the meaning of the ideas in the law should match common understanding, the assumption in the law should not falsify or mystify experience, and the law should protect those interests that are most critical subjectively to maintenance of dignity.[35]

---

[33]   *Supra*, note 22, p. 262.

[34]   Albie M. Davis, "What Makes a Good Mediator? As a Middle School Student", *Negotiation Journal*, Vol. 10, No. 1, January 1994, p. 88.

[35]   *Supra*, note 25, p. 385.

## (i) Humour and Mediation

The mediator tries to get rid of all the formalities and side issues by enabling the parties to focus on what they really want to resolve. Mediation is not about law — mediation is about people in conflict. To mediate one must be learned in the art of human behaviour and group interaction. The mediator resembles the therapist because both use mirroring techniques to enable people to find the answers to their questions. Therefore, a mediator is someone who has observed human beings and simply lends his or her expertise to the parties who may be too involved in the process to be able to see it from a different perspective — the neutral third party permits the parties to see their conflict in a new light. One way of rendering the mediation process more enjoyable is by utilizing humour as a quality for successful mediation.

> The use of humour during the dispute resolution, whether the topic is family mediation, labour arbitration, public policy dispute settlements, or whatever can reduce tension, as well as create social cohesion among the parties. It can also encourage creativity, thereby resulting in other positive effects on the progress and outcome of the session.[36]

When thinking of mediation or skills necessary to be a successful mediator, one may not think of the importance of having the ability to make people laugh. It would seem though that humour can be strategically employed in the mediation process to help reduce the tension level between the parties, create a bond between them, and help them reach an agreement. In addition to relieving tension and creating bonds between individuals, humour can also be used to ease the psychological pain of the parties as well as serving as a coping mechanism.[37]

> One of the main social functions of humour in a group is the lessening of tension and conflicts" (Ziv 1984, 32). The relief of tension not only serves the parties, it also can help the process as well as the mediator.[38]
>
> . . .

Another recognized function of humour is that of building social relationships.

---

[36] Karen N. King, "But I'm Not a Funny Person . . . : The Use of Humor in Dispute Resolution", *Negotiation Journal*, Vol. 4, No. 2, April 1988, p. 119.

[37] Ansgar M. Wimmer, "The Jolly Mediator: Some Serious Thoughts About Humor", *Negotiation Journal*, Vol. 10, No. 3, July 1994, p. 194.

[38] *Ibid.*

> When one person shares a humorous observation with another, a feeling of closeness is created that tends to reduce the divisions that separate them . . . Humour that bonds individuals together in a dispute resolution setting increases the likelihood of a positive outcome.[39]

It has also been shown that laughter broadens the parties perspective by allowing them the opportunity to distance themselves from their immediate conflictual situation.[40] When a humorous incident arises during mediation, it can serve as an emotional break for the parties and help the mediation process to continue. "It is a way of inviting people to distance themselves, to separate their ego and their self-esteem from that issue."[41]

Another benefit of humour is that because it creates a break in the process, it can actually be used not only to diffuse tension, but also give the parties time to collect their thoughts and to gain a new perspective. As one mediator puts it: "I know that I use stories or change the subject to give the parties a break to think about something. It may be that, at the back of their minds, they realize they have to give that concession and they are not ready to give in."[42] It has also been noted that humour can be used to help parties distance themselves from their counter-productive emotions such as anger and frustration. Humour can therefore also be beneficial as a "strategy mediators can use to help parties vent their anger and therefore limit its negative impact."[43] Humour is an effective method of reducing the threat level of the mediation while providing security for its participants. Positive humour creates bonds between people which leads to a lowering of the protective armours one wears when confronted with a conflictual situation.

> A mediator is most successful when he or she has the trust of the participants and trust comes with a sense of connection and commonality. Whether it's a joke that you all laugh about together or something else, it just sort of brings out the humanity and the connection between people.[44]

Although humour has many advantages, we must also focus on the shortcomings of using humour during mediation. Let it not be forgotten that humour "is a double-edged sword, and it is generally sharp on both sides".[45] Therefore, one must use humour in a thoughtful and insightful way.

---

[39] *Supra*, note 36, p. 120.
[40] *Supra*, note 37, p. 194.
[41] *Ibid.*
[42] *Ibid.*
[43] *Ibid.*
[44] *Ibid.*, p. 195.
[45] *Ibid.*, p. 196.

As previously mentioned, humour has the ability of creating a bond between the parties, but it can be detrimental to the resolution of the issue if it is used to exclude certain parties to the mediation. Therefore, "if used improperly and to the detriment of the weaker party, such a technique can invalidate and discredit the whole concept of mediation."[46]

Humour should also never be used to ridicule someone's rationale or to make fun of his or her personality. Therefore, the mediator must be quite sensitive to the group dynamic, and humour should be employed accordingly. For example, when "the level of hostility is high, the tension-reducing capability of humour disappears and its use will only increase anger."[47]

The type of humour which works well in mediation is one that makes people feel good about themselves and helps them cope with the stress of resolving their conflict. It is a humour which is liberating and entertaining. It is not a humour which degrades or ostracizes the participants. It is not funny if it excludes people or makes them feel defensive. This is why it is important to understand the psychology of human dynamics when dealing with humour in a conflict resolution situation. It takes timing, sensitivity and a sense of humour adapted to the audience.

The psychology of humour shows us the "importance of humour in identifying the ability to distract and entertain as one qualification for mediators in addition to such talents as empathy, investigation, innovation, and the capacity to persuade."[48]

As we have seen, although mediation is not therapy, it does empower itself in the depths of human psychology. In mediation the solution lies in the creativity of the players. When the parties embark upon the road to reconciliation, they are guided by the mediator who will enable them to see the possibilities which are open to them. Mediation is not about preconceived ideas, precedents or legal expectations.

Mediation allows the parties to explore the unchartered waters which are found outside the realm of the legal system. Therefore, it is important to understand people when one is involved in the mediation process because the focus is on the parties and the resolution is in their hands. The journey of mediation involves understanding on the part of its guide and acceptance on the part of its players.

---

[46] *Ibid.*, p. 198.
[47] *Supra*, note 36, p. 122.
[48] *Supra*, note 37, p. 193.

## 13. LAWYERS AND THE PSYCHOLOGY OF MEDIATION

The psychological nature of mediation often means that lawyers are uncomfortable in the process. The most carefully drafted mediation brief and "opening statement" can be quickly subsumed as the parties unleash emotional barrages. As the lawyer watches a carefully constructed mediation strategy unravel, he or she is doubly concerned that the mediator is encouraging the unravelling to "arrive at the parties' true interests". Lawyers must be prepared to take charge and stop mediation if they perceive that hostility — not healing, ruthlessness — not resolution, are evident. This requires a sensitivity and perceptiveness since, ironically, the clash and din of the outbursts may be the very catharsis required to break the logjam of dispute.

## 14. THE MEDIATION BRIEF

What a great advocacy opportunity the drafting of the mediation brief provides! The thorough, well-constructed and persuasive brief can have a very direct impact on whether the mediation session leads to a settlement, perhaps on the conclusion of the session or perhaps later, or not at all.

Whereas a trial allows parties in conflict an opportunity to try to persuade a judge or jury to accept their respective versions of a set of facts behind a dispute, the mediation session allows parties in conflict an opportunity to come face to face, together with an impartial mediator, to present to each other their own respective version of the facts out of which the conflict arose and their particular interests relating to it. The goal is that they will be able to mutually decide on a course of action to bring closure to the conflict without the involvement, or further involvement, of the state through the vehicle of the courts. Though the mediation session may explore the parties' respective legal rights, the greater emphasis is on the points where the parties' needs and concerns with respect to the outcome of the conflict converge to create a mutual base in which to ground a settlement of their differences. The mediation brief attempts to set the stage for an interest based or principled negotiation. It serves as an important tool in facilitating the achievement of the ultimate goal of a collaborative resolution.

The mediation brief lays out the playing field for the mediation session itself, especially when it is first to be served on various parties and the mediator. The process of preparing the mediation brief will focus the drafter's attention on the questions of fact and the major legal issues that will have to be resolved before the dispute between the parties can be concluded, either through settlement or by judicial determination if the matter goes that far, as well as on the strategies that the circumstances of the particular dispute will require. Examples of strategies requiring consideration in this regard might be the best manner in which to handle multiple plaintiffs or multiple defendants or perhaps the impact that an insurance coverage dispute may have on achieving settlement between the plaintiff and the defendant.

As well, the preparation and serving of a mediation brief in advance of the mediation session allows the time during which the parties and mediator are together in the mediation session to be dedicated to focussed discussion and negotiation without much time being consumed in establishing the basic facts of the dispute or the positions being held by the parties. The effective use of mediation session time will always be a concern because, as in most areas of business, time is money. This is particularly so when the mediation session is being conducted as part of a litigation process where a certain number of mediator hours are available at a reduced hourly rate that is prescribed by a jurisdiction's rules of civil procedure and which will increase once the statutorily required hours have been maximized, allowing the mediator's normal professional billing rate, which is always higher, to apply.

Further, the mediation brief also establishes the groundwork for the future litigation process, should litigation even be necessary after the mediation session has been concluded. Once prepared in electronic format, the facts and issues drafted in the mediation brief can be rejigged easily into any required form because the basic facts and issues requiring consideration will not change. Such further steps may well include everything from the drafting of a statement of claim or defence to the conducting of examinations for discovery and to the drafting of *facta* on motions, the settlement conference brief and the pre-trial conference brief right through to the drafting of written or oral submissions at the end of the trial. Therefore, the time taken to prepare an excellent mediation brief can be leveraged over the remainder of the file to both counsel's and client's benefit. This obviously depends on the stage at which the mediation is being held in the dispute resolution process.

The KISS (Keep It Simple, Sweetie) rule of writing works well for mediation briefs as it does for all legal writing. The brief needs a beginning, a middle and an end with a point of view that is compelling but not exaggerated. It needs human elements in ordinary language that create a visual picture. It needs comprehensible sentences that are short and are written in plain English without legalese. It is critical to remember to tailor your brief to those you are trying to persuade. For example, a defence brief in a case where the plaintiff is an individual with a Grade 10 education should be geared to that plaintiff. The mediation brief is designed to impress both opposing counsel and their clients.

The format and content of the mediation brief are very much at the call of the drafter unless they have been statutorily prescribed and are susceptible to official sanction for non-compliance. Even where that is the case, the very nature of mediation as a process to bring the parties together to resolve their dispute demands flexibility and requires that the parties be allowed to personalize their own brief to meet their particular needs. Therefore, prescribed mediation brief form and content requirements are usually neither onerous nor rigorous. The Ontario *Rules of Civil Procedure* provide an example of a prescribed mediation brief. Rule 24.1.10 and its related Form 24.1C of the Ontario Rules require:

## PROCEDURE BEFORE MEDIATION SESSION

24.1.10 (1) *Statement of issues* — At least seven days before the mediation session, every party shall prepare a statement in Form 24.1C and provide a copy to every other party and to the mediator.

(2) The statement shall identify the factual and legal issues in dispute and briefly set out the position and interests of the party making the statement.

(3) The party making the statement shall attach to it any documents that the party considers of central importance in the action.

(4) *Copy of pleadings* — The plaintiff shall include a copy of the pleadings with the copy of the statement that is provided to the mediator.

(5) *Non-compliance* — If it is not practical to conduct a mediation session because a party fails to comply with subrule (1), the mediator shall cancel the session and immediately file with the mediation co-ordinator a certificate of non-compliance (Form 24.1D).

**Form 24.1C**

**STATEMENT OF ISSUES**

*(To be provided to mediator and parties at least seven days before the mediation session)*
1.   *Factual and legal issues in dispute*
The plaintiff (*or defendant*) states that the following factual and legal issues are in dispute and remain to be resolved.

*(Issues should be stated briefly and numbered consecutively.)*

*2.   Party's position and interests (what the party hopes to achieve)*
*(Brief summary.)*

*3.   Attached documents*
Attached to this form are the following documents that the plaintiff (*or* defendant) considers of central importance in the action: *(list)*

*(date)*                                    *(party's signature)*
                                          *(Name, address, telephone number and fax*
                                          *number of lawyer of party filing statement of*
                                          *issues, or of party)*

NOTE: When the plaintiff provides a copy of this form to the mediator, a copy of the pleadings shall also be included.

NOTE: Rule 24.1.14 provides as follows:
> All communications at a mediation session and the mediator's notes and records shall be deemed to be without prejudice settlement discussions.

The Ontario Rules allow for a fair amount of flexibility as this prescribed form establishes only the scantiest of requirements. Further, the mediation brief that does not comply with even these basic requirements will not attract sanction unless it becomes impractical to conduct the mediation session as a result of non-compliance. The sanction established by the Ontario Rules is the filing by the mediator of a certificate of non-compliance with the court which could be used by the opposing party to seek costs thrown away for that party's mediation preparation and attendance time and share of the mediator's fees. The costs of sanction could be sought either on a motion specifically brought in this regard or when making submissions with respect to costs at the conclusion of trial.

Some disputes call for the creation of an extensive mediation brief. The personal injury matter where both liability and damages are at issue, where contributory negligence must be factored into the equation and where there are claims for damages by family members would be one example of a situation where the mediation brief will have to cover a lot of ground. The commercial litigation resulting from the theft of a partnership by one of the partners is another such example. Some disputes will call for a simpler brief — the wintertime slip and fall in a Canadian parking lot left unsanded which results in a broken wrist, for example. Counsel must bring their professional judgment to bear on the determination of the extensiveness of the mediation brief required by the facts and circumstances behind the dispute. One consideration obviously to be kept in mind is the value of the claim. Plaintiff clients simply cannot afford to pay for the costs of preparing an extensive mediation brief when the real damages value of the claim is low and most of the settlement funds received would in actual fact go to cover the cost of preparing the brief. Another consideration in the preparation of a plaintiff client's brief is whether there is in reality any liability on the part of the defendant. The costs for the preparation of a mediation brief in a circumstance where the defendant's liability is significantly uncertain will have to come either from a client unable to obtain settlement funds or from counsel's pocket as fees and, potentially, disbursements are written off.

Whether the circumstances demand an extensive mediation brief or an abbreviated brief, the mediation brief should present an overview of the fact situation out of which the dispute between the parties arises. The mediation brief should tell your client's story of the event or events out of which the dispute arises: the what, the where, the how and the when of it. It should also present the party's thoughts on why the event occurred: the defendant rear-ended your client's car because she was distracted while talking on a cell phone; the plaintiff braked suddenly and, without signalling, attempted a left turn into a driveway causing your client, the defendant, to rear-end her. Although each of the parties will already have a good idea as to the matter in contention, the mediator will not, and this overview allows the mediator to consider the parties' issues and interests within the context of the events that have led to the dispute in advance of the mediation session. It will also allow your clients the opportunity to gain some empathy, or even sympathy, for the position in which they find themselves.

The mediation brief should also state the factual issues in dispute, the legal issues in dispute, and the drafting party's position on those factual and legal issues. A lengthy legal brief of all relevant case law is neither necessary nor desirable as the point of the mediation session is not to establish the strict legal rights of the parties in the matter but to move the parties away from focussing on their strict legal rights toward the compromises that will allow for settlement. However, where there is a judicial decision or other authority upon which a legal position is based, it may be helpful for the case citation and a synopsis of the case to be included in the brief along with a statement as to the applicability of the case to the facts at hand. For example, if there are key issues of contributory negligence, counsel would do well to include in their mediation briefs their understanding of the leading case law. Stressing the supporting case law will, at the very least, underscore the risk and uncertainty of the litigation process and for this reason is helpful in the mediation context.

As well, any documentation of significance with respect to the dispute upon which the party is relying should be attached to the brief, together with a notation as to the respective document's significance.

A party will want to consider carefully how much of its actual position is to be disclosed to the opposing party. Potentially, where a plaintiff announces the lowest bottom line figure it will accept for a settlement and a defendant announces its actual highest limit past which it will not pay one penny more, there is no room for further discussion or negotiation. Further discussion, however, could result in a settlement which provides the plaintiff with more than its bottom line figure and also allow the defendant to pay less than its uppermost limit. The party would be better off to include in its brief a declaration of interests and positions allowing for flexibility and giving the mediator scope to broker a deal between the parties that will be more mutually beneficial than a hard and fast statement of firm positions would allow. However, where a defendant truly denies any liability whatsoever with respect to a plaintiff's loss, that fact should be made patently clear, together with the reasons for the denial in the mediation brief. Where the defendant is willing to concede that there may be liability but does not wish to prejudice its right to plead no liability in the future, the defendant can indicate in its brief: "For the purposes of this mediation and on a without prejudice basis only, liability is not denied". This should allow the parties to avoid wasting time on an issue that, in fact, is secondary to the greater issue of establishing a settlement figure that will allow plaintiff and defendant to walk away from the dispute. In most cases, it is helpful to at least set the stage with precise numbers and basis of calculation (including, where applicable, interest calculations and net present value assumptions). For example, in the Statement of Claim, counsel have claimed $150,000.00 non-pecuniary damages. In the context of the mediation brief there is little danger in counsel setting forth a reduced yet assertive and realistic assessment of general damages. This can set the stage for meaningful discussions at the mediation and can also be seen as the "first offer" from which one could expect to draw a response from the other side. If an expert's reports have been obtained to support damage claims these should be included in the brief so that the mediator can have something to work with.

The one thing that has no place in a mediation brief is sniping directed at the opposing party or counsel. Whereas the tone of a mediation brief need not be conciliatory, it must at least not present a highly-charged negative attitude either against other parties or against the mediation process if it is to aid the parties to achieve settlement. Comments such as "Mr. Plaintiff is intensely resentful of the insulting offers of settlement previously put forward by the defendants" detract from any positive sense of mutual commitment to work toward settlement or even from a position of neutrality. A statement of this nature is like throwing down the glove, if not a call to battle, rather than a simple shaking of hands, as the parties prepare to try to resolve their differences in a non-litigious setting.

There are powerful mediation briefs of seven pages and powerful mediation briefs of 65 pages. There are also ineffective mediation briefs of seven pages and ineffective mediation briefs of 65 pages. The ineffective mediation brief, no matter of what length, is frequently one that has been drafted on the morning of the day on which it is due, if not later. It often follows a *pro forma* precedent of a mediation brief prepared in an earlier file without giving any flavour of the particular parties and the particular circumstances underlying the dispute to be mediated in the present instance. And it has usually been prepared without any sense of the opportunity it presents to move the parties forward to settlement.

The mediation brief will be a success if it moves the other side to come to some empathy for the position in which your client finds itself with respect to the dispute. This allows the parties to go into the mediation session in a positive atmosphere of decreased litigation tension and with a sense that compromises can be made and settlement achieved by the parties themselves without the assistance of the courts or other adjudicative bodies.

# 7

# Mediation in Real Life

## 1. CONDUCT OF A MEDIATION

Mediation actually involves a continuous flow of activity and interaction. Nevertheless, as part of preparing for mediation it is important for the lawyer to describe the typical conduct of a mediation to the client.

### (a) Mediator's Opening Statement

The content of the mediator's opening statement will vary depending on the complexity of the dispute, the sophistication of the parties, and whether or not an initial meeting was held. However, the common objectives are to introduce the parties to each other and to the process, discuss the ground rules, answer any questions and obtain a commitment to begin the process. The following list prepared by the ADR Institute of Canada outlines the common objectives of the mediator's opening statement in more detail:

### Purpose

- To make face to face introductions.
- To establish a positive tone.
- To educate the parties about the negotiation/mediation process.
- To reach an agreement on rules/protocol/standards of behaviour.
- To obtain a commitment to begin the process.

### Procedure

- Introduce yourself as the mediator.

- Welcome the parties and affirm their willingness to discuss the issues or negotiate a settlement.
- Review why people are there in neutral terms.
- Explain that the mediation process is:
    - An attempt by the parties to reach their own agreement through discussions or negotiations.
    - Voluntary.
- Explain your role:
    - Neutral/Impartial — Process assistance.
    - You are not the decision maker.
- Explain the limits of confidentiality.
- Describe the problem-solving process:
    - Each person will make an opening presentation.
    - Participants will agree on topics for discussion.
    - Participants will create an agenda.
    - Participants will educate each other about their interests or needs.
    - Participants will discuss agenda items one by one.
    - Participants will look for solutions that are mutually satisfactory.
    - Any agreement will be written down and formalized according to disputants desires.
- Describe the process and desirability of legal counsel and review prior to, during and at the end of negotiations.
- Describe the use of private meetings (caucus).
- Identify with the parties procedural guidelines that will help them negotiate more effectively.
- Ask for and answer questions raised by parties.
- Obtain the whole-hearted consent to begin from each party.[1]

The mediator's opening statement in the joint session serves as the foundation upon which the parties can start to build the resolution of the conflict. Typically the mediator will be attempting to establish a relaxed, informal tone and put parties at ease. There is no one perfect statement for all occasions but the following is a list of matters to consider for the opening statement:

---

[1] *The Commercial Mediation Practice Handbook*, Arbitration and Mediation Institute of Canada Inc., February 1998, p. 10-5.

## Welcome participants

- Introduce mediator (perhaps a word or two about mediator's background).
- Introduce everyone else — names and roles in the mediation.
- Congratulate the parties on undertaking this process.
- Thank them for the opportunity to assist them.
- Comment on facilities, temperature, washrooms, refreshments, etc.
- Get the parties OK to spend a few moments to describe the mediation process.
- Describe the process and the mediator's role.
- Confirm time arrangements.
- Suggest guidelines (listening, no interruptions, civility, respect, etc.).
- Ask if the parties have other guidelines.
- Confirm provisions of agreement to mediate (confidentiality, no prejudice, voluntary, authority to settle, fees — if appropriate).
- Discuss caucus — why, how, when — confidentiality.
- Tell the parties they have every right to be optimistic that this matter can be resolved in a way that meets their interests — and, it will be up to them.
- If agreement is reached it can be documented here today.
- Ask the parties if they have any other suggestions or questions about the process.
- Get them to buy-in — "Are you willing to proceed with this session in the manner I've described?"
- Call for opening statements from the parties.

## (b) Parties' Opening Statements

Following the mediator's opening statement, each party is invited to present their understanding of the matters in dispute. In other words, the parties are to tell their side of the story. The presentation should be objective and include all supporting evidence. If there are collaborating presenters, such as lawyers, witnesses or neutral experts, they should be included as part of the opening statement.

The decision on who speaks first may vary depending on the type of dispute, the temperament of the parties, or the policy of the mediator. However, the mediator should ensure that the person speaking second understands that he or she should not present his or her story in the form of a response to, or critique of, the first presentation. The second party should present their story in the same independent manner as the first party. The opportunity for rebuttal will come after the storytelling is finished.[2]

These opening statements are important because they give the parties an opportunity to vent their feelings and to have their uninterrupted say. They also provide the other party with an opportunity to hear the "other side of the story".

### (c)  Exploring Interests

Next, the parties will discuss the issues in detail and communicate their interests and underlying positions. This way the parties can gain mutual understanding of what is important to each of them, their motivations, and concerns. Here it is important for the mediator to break the issues down into manageable components, and help avoid reaching premature assessments and agreements.

### (d)  Generating and Assessing Options for Settlement

At this stage, also known as brainstorming, the parties begin to focus on possible options. Multiple options are generated at first without judgment or analysis. As many ideas as possible should be generated. The more ideas the better the chances are of coming up with a final product which meets everyone's needs. When properly facilitated, brainstorming stimulates a greater range of higher quality creative thinking than those involved would generate on their own.

Once the creative process is complete, the parties should review and confirm their stated interests and determine how well the options satisfy those interests. The options are assessed in terms of how they benefit one party without detracting from the interests or benefits received by the other. The options are modified and eliminated based on the ability to satisfy interests.

### (e)  Caucusing

"Caucus" refers to the separate meetings that mediators will have with parties during mediation. In mediation it is generally preferable to have direct discussions take place with all parties present for the following reasons:

---

[2] *Ibid.*, p. 10-6.

- The communications are more effective.
- Clarification is easier.
- There is an opportunity to develop an "acknowledgment/empowerment" loop which can lead to transformation.
- There are no secrets — nothing is hidden.

## (f)  Reasons for Caucus

There may be times when the mediator or the parties will feel that the interests of effective conflict resolution are best served by a caucus or separate meeting. These separate meetings serve to:

- **Maintain confidentiality.** Some parties are reluctant to talk in front of the other party. The confidentiality of the private session allows parties to tell you sensitive information that may be critical to finding a solution to the dispute.

- **Divert hostility.** Sometimes people are afraid to show their hostility to the person with whom they are having a dispute. Nevertheless, it is important to express the hostility in order to move on to more productive work. During private meetings, the mediator may draw out this hostility and create a safe place for venting.

- **Filter out negatives.** Often important information is overshadowed by the negative manner in which it is delivered. The mediator can separate the information from negative connotations.

- **Explore settlement possibilities in safety.** The mediator can explore possibilities more safely with each party alone. This way a party is not "put on the spot" in front of the other party.

- **Educate the parties.** Sometimes the mediator can assist the parties in negotiating more rationally so that settlement can be achieved.

- **Stroke the parties.** The parties can be complimented and made to feel good about the progress they have made so far.

- **Refocus the parties.** Joint sessions sometimes are taken up with discussions or arguments over issues that are not relevant to the dispute. If this cannot be controlled in the joint session, separate sessions can be used to focus the parties on the dispute.

- **Overcome an impasse.** When parties find that they simply cannot talk to each other anymore, private meetings help to keep the discussion moving.

## (g)  Risks of Caucusing

The mediator and the parties need to be aware of some of the risks associated with caucusing, including:

*   Negotiations slow down or become disjointed.
*   Suspicion and paranoia increase.
*   Mediator appears to lose impartiality.
*   Parties feel ganged up on.
*   Mediator has challenges with confidentiality.

## (h)  Some Basic Guidelines for Caucusing

There are many different models of mediation and the attitude towards caucusing is different for each model. The following "default" guidelines are offered for your consideration:

*   Don't caucus too soon.
*   Don't caucus too long.
*   Don't caucus too often.
*   Generally, caucus with both parties.
*   Be clear on confidentiality "defaults".
*   Give reasons for caucusing — make sure everyone knows that anyone can call.
*   Summarize the caucus when joint session resumes.
*   Generally, don't negotiate between parties in caucus — don't play "shuttle diplomacy".

Caucusing entails the mediator holding separate private meetings with each of the parties. A caucus may be held at any time at the request of either the mediator or one of the parties. Not all mediations call for the use of caucusing. For example, where there is a high level of trust and respect between the parties and full disclosure has been made, a caucus might not be necessary. However, in the majority of mediations caucusing is not only productive but necessary.

The caucus can be used for a variety of reasons such as to:

- seek, impart, or clarify sensitive information in a secure and safe environment;
- educate, re-educate the mediator, parties or counsel;
- deal with confusion in the process;
- allow the participants to vent without jeopardizing the mediation process, defuse excessive anger;
- allow each party to develop settlement options in private;
- provide an opportunity for the parties to ask for help which they may be reluctant to do in a joint session; and
- facilitate a "meeting of minds" between and among negotiating teams whose members are not seeing eye to eye.[3]

## (i)  Termination

The mediation session generally ends with an agreement, a need for further mediation, or termination of the process. Following a successful mediation session where a mutually acceptable agreement is reached, a settlement agreement must be drafted. It is important that lawyers ensure that their client's interests are properly represented in the mediation agreement. It may be useful for the lawyer to keep accurate notes of what transpires during the mediation and draft the details of the agreement as soon as possible following the mediation.

Typically, postponement or adjournment of a mediation session is to be avoided. Mediations develop a "momentum of agreement" that facilitates settlement.[4] If it is necessary to adjourn, the lawyers should ensure that the next session will be held as soon as possible. This will ensure that the momentum is not lost, and will reduce the need for the mediator to re-establish a relationship with the parties.

Either party has the right to withdraw from the mediation at any time. To terminate a mediation, the lawyer and client should be certain that the parties are deadlocked and unwilling to move.[5] This reinforces the need to seek the opinion of the mediator who may have an enhanced perspective as a result of private caucuses. As well, if a mediator feels that the decision to withdraw is unwarranted, premature or the result of a misunderstanding, then the mediator should attempt to reverse the decision.

---

[3] *Ibid.*, p. 6-9.
[4] Norman Brand, "Learning to Use the Mediation Process — A Guide for Lawyers", December 1992, *Arbitration Journal*, Vol. 47, No. 4, p. 12.
[5] *Ibid.*, p. 13.

A useful technique that the mediator may use to accomplish this is to call a recess and ask the withdrawing party to "Please give me 10 minutes in caucus before making the decision final." The mediator will use this time to give the party an opportunity to "cool down" and use empathy and persuasive skills to try and get a reversal of the decision to withdraw.[6]

## 2. THE CIRCLE OF CONFLICT: A TOOL FOR MEDIATORS

Conflict can be confusing. What is causing this conflict? What is the next right step towards the resolution of this conflict? These are questions that confront a mediator as he or she attempts to assist the disputants move towards settlement.

Effective mediators use tools to assist them in addressing these questions. The "Circle of Conflict" is such a tool. It has a dual purpose: diagnostic and strategic. It is a diagnostic tool because it can help mediators develop hypothesis about what is causing the conflict. It is a strategic tool because it can suggest a way forward — a strategy — that can assist in the resolution of the dispute.

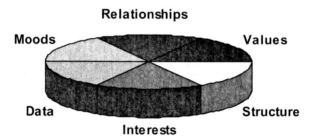

The Circle of Conflict is divided into six wedges — each wedge represents a potential cause or "driver" of conflict. These drivers are labeled, "Values", "Relationships", "Moods", "Data", "Structure" and "Interests".

The fact that the Circle of Conflict contains six drivers of conflict does not mean that each driver is present in each conflict. It may be that only one

---

[6] *The Commercial Mediation Practice Handbook, supra,* note 1, p. 10-12.

driver is the real cause of the dispute, or perhaps two or more drivers are operating in combination.

Let us review each of the drivers of conflict:

## (a) Values

This refers to people's belief systems about what is right and wrong, what is good and bad, just and unjust. Differing values or a perception of differing values can be a significant driver of conflict. It is the rare conflict that does not involve a difference of "values".

In the world at large, examples of values driving conflict might include examples such as:

- Communism vs. Capitalism
- "Life" vs. "Choice" in the abortion issue
- Pornography vs. Freedom of Speech

There are many other examples. But value differences also play a part in everyday commercial, consumer and labour disputes. In any situation where one of the disputants is saying, in effect, "We are the good guys and they are the bad guys", we can see an example of how values drive conflict.

## (b) Relationships

This refers to the past relationship between the parties. In many conflicts the present dispute is just the current manifestation of relationship problems from the past. Negative interactions in the past lead to negative stereotyping combined with strong negative emotion. Communication is usually poor or non-existent.

Relationship problems often play a role in smaller scale disputes as well. For example, in a labour/management dispute, it may be that problems from the past such as unresolved resentments will surface in the negotiation of a new issue. In consumer disputes, a negative experience of a customer in the past may be a factor in a fresh dispute occurring in the present. In a commercial setting, past unresolved disputes among shareholders will carry forward into a new issue.

The essence of the relationship driver is the past impacting heavily on the future and preventing parties from moving forward.

**(c) Moods**

This driver invites us to consider whether there may be factors unrelated to the present dispute that are affecting someone's ability to deal with the situation. This refers to psychological or physiological issues — minor or serious — that are impacting on someone's ability to deal with a dispute. It could be as minor as a quarrel at home with a spouse or child to something as serious as a life-threatening disease. Mediators must be aware that there may be other factors, unrelated to the dispute, which are affecting a party's ability to move towards resolution.

These three drivers: Values, Relationships and Moods are sometimes referred to as the "Hot 3" because they tend to generate most of the heat and frustration in a dispute. Let us move on to consider the three drivers in the bottom half of the Circle of Conflict.

**(d) Data**

Data problems can be a significant driver of conflict. These problems take many forms:

- Too little information.
- Too much information.
- Issues about relevance of information.
- Concerns about how data was collected.
- Concerns about how data was assessed.
- Differing expert opinions, including legal opinions.

Most disputes will have a data component.

**(e) Structure**

Some disputes are driven by the structure or environment within which they occur. Structural problems often have to do with a shortage of resources: not enough money; not enough time; not enough people. Other examples of structural problems include communication constraints and issues of organizational governance.

The essence of this driver is that something about the structure of the situation is contributing to the dispute.

## (f) Interests

"Interests" refer to the wants, needs and concerns of those involved in the dispute. Obviously, actual or perceived differences of interests will tend to be a driver of conflict.

It is helpful to divide interests into three categories: substantive, procedural and psychological.

- **Substantive interests** relate to the substance of the actual issue in dispute. For example, in a contract dispute the substantive interest of various parties is usually money. One party wants to receive more and the other party wants to pay less (or, even better, nothing). It will be seen that, generally, substantive interests are divergent.

- **Procedural interests** are interests related to the process by which the dispute will be resolved. There is often a joint procedural interest in having the dispute resolved quickly and inexpensively. This common interest is, in fact, one of the motivations for people becoming involved in mediation. In cases where the parties may have an ongoing relationship, there is often a common procedural interest in that relationship being harmonious.

- **Psychological interests** refer to human need for dignity and respect. For example, it is very difficult for people to admit they have been wrong. They will often have an interest in not having to admit they were wrong — in finding some way of resolving dispute without losing face. In other cases a heartfelt apology can go a long way towards resolving a dispute because it addresses the psychological interest (acknowledgement) of the party receiving the apology.

The mediator uses the Circle of Conflict as a diagnostic tool by reflecting on these drivers as they may relate to the dispute he or she is mediating. The mediator will develop a working hypothesis about what is really driving this conflict.

The Circle of Conflict also has a strategic purpose. It can help mediators plan the next right step in a mediation. The mediator will attempt to move the focus of the dispute from the top half of the circle to the bottom half. There are a number of reasons why the mediator will attempt this move in focus:

- The top part of the Circle is often more filled with emotion, whereas the bottom lends itself to a more rational approach.

- In the top part of the Circle, the focus is adversarial: one side versus the other; while in the bottom part of the Circle the focus can be on mutual problem solving: e.g., How do we obtain data that we can both rely on to resolve this dispute? What are the structural issues driving this conflict and how can we deal with them? How can we resolve this dispute in a way that acceptably addresses the interests of all parties?

- The focus in the top part of the Circle is on the past while the focus in the bottom part can be on the future. Successful mediations tend to focus on the future as opposed to the past.

The following are examples of what a mediator might say to try to refocus on the bottom part of the Circle of Conflict:

| Top of Circle | Bottom of Circle |
|---|---|
| If a disputant seems to be focused on relationships . . . | A mediator might say, "I can really appreciate how the history of this thing has left a bad taste for all parties. I'm sure there are things both parties wish hadn't happened. At the same time, we've got this present situation to deal with. Let's find an approach that will focus on the future—on finding a solution that will meet the real needs and concerns of all parties. Are you willing to work with me using that approach?" |
| If the disputant seems to be focused on values . . . | A mediator might say, "I'm hoping that all parties can move beyond 'right and wrong' – 'good guys/bad guys'. I'm sure you see that that kind of approach won't get us anywhere. Let's focus on what we need to move forward. Rather than focusing on who's right and who's wrong, let's ask the question, 'How can we resolve this in a way that will address the legitimate concerns of all parties?' Can we give that a try?" |
| If the disputant's moods seems to be an issue . . . | A mediator might say, "Look, it's obvious that you're upset or have something else on your mind today. You know that we've got to have a difficult discussion about these issues and we need to do it when everyone can focus on this situation in a positive way. Let's take a short break to reflect on what's been said and to see if we can come up with some strategies to move this issue towards resolution in a productive way. How's that sound to you?" |

## 3. RESPONDING TO CONFLICT

When we are involved in a conflict we often think we have only two choices: fight or flight. We can choose to stand up to the other person, be assertive and try to get what we want or we can choose to give in and allow the other person to win. We perhaps also believe that our own personalities make us more likely to choose one of these two options.

However, we can respond to conflict more effectively if we appreciate that there are five responses rather than just two. It is also helpful to know that while each person may have a response that is more natural to them, they also have the ability to use each of the five conflict handling modes.

The five conflict responses are as follows:

- **Competing** is assertive and uncooperative — an individual pursues his or her own concerns at the other person's expense. This is a power oriented mode in which one uses whatever power seems appropriate to win one's own position — one's ability to argue, one's rank, economic sanctions. Competing might mean "standing up for your rights", defending a position that you believe is correct, or simply trying to win.

- **Accommodating** is unassertive and cooperative — the opposite of competing. When accommodating, an individual neglects its own concerns to satisfy the concerns of the other person — there is an element of self-sacrifice in this mode. Accommodating might take the form of selfless generosity or charity, obeying another person's order when one would prefer not to, or yielding to another's point of view.

- **Avoiding** is unassertive and uncooperative — the individual does not immediately pursue its own concerns or those of the other person. It does not address the conflict. Avoiding might take the form of diplomatically sidestepping an issue, postponing an issue until a better time, or simply withdrawing from a threatening situation.

- **Collaborating** is both assertive and cooperative — the opposite of avoiding. Collaborating involves an attempt to work with the other person to find some solution that fully satisfies the concerns of both persons. It means digging into an issue to identify the underlying concerns of the two individuals and to find an alternative that meets both sets of concerns. Collaborating between two persons might take the form of exploring a disagreement to learn from each other's insights, concluding to resolve some condition which would otherwise have them competing for resources, or confronting and trying to find a creative solution to an interpersonal problem.

- **Compromising** is intermediate in both assertiveness and cooperativeness. The objective is to find some expedient, mutually acceptable solution that partially satisfies both parties. It falls on a middle ground between competing and accommodating. Compromising gives up more than competing but less than accommodating. Likewise, it addresses an issue more directly than avoiding, but doesn't explore it in as much depth as collaborating. Compromising might mean splitting the difference, exchanging concessions, or seeking a quick middle-ground position.

These five responses can be illustrated on the x/y axis shown below:

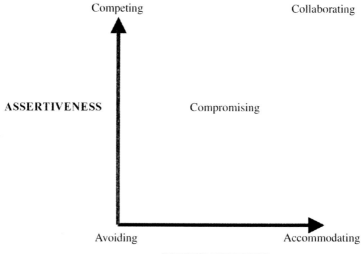

## (a)  The Appropriate Response

Now let us consider the circumstances in which it may be appropriate to use each of the five conflict handling modes:

The **Competing** response is appropriate:

- when quick, decisive action is vital, e.g., emergencies;

- for important issues where unpopular courses of action need implementing e.g. cost cutting, enforcing unpopular rules, discipline;
- for issues vital to organizational welfare when you know you are right; and
- to protect yourself against people who take advantage of non-competitive behavior.

The **Accommodating** response is appropriate:

- when you realize that you are wrong — to allow a better position to be heard, to learn from others and to show that you are reasonable;
- when the issue is much more important to the other person than to yourself — to satisfy the needs of others, and as a goodwill gesture to help maintain a cooperative relationship;
- to build up social credits for later issues which are important to you;
- when continued competition would only damage your cause — when you are outmatched and losing;
- when preserving harmony and avoiding disruption are especially important; and
- to aid in the managerial development of subordinates by allowing them to experiment and learn from their own mistakes.

The **Avoiding** response is appropriate:

- when an issue is trivial, of only passing importance, or when other more important issues are pressing;
- when you perceive no chance of satisfying your concerns, e.g., when you have low power or you are frustrated by something which would be very difficult to change (national policies, someone's personality, structure, etc.);
- when the potential damage of confronting a conflict outweighs the benefits of its resolution;
- to let people cool down — to reduce tensions to a productive level and to regain perspective and composure;
- when gathering more information outweighs the advantages of an immediate decision;
- when others can resolve the conflict more effectively; and
- when the issue seems tangential or symptomatic of another more basic issue.

The **Compromising** response is appropriate:

*   when goals are moderately important, but not worth the effort or potential disruption of more assertive modes;
*   when two opponents with equal power are strongly committed to mutually exclusive goals — as in labor-management bargaining;
*   to achieve temporary settlements to complex issues;
*   to arrive at expedient solutions under time pressure; and
*   as a backup mode when collaboration or competition fails to be successful.

The **Collaborating** response is appropriate:

*   to find an integrative solution when both sets of concerns are too important to be compromised;
*   when your objective is to learn, e.g., testing your own assumptions, understanding the views of others;
*   to merge insights from people with different perspectives on a problem;
*   to gain commitment by incorporating other's concerns into a consensual decision; and
*   to work through hard feelings which have been interfering with an interpersonal relationship.

## 4.  ENFORCEMENT OF THE RESULTS

As a result of the current unregulated state of mediation, enforcement, as with structuring the mediation environment, remains a matter of contract. In agreeing to participate in the process of mediation, the parties do not, in any way, affect their rights to subsequently litigate the issues. In fact, it is often best that a party pursue both avenues — mediation and litigation — contemporaneously in order to best serve its interests. A successful conclusion to the mediation is enforceable in a court of law. In order for the mediation to have a binding effect, both parties must sign a binding settlement stating that the mediated agreement will be enforceable and will effectively destroy the parties' rights to reopen the matter in court.

As with other settlement agreements, the parties must sign the agreement willingly and freely, without duress or fraud being exerted upon either of them. Both parties must also be given the opportunity to obtain independent legal advice before executing the agreement. If these steps are not followed, the agreement may be viewed as null and void on grounds of unconscionability.[7]

## 5.  ARE COURTS UPHOLDING THE COMMITMENT TO MEDIATION?

After looking at the cases since 1998 that have mentioned mediation, it is apparent that the courts are upholding the commitment to mediation.

### (a)  Courts Ordering or Suggesting Mediation

Even where mediation is not mandatory, the courts are recognizing the benefits of mediation and encouraging parties to resolve their disputes outside of the traditional litigation process. For example, in *Meenink v. Meenink*,[8] a custody dispute, the judge ordered that any concerns about the child's safety while in custody with the other parent are to be discussed directly with the other party. And, if no satisfactory resolution is achieved, the parties will enter into mediation before resorting to litigation.

In another custody dispute, *Petrocco v. Von Michalofski*,[9] Métivier J. ordered that the parties attend three mediation sessions to discuss details of improving communication, expanding access and easing current problems over access.

In *Union culturelle des Franco-Ontariennes c. Bessette*,[10] Master Beaudoin pointed out that the legal costs of the motion were almost as much as the property in dispute. He then went on to suggest that he hoped that his decision would encourage the parties to come to a solution by way of mediation in order to avoid the costs of a trial.

In *Barber Sport Surfaces Ltd. v. F.G. Soccer Enterprises Inc.*,[11] Ground J. proposed the use of mediation to solve a commercial dispute. After dismissing Barber Sport Surfaces' application to repossess the Astro Turf Trademark, Ground J. commented that:

---

[7] Neidermayer, P. "Are Mediated Agreements Enforceable?", Supplement to the *Community Justice Report*, September 1987, p. 1.

[8] [1998] O.J. No. 2102, 1998 CarswellOnt 2183 (Gen. Div.).

[9] [1998] O.J. No. 200, 1998 CarswellOnt 336 (Gen. Div.), affirmed (1998), 1998 CarswellOnt 4813 (Div. Ct.).

[10] [1998] O.J. No. 2284, 1998 CarswellOnt 2567 (Gen. Div.), additional reasons at (1998), 1998 CarswellOnt 2568 (Gen. Div.).

[11] [1998] O.J. No. 2641, 1998 CarswellOnt 2573 (Gen. Div.).

This seems to me to be a classic case where commercial mediation should be entered into with the hope of coming up with some method of providing the applicant with security for the payment of the balance of the contract without serious disruption to the business of the respondent.[12]

### (b) Mandatory Mediation being Upheld

In addition to courts encouraging mediation, they generally uphold mandatory mediation when it is challenged. The courts have even been reluctant to defer mandatory mediation to a later date. An example of this is found in *Rundle v. Kruspe*.[13] In this case the plaintiff sought to defer the proceedings from mandatory mediation until such time as oral examinations for discovery are complete. The plaintiff argued that she had yet to have an opportunity to tell her side of the story and that she had yet to be heard in the dispute. She also submitted that the she cannot be forced to settle in mediation. The Court denied the motion and ordered that the parties proceed with mandatory mediation.

In reaching this decision, the Court recognized that mediation is a more cost effective way of resolving this dispute. In addition, Master Beaudoin stated that if the plaintiff is looking to confront the defendant and convey her side of the story, this is precisely what can happen at a mediation. In supporting the mandatory mediation, Master Beaudoin also commented on how the contract is private and the atmosphere is less adversarial in a mediation. He further stated that a settlement is not the only successful outcome of a mediation. If the parties can narrow the issues in the dispute or, at the very least, can come away with a better understanding of the other side's position, the mediation can still be considered a success.

In *Mihichuk v. Allstate Insurance Co. of Canada*,[14] the plaintiff brought a motion for a determination before trial of whether the plaintiff is required to mediate the issue of loss of earning capacity benefits under the provision of sections 280 to 283 of the *Insurance Act*[15] where the insurer defendant is not in agreement with the assessment of the Residual Earning Capacity Designated Assessment Centre (R.E.C.D.A.C.). Pursuant to section 281(2) of the *Insurance Act,* no person may bring a proceeding in any court or refer a matter to arbitration unless mediation has first been sought and has failed. The plaintiff argued that the right to mediate has been restricted by section

---

[12] *Ibid.*, at para 4.
[13] [1998] O.J. No. 2078, 1998 CarswellOnt 2193 (Master).
[14] [1998] O.J. No. 897, 1998 CarswellOnt 775 (Gen. Div.).
[15] R.S.O. 1990, c. I.8.

23(5) of Statutory Accident Benefits Schedule (S.A.B.S.) since there is no specific provision of S.A.B.S. which gives the insurer the right to ignore the findings of R.E.C.D.A.C. or to mediate with respect to that specific issue.

The Court held that a recommendation report issued to the parties by R.E.C.D.A.C. is not a binding decision and, where a dispute arises from the R.E.C.D.A.C. report, the provisions of sections 279 to 283 of the *Insurance Act* require that the parties must attempt a resolution via mediation.

The Court remained unconvinced that the rights of the parties to mediate the findings of R.E.C.D.A.C. with respect to residual earning capacity pursuant to sections 279 to 283 of the *Insurance Act* have been restricted or curtailed by the provisions of section 23(5) of S.A.B.S. The wording of the regulation simply lacks the required clarity of meaning to meet the criteria of section 279(2) of the *Insurance Act* so as to deprive the parties of their right to mediate a dispute pertaining to the amount of statutory accident benefits payable to an injured person. The Court ordered the plaintiff to mediate the issue as a condition precedent to the commencement of the action.

### (c) Exemption from Mandatory Mediation

The one case where the Court did not uphold mandatory mediation dealt with a *Charter* issue. The applicants in the main proceedings were seeking a declaration that section 25(4) of the *Public Services Act* violates section 15 of the *Charter*. In *Wilson v. Canada (Attorney General)*,[16] the moving parties sought leave to have the proceedings exempted from a mandatory referral to mediation.

In this case the Court held that Constitutional cases which involve issues paramount to societal concern must have the ability to influence and shape future conduct and to prompt necessary behavioural changes. This requires adjudication within a public forum where the public interest is represented and binding decisions are rendered. Since the ultimate disposition of this application will have implications for same sex couples throughout the country, the Court exempted the moving party from mediation.

---

[16] [1998] O.J. No. 1780, 1998 CarswellOnt 1836 (Master).

## 6. CO-MEDIATION

The use of two or more mediators in a dispute is called co-mediation. While the basic principles of mediation remain the same in a co-mediation setting, co-mediation requires different type of advance planning and additional procedures for the mediation team.

There are basic guidelines for co-mediation.

- Choose a partner with a similar vision of mediation's goals and compatible strategies for executing the mediator's job.

- Co-mediators must share similar approaches and strategies. While it may be productive to observe a mediator with a different orientation and basic strategies, an effective partnership requires a consonance in goals, objectives, and strategies.

- Work out a way of communicating with each other before the mediation session starts.

- Co-mediators must develop communication signals ahead of time, including signals that address both procedural decisions and tactical moves.

- Give leadership roles to co-mediators.

- To avoid a power vacuum, one member of the co-mediation team should be in charge at any given point. Particularly where mediators have not mediated in the past, allocating leadership roles should minimize the chance of conflict among mediators.

- Either one of the mediators can be the lead for the entire session, or the session can be divided into discrete segments with leadership changing for various segments. The latter approach can maximize particular strengths of each mediator and give the mediators a more equal voice.

Strategically use the seating arrangement to maximize opportunities for success. The seating arrangements, like other aspects of planning and executing an effective co-mediation, are important and must be done thoughtfully. Important goals in structuring the seating arrangement include:

- Maximizing the co-mediators' ability to communicate with each other.

- Taking advantage of the diversity of the mediation team to balance the room.

- Unifying the parties' focus.

- Providing for mediator breaks.

- Assigning specific tasks to each mediator to make the mediation as efficient and productive as possible.

- Assigning one person to write agreements as they emerge, manage paperwork, check on resources or obtain special information, while the other focuses solely on the parties' interaction, to maximize mediator resources. Whenever one mediator is not undertaking a specific task or is less active than the other, he or she should use the opportunity to become an astute process observer, tracking both the subtleties of parties' interactions, as well as substantive developments in the session.

- Using the opening statement to set the tone for co-mediation. Co-mediating mediators should thoughtfully present their opening remarks in a manner that reinforces their being perceived as a team. The pronoun "we" should be routinely used to describe the mediation team's goals, roles and ground rules, instead of the pronoun "I". If the mediators divide the components of the opening statement, they should have a transition strategy that they convey to the parties (e.g., "I will explain the goals for our session, and my colleague will review the ground rules for our discussion.").

- Adopting the principle of non-competition among mediators. There is no need for co-mediators to have equal time. The dictum — whatever works best — should be the guiding principle for determining which mediator is most active.

- Remembering to consult your co-mediator before any important decisions. Important decisions such as structuring the discussion agenda or declaring a caucus should be made with the consensus of co-mediators.

- Maintaining a unified focus so that common understandings are reached. Mediators should not split conversation with parties. That is, while one party is addressing the active mediator, the other party should not be allowed to have a private conversation with the less active mediator. To maintain a unified focus, the less active mediator can rivet his or her attention to the party who has the floor and refuse to be distracted by the other. In addition, a mediator should be careful not to jump in and initiate conversation when his or her partner is exploring a topic or pursuing a line of questions.

- Using the diversity of the mediation team to maximum advantage. Be certain to use the strengths of your team to support the process. If a co-mediator has more information about the working of an agency, you may wish to highlight the co-mediator's expertise in a certain area to demonstrate your team's knowledge of contributing factors to the situation.

- Having a fallback or "fail-safe" plan if co-mediation is not working. Should co-mediation not work, the co-mediators should decide in a private meeting whether they can alter their strategy to make it work or whether they should switch to "solo" mediation.

- Being flexible. All mediation is subject to shifting circumstances, and co-mediators must have "built-in" flexibility that allows them to alter plans seamlessly when the situation requires.

- Supporting your co-mediator. For co-mediation to succeed, all parties must see the co-mediators as a team. It is important that co-mediators support each other by:

  - Modelling active listening body language when the other is speaking.
  - Reinforcing the points that the co-mediator has made when you are speaking.
  - Allowing the co-mediator to be part of all conversations. In other words, do not "freeze out" your co-mediator.
  - Debriefing after each co-mediation.

Following each co-mediation, each mediator should invite comments about individual and team strengths, individual and team areas for improvement, and the plan of the next mediation session.

To conclude, co-mediation can be very useful in a variety of situations if the foregoing guidelines are kept in mind.

## 7.  BARRIERS TO SETTLEMENT IN MEDIATION

Negotiators often fail to reach an agreement. A growing body of research and writing focuses on the reasons for failed negotiations.[17] Although there are many reasons why negotiations fail, the following four barriers to settlement are seen frequently by negotiators and mediators:

• Strategic Barriers

• Principal/Agent Divergence

• Cognitive Barriers

• Reactive Devaluation

Effective mediators are aware of these barriers and develop strategies to overcome them. Let us examine the nature of each of these barriers and some things mediators can do to assist negotiators overcome them.

### (a)  Strategic Barriers

This barrier relates to the underlying dilemma in the negotiation process. On the one hand, negotiators would like to discover shared interests and maximize joint gains. On the other hand, every negotiator wants to maximize his or her own gains.

While "interest based" approaches to negotiation encourage negotiators to take an "integrative" or "win/win" approach, in the real world negotiators understand that there are limited resources, and for one person to get more sometimes necessarily means that the other person will get less. Thus, in some cases, one must take a "distributive" approach to negotiation. This approach is characterized by secrecy, game playing tactics and value claiming behaviours.

This focus on the distributive aspects of bargaining can often lead to unnecessary deadlocks and, perhaps more importantly, failure to discover solutions that could truly leave all sides better off.

Mediators can help overcome strategic barriers in the following ways:

• Encourage parties, in caucus, to reveal information about their under-

---

[17]  See, for example, Arrow, Mnookin et al., *Barriers to Conflict Resolution*, W.W. Norton & Co., London, 1995.

lying interests, needs, priorities and aspirations. This information, which a party would not disclose to their adversary directly, can be used by the mediator to help expand the pie.

- Foster a problem solving atmosphere in mediation as opposed to an adversarial contest.

## (b) Principal/Agent Divergence

In many negotiations, principals do not negotiate directly on their own behalf. Rather, agents who may have certain interests that diverge from those of the principal carry on negotiations. Lawyers negotiating for clients, executives negotiating for businesses and civil servants negotiating for governments are all examples of principal/agent relationships which may give rise to this divergence.

Mediators, sensitive to this barrier, can help in the following ways:

- **Name the problem.** Gently and appropriately suggest to the agents that this may be a perceived problem in a particular negotiation.

- **Get the principals to the table.** Have clients personally attend the negotiations along with lawyers.

- **Get more senior people involved.** Often individuals with higher positions in an organization will have a keener awareness of the true best interests of the organization.

## (c) Cognitive Barriers

Drawing on the field of psychology, this barrier refers to the way that the human mind processes information, deals with risks, loss and uncertainty and makes inferences and judgments. Research[18] has indicated several ways that human reasoning often departs from that suggested by theories of rational judgment and decision making. In particular, "loss aversion" and "framing effects" can present significant barriers to reaching a settlement.

Loss aversion refers to the fact that people will generally gamble to avoid a sure loss even when the amount risked is significantly greater than the sure loss.

---

[18] Amos Tversky et al., "Contingent Weighting in Judgment and Choice", 95 Psychology Review, July 1988, pp. 371-384.

Framing effects refer to whether a situation is seen as a gain or a loss. This will depend on the individual's reference point and this reference point may be manipulable. This reflects the old question, "Is the glass half empty or half full?".

Mediators aware of these cognitive barriers can assist negotiators in the following ways:

- **Helping parties to see that there are at least two sides to the story**. Mediators can encourage one side to acknowledge the perspective of the other side (without agreeing with it).

- **Helping parties to rationally compare choices**. Mediators can help make apparent the gamble being taken to avoid ultimate loss and the consequences if that gamble is unsuccessful.

- **Helping parties to focus**. Mediators can help focus parties not so much on how much they have given up in a negotiation, but how much closer the parties are to achieving a resolution of all issues in a way that acceptably meets their underlying interests.

## (d) Reactive Devaluation

This relates to the way that one side sees proposals made by the other side during negotiation. Negotiation is an interactive process in which each side is continually drawing inferences about the intentions, motives and good faith of others. When one side offers a particular concession or proposal the other side may view the attractiveness of that offer as diminished simply because it originated with the perceived opponent.

In mediation there is an obvious opportunity to avoid reactive devaluation if the source of a proposal is perceived as neutral. For this reason the mediator will often take responsibility as the source of an offer thus allowing a party to accept an otherwise sensible and acceptable proposal which otherwise they may have rejected.

To conclude, through an awareness of the existence of these barriers to settlement and a knowledge of strategies for overcoming them, mediators can add significant value to the negotiation process for all parties.

## 8.  TELEPHONE MEDIATION

It is always preferable to conduct mediation sessions in person with the parties and the mediator physically present at the same place and time. However, this is not always possible or practical. Sometimes mediators will be called upon to conduct mediations by telephone. This could either be a conference call in which all parties are present by phone at the same time or it could be a situation in which the mediator is contacting each party by phone separately — similar to a caucus situation.

It is important for the mediator to be aware of the unique challenges associated with phone mediations. One mediation organization notes that while approximately 90% of their face to face mediations result in settlement being reached, that figure drops to approximately 30% for telephone mediations.

In telephone mediation, a mediator cannot rely on traditional cues like body language and eye contact to build trust. Nor can the mediator use appearance or physical settings to establish authority or credibility.

However, the goals of mediation remain the same. They are:

- Identifying and mitigating communication barriers.
- Defining the problem or dispute.
- Moving parties away from positions and toward mutual interests.
- Facilitating joint problem solving.
- Bringing the mediation process to closure through an agreement or by outlining other options.

### (a)  Guidelines for Telephone Mediation

These guidelines will help establish effective communication in telephone mediation:

### Prior to the conference

- Be familiar with all material and background information prior to the meeting.
- Schedule a specific date and time for the telephone mediation.
- Insist that the parties are in rooms that are free from distractions and interruptions during the scheduled time.

- When teleconferencing, do not hold any conversation until all parties are on the line.
- Establish ground rules and secure agreement with all parties to abide by them.

### During the conference

- Have all written material available, clearly marked and identified.
- Have all appropriate written material to the parties prior to the call and do an "inventory check" with them before beginning the meeting.
- Speak succinctly and clearly. Voice control is important — speak slowly, clearly, and do not drop voice at the end of sentences.
- Discourage the use of technical language or jargon.
- Have people introduce themselves at the beginning and identify themselves when they speak.
- Repeat and paraphrase comments made by the parties to make certain that everyone has heard them.
- Summarize each point to assure that the point has been understood.
- Take extensive notes.
- Inform the parties of next steps (e.g., separate telephone calls).
- Hang up the telephone first so as not to be alone with either party.

While telephone mediation is always "second best" to in person mediation, following these guidelines can help the mediator maximize the opportunity for success.


## 9.  MANDATORY MEDIATION

### (a)  Basic Components

The advent of mandatory mediation programmes will fundamentally alter the practice of litigation. The cultural impact of such programmes has already been described by Professor Macfarlane.[19] In fact, if the essence of mediation is the voluntary entry by disputing parties into a settlement process, mandatory mediation is an oxymoron. Ironically, U.S. mandatory mediation programmes have roughly the same settlement rates as voluntary

---

[19] Macfarlane, J., "Culture Change? Commercial Litigators and the Ontario Mandatory Mediation Program", Canadian Law Reform Commission Paper, May 2000.

mediation. This statistic means that the litigation bar will be forced to make the greatest accommodation to the new process.

Mediators in mandatory mediation programmes will exercise their craft in accordance with classic mediation principles described below. Further parties will in particular move towards or away from settlement on the basis of their interests. In mandatory mediation, the complexity of the relationships (as described by Mnookin) is aggravated by the tension of the litigation process.

- The mandatory mediation process puts more pressure on the litigants to effect a settlement when litigators are really trained to drive cases to court victory.

- Litigators are accustomed to the lengthy discovery process which enables them to prepare strategies which often depend on the evolving nature of the litigation. However, mandatory mediation demands an abrupt early discussion of the case before theories can evolve.

How can complex legal theories evolve if the mandatory mediation is ordered within 90 days of the closing of the pleadings? In order for a litigator to prepare advice for the client during the mandatory mediation, the lawyer must radically accelerate the analysis to arrive at the basis of his or her theory or seek a court deferral of the mandatory mediation session.

The mandatory mediation rule provides that documentation of central importance must be produced prior to the mediation. This concept of "central importance" means that a litigator must develop the central theories of the case prior to mediation. Clients must appreciate the demands this places on litigators. Legal issues will be more concentrated in the early stages of the case.

Mandatory mediation is placed directly within the adversarial system. Lawyers and clients must be extremely cautious in statements made in the presence of opposing parties and clients, notwithstanding the gentle efforts of mediators to persuade "everyone" to disclose their true interests. Mandatory mediation is part of an adversarial system and this system is designed to create a court winner and a court loser.

## (b)  Tension between Victory and Peace

Litigators perceive themselves as a warrior class somewhat between samurai and knights. It is the dream of victory that drives the innermost emotional springs of the litigation class even though 97% of cases eventually settle. The tension between victory and peace is described by Kershaw.[20]

The drive to win creates an "edge" in litigation. At its best, this edge creates the excitement for, and drama of, trials. At its worst, the litigation edge causes a destruction of civility and manners between opposing counsel and opposing parties.

Mandatory mediation drives the litigation bar to the peace table. The abrasiveness of litigation must be exchanged for the dulcet tones of the peace maker.

## (c)  Don't Settle if You don't Want to

The ethics of mediation demand that the parties and counsel wear a more candid and friendly face than traditional adversarial procedures. Yet, there are many reasons why cases will not settle at this stage.

- Big powerful parties will not settle with weaker parties if they can drag the case out longer. Parties may be gravely concerned that "easy resolution of disputes" will encourage others to start lawsuits.

- Parties who perceive their case to be legally strong will not settle with the legally weak.

- Plaintiffs may have an over-inflated view of their case.

---

[20] Ian Kershaw, *Hitler: 1936-1945 Nemesis*, Penguin Press, p. 577:
When President Roosevelt, at the end of his meeting to discuss war strategy with Churchill and the Combined Chiefs of Staff at Casablanca in French Morocco between 14 and 24 January 1943, had — to the British Prime Minister's surprise — announced at a concluding press conference that the Allies would impose 'unconditional surrender' on their enemies, it had matched Hitler's Valhalla mentality entirely. For him, the demand altered nothing. It merely added further confirmation that his uncompromising stance was right. As he told his Party leaders in early February, he felt liberated as a result from any attempts to persuade him to look for a negotiated peace settlement. It had become, as he had always asserted it would, a clear matter of victory or destruction. Few, even of his closest followers, as Goebbels admitted, could still inwardly believe in the former. But compromises were ruled out. The road to destruction was opening up ever more plainly. For Hitler, closing off escape routes had distinct advantages. Fear of destruction was a strong motivator.

For many good reasons, the parties must be more cautious in mandatory mediation.

### (d) The Ontario Mandatory Mediation Program

Rule 24.1 of the Ontario *Rules of Civil Procedure*, which came into force on January 4, 1999, established mandatory mediation for all civil, non-family, case managed actions. Rule 75.1, which came into force on September 1, 1999, added estates, trusts and substitute decisions matters within the Ontario Mandatory Mediation Program. These two Rules were first introduced as pilot projects in Toronto and Ottawa, which ended on July 4, 2001 with an independent assessment evaluation, recommending it be expanded to all of Ontario.

Under this Mandatory Mediation Program, cases are referred to mediation very early in the process in order to give the parties an opportunity to discuss the issues in dispute and explore the settlement options available. According to Roger Beaudry, head of the local mediation committee in Ottawa, the idea was not to have more cases settle, since 95% of the cases already settle before trial. The idea was to have these 95% of cases settle much earlier in the process and hence be cheaper for the litigants.[21]

### (i) *Rule 24.1 — Mandatory Mediation*

Subrule 24.1.09(1) provides that a mediation session must take place within 90 days of the filing of the first defence. However, this provision goes on to give the court the discretion of extending the time limit for initiating the mediation. Subrule 24.1.09(2) lists the circumstances which the court must take into consideration in exercising its discretion. These are (a) the number of parties and complexity of the case; (b) whether a party intends to file a motion for summary judgment (Rule 20), determination of an issue before trial (Rule 21) or special case (Rule 22); and (c) whether the mediation is more likely to succeed if a postponement is granted in order to allow the parties to acquire more information. An order for extension will be granted only if the reasons advanced in support of the motion fit within one of these factors. Mere consent of all parties involved is not sufficient in

---

[21] See "Confusion over Flaherty's Mediation Speech", *The Law Times*, Vol. 12, No. 7, February 19, 2001, p. 4.

order to grant a postponement of the mediation.[22] However, for standard track cases, parties are allowed to consent to a postponement of up to 60 days.[23]

Rule 24.1.05 also confers the court with the discretion of granting an order, on a party's motion, exempting an action from mandatory mediation. Such orders for exemption are rarely granted. Master MacLeod observed in *Slater* v. *Amendola* that this discretion for complete exemption should be exercised sparingly.[24] In the case of *O. (G.)* v. *H. (C.D.)*,[25] Justice Kiteley provides an analysis of circumstances under which orders for exemption from mandatory mediation could be granted. The criteria which are relevant in deciding whether to grant an exemption are:

- whether the parties have already engaged in a form of dispute resolution, and, in the interests of reducing cost and delay, they ought not to be required to repeat the effort;

- whether the issue involves a matter of public interest or importance which requires adjudication in order to establish an authority which will be persuasive, if not binding on other cases;

- whether the issue involves a claim of a modest amount with little complexity which is amenable to a settlement conference presided over by a judicial officer, without examination for discovery;

- whether one of the litigants is out of the province and not readily available;

- whether the exemption for any other reason would be consistent with the stated objective of reducing cost and delay in litigation and facilitating early and fair resolution.[26]

For example, in *Garneau v. Allstate Insurance Co.*,[27] Master Beaudoin granted a complete exemption while considering that the parties had already conducted an unsuccessful mediation pursuant to the *Insurance Act* and had also attempted a second private mediation, still unsuccessful. He recognized that the mandatory mediation Rule was put in place to reduce the costs and

---

[22] See, for example, *Dick v. Toronto (City)*, [1999] O.J. No. 5637 (Ont. S.C.J.); *Rokicka v. Mechel*, [2000] O.J. No. 589 (Ont. S.C.J.); and *Dicaro v. Wong*, [2001] O.J. No. 347.

[23] Subrule 24.1.09(3).

[24] [1999] O.J. No. 3787, 1999 CarswellOnt 3049 (Master) at para 16.

[25] (2000), 50 O.R. (3d) 82 (S.C.J.).

[26] *Ibid.*, at para 13.

[27] [1999] O.J. No. 3756, 1999 CarswellOnt 3211 (Master).

delays of litigation and that in the circumstances the most efficient thing to do was to "establish a timetable to bring this matter to a conclusion either at the settlement conference or at trial".[28]

Each county has a mediation co-ordinator, named by the Attorney General or his or her delegates, who is responsible for the administration of the Mandatory Mediation Program in the county.

The parties to mediation may choose any mediator on the list of mediators maintained in each county or may agree to name a mediator who is not on the roster. This nomination, along with a date of the mediation session, must be submitted to the mediation co-ordinator within 30 days after the filing of the first defence. If a mediator is not assigned by the parties within 30 days, the mediation co-ordinator will assign a mediator from the list. The assigned mediator will be responsible for fixing a date for the mediation and will serve a notice on the parties, at least 20 days before the session, stating the place, date and time of mediation.

Under Rule 24.1.10, each party shall, at least seven days before the mediation session, provide every other party and the mediator with a Statement of Issues identifying the factual and legal issues in dispute and setting out its position and interests. A copy of any documents that the party considers of central importance to the action is to be attached to this statement.

Unless the court allows otherwise, every party to the dispute and their lawyers (if they are represented) are required to attend the mediation session. However, it is not essential that the mediation session occurs in the presence of all the parties simultaneously.[29] In *O. (G.) v. H. (C.D.)*, which concerned a case of sexual assault and indecent assault, it was argued that if the defendant was to be in the same room as the plaintiff she would suffer a setback in her progress of getting over her psychological trauma. Justice Kiteley, faced with the request of authorizing an exemption from mediation, ordered instead that the parties select a mediator competent in addressing issues of violence and analyse with that mediator the possibility of proceeding without the plaintiff and defendant being present in the same room.[30]

Under the Ontario Mandatory Mediation Program, the parties are not required to continue mediation for more than three hours. However, the mediator has the right to end the mediation before the three hours have expired if the case is settled or if he or she concludes that the session is not constructive for the parties. If the mediation is being beneficial but it is not

---

[28] *Ibid.*, at para 1.
[29] See *O. (G.) v. H. (C.D.), supra,* note 25, at para 15.
[30] *Ibid.*, at para 19.

terminated in three hours, the mediator may, with consent from all the parties, continue the session.

If a settlement is reached resolving some or all of the issues, a written agreement must be signed by the parties and the defendant must file a notice with the court advising of the settlement, within 10 days of the agreement being signed, or within 10 days of the condition being satisfied in the case of a conditional agreement. If a party fails to comply with the settlement agreement, any other party may file a motion for judgement or continue the legal proceedings as if there had never been an agreement.

According to Rule 24.1.12, if a mediation cannot be conducted because a party fails to submit a Statement of Issues or fails to attend the session in the first 30 minutes of the time appointed, the mediator shall cancel the session and immediately file a certificate of non-compliance with the mediation co-ordinator. The mediation co-ordinator then refers the matter to a case management master who may, amongst other things, dismiss the action, if the non-complying party is the plaintiff, or strike out the statement of defence, if that party is a defendant.

(ii) *Rule 75.1 — Mandatory Mediation — Estates, Trusts and Substitute Decisions*

Rule 75.1 is structured and functions similar to Rule 24.1, with a few minor differences. For proceedings related to estates, trusts and substitute decisions, applicants are required to bring a motion for directions relating to the conduct of the mediation within 30 days after the last day for serving a notice of appearance. At this motion, the court may direct the issues to be mediated, who has carriage of the mediation, the time frame for conducting the mediation, who shall attend the mediation, how notice is to be given to the parties and how the cost of the mediation is to be shared.

Again, the parties have 30 days following the court order giving directions to appoint a mediator. If none is designated within this period, the party with carriage of the mediation shall file with the mediation co-ordinator a request to assign a mediator. The party with carriage of the mediation is required to provide the mediator with a copy of the order giving directions.

All other Rules and established time frames of Rule 75.1 are equivalent to those formulated in Rule 24.1.

## (e) Cultural Shift: the Impact of Mandatory Mediation

The future of the Ontario Mandatory Mediation Program beyond July 4, 2001 depended on the outcome of a 23-month evaluation that was published on March 12, 2001. This report found that the program demonstrated a general positive impact on the pace, costs and outcomes of litigation and must be considered a success. The overall conclusion was that with this Program in place, cases really did proceed to disposition faster. (See chart*)

**Figure 1.1**

% of Cases Disposed Within 6 Months of 1st Defence: Control Group vs. Rule 24.1 Cases

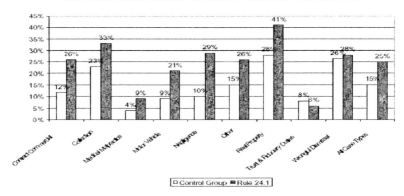

*Taken from Hann, R. and Baar, C., *"Evaluation of the Ontario Mandatory Mediation Program (Rule 24.1): Executive Summary and Recommendations"*, Queen's Printer 2001.

According to this report, about four out of ten cases settle completely within seven days of mediation and another two cases out of ten reach a partial settlement. However, the evaluation reveals that the lawyers' satisfaction with the Program is not as high in Toronto as in Ottawa. Lawyers in Toronto were more likely to point out that mandatory mediation can in fact increase the overall cost if the case does not settle at mediation. Moreover, a substantial number of lawyers and litigants in Toronto expressed concerns with the whole program and disagreed with the statement that "justice was served by this process".

However, there are rational explanations for this less enthusiastic view of the Program in Toronto than in Ottawa. First, Rule 24.1 was not a new concept in the county of Ottawa-Carleton since a Practice Direction had already been in place for two years which introduced a similar program of mandatory mediation. In Ottawa, about 90% of non-family civil cases were subject to mandatory mediation while only about 14% of the cases in Toronto were subject to this Program. This is because almost all the civil caseload in Ottawa is case managed while only a small percentage of the Toronto civil caseload was case managed at that time. Also, in Ottawa the cases under the simplified procedure rule qualified for the Mandatory Mediation Program, while these cases were excluded in Toronto where they were being evaluated under another project.

The Evaluation Committee for the Mandatory Mediation Pilot Project noted that lawyers in Toronto allowed the local mediation co-ordinator to appoint a mediator in a greater number of cases than in Ottawa. They also concluded that this factor was significant in that the selection of the mediator by the parties increases the likelihood of a successful mediation session.[31] Another factor that increases the success of a mediation, according to the Evaluation Committee, is the experience of the mediator. This means that as mediators conduct more mediation sessions and gain more experience, the results of the Mandatory Mediation Program are likely to improve. This may also help explain the fact that more lawyers and litigants are satisfied with the program in Ottawa, where mediators have been conducting mediation sessions for a longer period.

It therefore seems promising that, as more mediation sessions are conducted and mediators gain further experience, such a project will become more beneficial as an additional percentage of disputes will settle earlier in the process and lawyers will develop a better impression of its benefits.

However, as lawyers get accustomed to mandatory mediation and it becomes a more standard element in our legal system, many aspects of their practices, attitudes and strategies will be affected. The current culture amongst lawyers is based on an adversarial system, where one party emerges victorious and where, during this confrontation, the lawyer is the controlling player, without much participation from his or her client. This issue is described by Professor Macfarlane as follows:

> The dominant cultural context for lawyering practice assumes win/lose outcomes which are substantially determined by the expertise of those versed in the normative principles of law ... The relationship between counsel and

---

[31] See *Report of the Evaluation Committee for the Mandatory Mediation Rule Pilot Project*, March 12, 2001, available online at: http://www.attorney general.jus.gov.on.ca/html/SERV/sermed.htm.

client in a predictive bargaining model is one of (substantive) expert/naif and this is reflected in assumptions about decision-making, judgement and autonomy.[32]

Therefore, the introduction of a mandatory mediation program where direct participation of a client is required and the outcome has a possibility of resulting in a win-win compromise can be a considerable challenge to the traditional role of a lawyer. For many, the introduction of this Rule has an impact on their conventional file management methods. This change is described in Professor Macfarlane's report as "front end loading", which means that a bigger part of the work on a file is now done at the beginning of the process in order to prepare for mediation. Lawyers now tend to gather as much information as they can on a file and spend a considerable amount of their time working on it from the beginning since they know they will be ordered to attend mediation within 90 days of the defence being filed. If cases settle earlier, litigators will now have to undertake a greater number of files and will not be able to rely as often on the large files that can last for years.

This also means that the major role of lawyers will have to change drastically. If a greater number of cases end up in mediation and get settled, lawyers will have to divert their efforts to negotiation rather than litigation. Whereas, traditionally, lawyers adopted an adversarial attitude towards the adverse party, now they will have to learn to be aware of the other side's needs and interests — two very important elements in mediation. As one commercial litigator from Toronto described his experience:

> I used to think my role as a lawyer was to go take cases to trial and win. And I think that because I was called in 1979 in the area I practiced in that's what the first sort of 10 years in my existence was like. I did lots and lots of jury trials and we took every case to trial that we could and that's what I felt was my duty. And I loved it. It's cases that become more complex and it's larger sums of money are at stake with the increasing costs of litigation. My role now appears to be as a settler.[33]

This means that litigators will have to develop a whole new set of skills. They will have to depart from the traditional adversarial attitude and shift towards becoming masters of dispute resolution.

While some lawyers are using this mandatory mediation appropriately to settle their clients' cases, others, who are more cynical of its benefits, are using the program in other strategic ways. Many, who have little or no

---

[32] *Supra*, note 19, pp. 6 -7.
[33] *Ibid.*, p. 66.

intention of settling, use this process to gain further information on the other side's case and will even take advantage of the fact that, in mediation, statements are not sworn under oath. Another approach is to use mediation in order to further delay the proceedings.[34]

Many lawyers and litigants perceive an early offer of settlement as a weakness. Litigants and their lawyers appear willing to spend all the time and money it takes in order to win. They feel that suggesting a settlement agreement will appear as a sign of weakness in their case and that the other party sensing this weakness will be less likely to accept the offer. Therefore, often both parties keep on bluffing rather than negotiating a reasonable agreement. As stated by Mnookin:

> Lawyers and clients in litigation fear that unilateral disclosure risks exploitation. "If I admit the weaknesses in my case, they'll take advantage of the honest assessments without acknowledging the holes in their own argument." Neither side wants to look weak to the other. To admit doubt about one's case seems tantamount to handing money to the other side. As a result, each side holds its cards close to the chest, blathers loudly about strength of its hands, and possibly bets more on the outcome that its case was worth to begin with.[35]

With mandatory mediation, it can be a lot easier for a party to propose a settlement. Parties should not feel this way because the mediation is mandatory so while the parties are in mediation they may as well try to settle. Also, there is a third party available to help them in their negotiations.

### (f) The Tension between Mandatory Mediation and Litigation

Although mediation seems to be perceived as beneficial by a significant number of litigants and lawyers for its ability to reduce costs and delays, there is also those who consider it as a threat or a burden to our legal system.

First, there are arguments to be made that as mediation evolves and the range of cases submitted to it continue to expand, it will have an impact on our legal system and more importantly on the rule of *stare decisis*. A significant number of important cases in our common law system started as small and seemingly meaningless law suites, which in fact had important

---

[34] *Ibid.*, pp. 28-29.
[35] Mnookin, R., *Beyond Winning: Negotiating to Create Value in Deals and Disputes*, Belknap Press of Harvard University Press, Cambridge, Massachusetts, 2000, p. 116.

questions of law that needed to be addressed.[36] If these cases had been mediated instead of litigated in the courts, we wouldn't have these important decisions on which to rely on. In fact, our legal system is dependent on the public adjudication of disputes. To a certain extent, people plan their decisions and arrangements by relying on the public explanations of the law through legal precedents. Authors Ralph Nader and Wesley Smith argue that:

> In order for people to make informed decisions about how they will conduct their lives, about which products to purchase and which to avoid, about which companies to patronize, and the like, they need access to information . . . A secret settlement may have swept the potential danger under the rug.[37]

There are also concerns about the disclosure of information and the need for confidentiality in the mediation sessions. In mediation, where parties are encouraged to discuss their motives, interests and needs, information usually comes out which may not be legally relevant to the issue in dispute. In order for the mediation to be effective, parties need some type of protection from this information being used against them in future legal proceedings. It has been advanced that:

> The parties may fear that if they do not reach agreement, anything they say may be reported back to the court or agency. This fear may be caused by the compulsory nature of mediation as well as by its placement as a step in legal proceedings.[38]

If the mediators cannot guarantee to the parties that the communications made during the session will be confidential, the parties may be more reluctant and cautious in what they reveal. This fact is probably more pertinent to mandatory mediation where the parties are already involved in an adversarial relationship having previously filed legal claims and defences, whereas in voluntary mediation, the parties, by choosing to meet

---

[36]  See, for example, discussion on this subject in: Munro, M., "Musings on the Consequences of Mandatory Mediation", *The Advocate*, March 1999, Vol. 57, part 2, p. 195, listing as examples the cases of *McAlister (Donoghue) v. Stevenson*, [1932] A.C. 562 (U.K. H.L.); *Palsgraf v. Long Island Rail. Co.*, 248 N.Y. 339 (U.S. N.Y. Ct. App., 1928); and *Queen v. Cognos Inc.*, [1993] 1 S.C.R. 87.

[37]  *No Contest: Corporate Lawyers and the Perversion of Justice in America*, New York: Random House Publishing, 1996, p. 61.

[38]  Hamilton, J.W., "Protecting Confidentiality in Mandatory Mediation: Lessons from Ontario and Saskatchewan", *Queen's Law Journal*, Spring 1999, Vol. 24, No. 2, p. 570.

and negotiate the resolution of their dispute, have indicated some sense of trust in each other. However, Rule 24.1 in Ontario specifically states that communications at a mediation session and all notes taken by the mediator are deemed to be without prejudice settlement discussions. This concept and its practical applications are discussed in more details in chapter 4 — Privilege and Confidentiality in ADR.

## (g)  Lawyers' Concerns with Early Mediation

Most litigators, accustomed to turning to negotiations only after discoveries, seem to feel that the Mandatory Mediation Program orders a mediation session to be held too early in the process. Rule 24.1 compels the parties to hold a mediation session before discoveries, which many lawyers complained forced them to rely more on the participation and expectations of their clients. As one lawyer remarked:

> [T]he client has to be more involved because you have to rely on the client more to determine what their expectations should be. Whereas you can tell them after the other stages what you think they should be expecting, when it's really just at the pleadings stage you have to rely on them for what a reasonable attitude should be.[39]

Many lawyers express concerns that the fact that mediation is to be held before discoveries renders it useless because they do not have enough information on the other side's case in order to negotiate an appropriate settlement for their clients. They argue that before discoveries they do not have sufficient information on which to evaluate the best settlement offer for the client or to assess the strengths and weaknesses of their case. Negotiating and reaching a mutually beneficial agreement can be much easier after discoveries because both parties have a lot more, if not all, pertinent information.

In his book on negotiation, Robert Mnookin talks about a tension that is perceivable between distributing value and creating value.[40] He notes, for example, that people who are negotiating on the price of an item are negotiating on a purely distributive issue. However, as each party gains information on the needs and expectations of the other, they may become aware that the issue might not be only related to the fixing of a price. An exchange of items might be a more appropriate agreement considering the needs and

---

[39] *Supra*, note 19, p. 35.
[40] *Supra,* note 35.

interests of both parties. The only way to get to such an agreement, however, is through discussion and for each party to disclose information.

In discoveries, the parties have an obligation to reveal all pertinent documents and answer the questions of the opposing party. Therefore, all the necessary information is exposed and lawyers may have a better perspective of the other party's case and its strengths or weaknesses. They can thus be in a better position to advise their client on what would constitute an acceptable and appropriate settlement. A lawyer's responsibility is to advise the client on the best course of action to take. Hence, an important task for a lawyer is to analyse a client's case and the other side's position and to recommend whether to pursue the action, to try to settle, or to simply drop the case. This is a lot easier when there is a reasonable opportunity to analyse the other side's case, and what better opportunity than during discoveries.

Another concern relates to the preparatory work lawyers do when they receive a new file. Usually, upon receiving a new file, lawyers start gathering documents, facts and other evidence that is critical to building a good case. However, sometimes this information is not as important to securing a good outcome at the mediation. Therefore there are concerns that all this preparatory work, that has to be done in case the dispute goes to court, is just a waste of time. One lawyer expressed his concern in the following manner:

> I personally am concerned that if only 3% of the cases actually go to trial, that means 97% of the time all the pre-trial stuff is wasted to a large extent, so therefore 97% of the money I make is from wasted time.[41]

In order to arrive at a suitable deal, negotiators have to share their information. However, there is a possibility that as negotiators share their information, they are also increasing the risk of exploitation by the other party. For example, one party may freely disclose information while the other side may not be inclined to do the same. This is a real dilemma that litigators are faced with, especially now with mandatory mediation being held so early.

In order to get to a proper settlement agreement that will benefit both sides, parties have to share as much information as possible. However, litigators are also concerned that if their client discloses too much information at the mediation session and the case does not settle, that information could be used against them in further proceedings.

---

[41] *Supra*, note 19, p. 61.

# 8

# Introduction to Arbitration

## 1. BASIC PRINCIPLES

*Okay, so we agree that Abercrombie, Brown and Smith are going to Heaven, Denning, Parker and Neilson are going to Hell, and Jones, Michaels and Teller are going to arbitration.*

Arbitration is a binding method of resolving disputes which depends on the existence of an agreement between the parties. Once a party has contracted to arbitrate, it cannot unilaterally withdraw. The arbitration process ends with a ruling by the arbitrator called an award.

## (a) Advantages of Arbitration

Parties to an arbitration agreement can choose their own tribunal. Procedure can be constructed to meet the needs of the individual case while the process can be quicker and may be cheaper than court proceedings. In international arbitration, awards can be enforced under the New York Convention, sometimes more easily than a court judgment.

## (b) Role of the Courts

The courts play an important role in staying court proceedings when there is a valid arbitration agreement. They are also responsible for supervising the arbitration proceedings to ensure that justice is done while leaving the parties and the arbitrators free to construct their own procedure. Finally, courts can also be called upon to enforce valid awards.

## (c) The Arbitration Agreement

An arbitration agreement can be made after the dispute has arisen for the resolution of that dispute but can also be drafted as a contract to arbitrate future disputes. Agreements must be clear and workable. They must specify *which* disputes are covered, *how* the tribunal is to be constituted, *what* procedure will be adopted and *when* an award must be rendered.

## (d) Opening Statement or a Statement of Case in Arbitration

These statements will permit lawyers to make a declaration about their case. Smart lawyers will use this opportunity to present their client's case in the best possible light and will attempt to simplify and explain intricacies. Arbitrators must be aware that this is a potent tool designed to impress them.

### (e)  Purpose of an Opening Statement

Opening statements define the issues and outline the facts adduced to establish allegations advanced by the party. They also describe the evidence and witnesses and provide an overview of the case as a whole. Their purpose is to educate, defuse weaknesses and persuade the arbitrator of the righteousness of one's case.

### (f)  Inside the Arbitration

The Arbitrator will have reviewed the documents filed with the Statement of Claim. Therefore, legal counsel will wish to address the following:

- Procedure
- Jurisdiction of the Arbitrator
- Outstanding Documents
- Issues
- Facts
- Law
- Amount of the Claim

### (g)  Jurisdiction

The arbitration agreement is the foundation of the powers of the arbitrator. Questions of jurisdiction are fundamental to the power of the arbitrator. The arbitration agreement may incorporate rules of an existing arbitration institution. In order to continue with the arbitration, the arbitrator must be satisfied that the dispute falls within the arbitration agreement.

If the arbitrator has jurisdiction, the arbitrator is governed by the following:

- The Arbitration Agreement itself.
- The Rules of the Arbitration Institution which govern.
- The Mandatory Provisions of the State Arbitration Law, if any.

Arbitrators may inquire into the merits of an issue for the purpose of satisfying themselves whether or not they ought to go on with the arbitration. In modern international arbitration, the arbitration tribunal has the power to rule on its own jurisdiction. This power is called Kompetenz-Kompetenz.

## 2. PRIVATE ARBITRATION

Private arbitration is triggered by the agreement of the parties. If the parties have previously agreed on an arbitration clause, then the parties by law will be obligated to conduct a private arbitration, either institutional or *ad hoc*. The arbitration agreement between the parties can be made after the dispute has arisen for the resolution of that dispute. The arbitration agreement can also be made as a contract to arbitrate future disputes.

The arbitration clause must be clear and workable. It should contain a clear description of the following:

- *which* disputes are covered;
- *how* is the arbitral tribunal to be constituted;
- *what* procedure will be adopted;
- *when* must an award be rendered; and
- the *Rules* to govern the tribunal hearing.

The arbitration clause sets out the legal parameters of the private arbitration and therefore is a critical document. The arbitrator must determine the legal rights of the parties. His or her award has the legal force of law, and it will be enforced domestically or internationally.

The parties may elect to use the rules of an institutional arbitration organization. The parties may also wish to combine their own rules with institutional rules. As a general rule, the arbitration clause will be negotiated at the time the parties enter into a contract and long before any dispute arises.

This idea that in a private arbitration the parties have almost complete control over the process is as old as arbitration itself. The parties had this freedom even in Ancient Greek arbitrations:

> If the parties chose to submit their dispute to private arbitration, then throughout the arbitration process they had almost unlimited freedom of choice. By their agreement they controlled the subject-matter in dispute, the selection of arbitrators, the limits of their jurisdiction, the rules of procedure and even whether they should decide the issue according to the law or should determine according to their sense of fairness (or, more likely, expediency) of whatever they thought was best for the parties. The Greeks took it for granted that the parties had control over their own private process of dispute resolution. That is one conclusion that appears to be universal throughout the period. That has two elements. First, the community did not compel the parties to a private dispute to bring it to its attention, so that the community could concern itself

with how the dispute was resolved. Secondly, the community would enforce the agreement to submit to private arbitration and the award of the private arbitrator. In classical Athens, at least, the law forbade a party to a dispute, which had been resolved by private arbitration, from bringing it before a dikasterion.[1]

## 3.  WHAT IS ARBITRATION?

Consider section 1 of the *English Arbitration Act 1996*:[2]

the object of arbitration is to obtain the fair resolution of disputes by an impartial tribunal without unnecessary delay or expense;

the parties should be free to agree how their disputes are resolved subject only to such safeguards as are necessary in the public interest in matters governed by [this part] the court should not intervene except as provided by this part.

**Note**:  Arbitration depends on the agreement of the parties. Such agreement can be made after a dispute has arisen or in advance to cover future disputes.

The public interest requires that the ability of the parties to agree on arbitration be limited. Some matters are not suitable for arbitration, e.g., criminal charges, marriage and divorce, public health and environmental rights, constitutional guarantees, etc.

As a general and fundamental principle, once the parties have validly agreed on arbitration the courts should not interfere in the process except in legally defined circumstances. But, arbitration depends on the courts for the enforcement of awards if a party does not obey the award voluntarily.

### (a)  The Arbitration Agreement

Most legal systems require that the arbitration agreement be in writing.[3] However, under the Ontario *Arbitration Act, 1991*, the agreement need not be in writing.[4]

---

[1] Roebuck, D., *Ancient Greek Arbitration*, Holo Books - The Arbitration Press, Oxford, 2001, pp. 347-348.

[2] *Arbitration Act 1996 (U.K.)*, 1996, c. 23, s. 1.

[3] For example, the *UNCITRAL Model Law on International Commercial Arbitration* specifies in article 7(2) that an arbitration agreement must be in writing.

[4] S.O. 1991, c. 17, s. 5(3).

The agreement must be clear and unambiguous. It must specify the disputes to be covered, the method of appointing the arbitrators and, if the arbitration is to be held under the rules of an institution, the institution agreed upon. If the arbitration is international, the place of arbitration should also be specified. The arbitration agreement should be broad – "all disputes arising from or connected with this contract" and the machinery which it sets up for procedure should be workable even if one party subsequently defaults, e.g., if a party fails to appoint an arbitrator, there should be a default mechanism.

Most modern legal systems specify that the arbitration clause is independent of the contract in which it is contained – thus, even if the contract is alleged to be void or unenforceable, the arbitration clause will survive and enable arbitration to take place. Most modern arbitration systems give the arbitral tribunal the power to rule on its own jurisdiction. Such power is, however, ultimately subject to the decision of the courts. Although the parties have agreed on arbitration, most modern laws and rules allow a party to go to the court for interim measures of protection, e.g., to preserve evidence, to dispose of perishable goods, etc.

Section 1 of the Ontario *Arbitration Act, 1991* defines the arbitration agreement as "an agreement by which two or more persons agree to submit to arbitration a dispute that has arisen or may arise between them". Therefore, both parties must have consented to the arbitration in order for the agreement to be valid. In *Simmons v. London (City)*,[5] it was decided that a by-law stating that a Minister may refer a certain issue to arbitration was not an arbitration agreement within the meaning of section 1 of the Act.

## (b)  The Arbitrators

The arbitrators must be impartial and independent. "Independent" means that they must have no connection — financial, business, family or otherwise — with any of the parties. "Impartial" means that they must have no prejudice in favour of any party and that they must try the case on the basis of the arguments and evidence actually presented to them by the parties. They must observe the principles of natural justice — they must (a) give to each party a full opportunity to make its case; and (b) allow each party a full opportunity to answer its opponent's case. However, they must not allow any party deliberately to delay the process. Most rules require arbitrators to sign a statement of independence before their appointment is

---

[5]  [1997] O.J. No. 3073, 1997 CarswellOnt 3085 (Gen. Div.).

confirmed and to disclose then, or later, any circumstance which could give rise to doubts about their independence.

The parties may challenge an arbitrator on the grounds of lack of independence or impartiality. Most sets of institutional rules give the power to decide upon a challenge to the court of the institution concerned. There are usually provisions that challenges must be brought within a short period of time after the challenger became aware of the facts supporting the challenge.

It is sometimes useful to have arbitrators who have technical knowledge of the matters in dispute, but the arbitrators must not make their decision using such knowledge without giving the parties an opportunity to comment. It is generally recognized that arbitrators are under a duty of confidentiality to the parties.

The arbitrators have a duty to the parties to complete the case — they may not resign except for serious grounds such as ill health. If the arbitration is being held under institutional rules, there will usually be provisions for the payment of arbitrator's fees which must be advanced by the parties. If the arbitration is *ad hoc* the arbitrators usually stipulate for their fees (and expenses) to be paid in advance, in instalments or as lump sum, depending on the case. Most arbitrators insist that their fees are fully paid up before releasing their award.

Save for the correction of clerical errors and, under some systems, for the giving of some limited interpretation, once the award is issued, the arbitrator is *functus officio*, that is to say, he has finished his task and he has no more power or duty (save for confidentiality) in respect of the parties or the dispute which he was appointed to resolve.


### (c) Procedure

Subject to any rules of law and any institutional rules to which the parties may have agreed upon beforehand, the procedure to be adopted may be determined by agreement between the parties. If the parties fail to agree or if they have made no relevant agreement, procedure is determined by the tribunal. The International Chamber of Commerce Rules require the parties and the arbitrators to agree to the Terms of Reference at an early stage. Along with details of the parties, the Terms require the claims to be specified and the issues in the arbitration to be identified and they may also contain any special procedural rules not covered by the ICC Rules themselves. Opinions differ about the utility of such Terms of Reference. It is to be noted that the Moscow Rules[6] require not only that the claims be specified but that they be quantified (II 16).

> Most modern international procedures now commence with the exchange of Memorials in writing. These contain the arguments, factual, technical and legal supporting a Party's case e.g. London Court of Arbitration Rules 15.3: ". . . The Claimant shall send . . . a Statement of Case setting out in sufficient detail the facts and any contentions of law on which it relies, together with the relief claimed against all other parties . . ."

> "All Statements . . . shall be accompanied by copies (or if they are especially voluminous, lists) of all essential documents on which the party concerned relies . . . and any relevant samples and exhibits."

Sometimes the parties agree that the case can be decided on written materials only.

Following the receipt of Memorials, the tribunal may sometimes order the production and exchange of further documentary evidence. In traditional United States and British practice this has required the production by each party of *every* document relevant to the dispute which is within its possession, custody or power. This includes documents which may not support the party's case. Nowadays, international arbitration practice tends to reflect a convergence with civil law practice in which "discovery" of documents is not so wide. The parties may be ordered by the tribunal to produce certain specified categories of documents or identified individual documents. If the party which was ordered to make such production fails to do so, the tribunal may draw adverse inferences. Recommended contemporary international practice on evidence is contained in the International Bar Association Rules of Evidence.

---

[6] Rules of the International Commercial Arbitration Court at the Chamber of Commerce and Industry of the Russian Federation, Moscow, 1998.

# 9

# Setting-up the Arbitration

## 1. INTRODUCTION

If all parties to the agreement are Canadian and the law governing the arbitration is that of Ontario, then Ontario's *Arbitration Act, 1991*[1] will apply. If one of the parties is foreign, i.e., non-Canadian, the *International Commercial Arbitration Act*[2] of Ontario applies. As a general rule, the arbitration rules and procedures selected by the parties themselves will govern, save for mandatory provisions of the applicable legislation. If the parties have not dealt with a matter (e.g., rights of appeal) then the applicable legislation will govern as an emergency tool kit. It is important not to "adopt" arbitration rules without reading them and appreciating their relationship to the underlying legislation. The *Arbitration Act, 1991*, came into force in Ontario on January 1, 1992. Mr. Justice Blair in *Ontario Hydro v. Denison Mines Ltd.* considered the new legislation as follows:

The Legislative Framework
The *Arbitration Act, 1991* came into effect on January 1, 1992. It repealed the former *Arbitrations Act*, R.S.O. 1980, c. 25, and enacted a new regime for the conduct of arbitrations in Ontario. This new regime is more sophisticated than that of the former Act and more consistent with international commercial arbitration practices. It is designed, in my view, to encourage parties to resort to arbitration as a method of resolving their disputes in commercial and other matters, and to require them to hold to that course once they have agreed to do so.

---

[1] S.O. 1991, c. 17.
[2] R.S.O. 1990, c. I.9.

In this latter respect, the new Act, entrenches the primacy of arbitration proceedings over judicial proceedings, once the parties have entered into an arbitration agreement, by directing the court, generally, not to intervene, and by establishing a "presumptive" stay of court proceedings in favour of arbitration.[3]

The courts have long acted with caution in interfering with arbitration.[4] The powers given to an arbitrator under the *Arbitration Act, 1991* are broad enough to enable the arbitrator to deal with preliminary questions that relate to the underpinning of the parties' agreement. For example, the arbitral tribunal may rule on its own jurisdiction (section 17(1)); it may determine questions of law arising during the arbitration (section 8(2)); and it may apply both legal and equitable remedies (section 31).

The *Arbitration Act, 1991* is a marked improvement over the previous Act which had been in force in Ontario for almost 100 years. Its enactment, coupled with the *International Commercial Arbitration Act* of Ontario, means that the Province of Ontario has implemented legislation which enables it to take its place as a jurisdiction friendly to domestic and international arbitrations. The Act has many important features, and arbitral tribunals are given many important powers. The Act codifies many common law principles and in doing so clarifies the role of the court in overseeing the arbitral process.

The parties can agree to submit future disputes to arbitration when entering into a contract or may decide to arbitrate a dispute when it actually arises. It is preferable, however, to negotiate an arbitration clause prior to a dispute arising, that is, during the negotiations leading up to a main contract before battle lines become drawn in the midst of an actual dispute.

The parties have the power and the freedom to select a procedure best suited to their individual needs: they select their own judge, the rules of evidence and the precise issues to be submitted to the arbitrator(s) for consideration. Although the arbitration process has rules of its own, the arbitrants can, and should, by agreement define the rules at the outset to accommodate the subject matter, the aspirations of the arbitrants and, perhaps more particularly, a timetable so that the benefits of arbitration will not be lost in procedural wrangles.

The framers of the Act have sought to reduce the ability of recalcitrant arbitrants to delay arbitrations through the court process by clearly outlining

---

[3] [1992] O.J. No. 2948 (Ont. Gen. Div.). See also *Ontario Hospital Assn. v. Timbrell*, [1998] O.J. No. 2187 (Ont. Gen. Div.) per Macdonald J.

[4] *Scotia Realty Ltd. v. Olympia & York SP Corp.* (1992), 9 O.R. (3d) 414 (Gen. Div.).

the court's powers. However, opportunities still exist for an arbitrant, with deep pockets, to challenge and seek to frustrate the arbitral process through court intervention. On the other hand, the issue most commonly litigated is whether or not the arbitration should be stayed. If the arbitrator does not have jurisdiction to consider the dispute referred to arbitration, the courts will stay the arbitration. Eliminating the potential for such delay can only be controlled by the most careful drafting of an arbitration agreement.

## 2. THE ARBITRATION AGREEMENT: THE FOUNDATION OF ARBITRATION

Arbitration is a binding process which, short of a substantial defect or reversal on appeal,[5] will be enforced by the court. The most important agreement, of course, is the arbitration agreement (formerly called the submission to arbitration in the former *Arbitration Act).*[6] The Act defines an arbitration agreement as "an agreement by which two or more persons agree to submit to arbitration a dispute which has arisen or which may arise between them".[7]

Incorporation of an arbitration clause can only be accomplished by distinct and specific words.[8] An example of an arbitration clause is found in *Angelo Breda Ltd. v. Guizzetti*:

> Any dispute, difference or question between the parties hereto which touches upon or concerns the validity, construction, meaning, performance or effect of this agreement, or the rights and liabilities of the parties hereto, or pertains to any matter arising out of or connected with this agreement, shall be subject to arbitration pursuant to The Arbitration Act of Ontario, R.S.O. 1980, as amended, in accordance with the overriding provisions hereinafter set out, and the arbitration decision so rendered shall be final and binding on the parties hereto on their respective successors and permitted assigns, and shall not be subject to appeal.[9]

---

[5] *Buck Brothers v. Frontenac Builders Ltd.* (1994), 19 O.R. (3d) 97 (Gen. Div.).
[6] R.S.O. 1990, c. A.24.
[7] S.O. 1991, c. 17, s. 1.
[8] *Dynatec Mining Ltd. v. PCL Civil Constructors (Canada) Inc.* (1996), 25 C.L.R. (2d) 259 (Ont. Gen. Div.). According to Chapnik J.:[para11] Incorporation of an arbitration clause can only be accomplished by distinct and specific words: Halsburys Laws of England, 4th ed. reissue (London: Butterworth, 1992), volume 4(2), at 390; *Lexair Ltd v. Edgar W. Taylor Ltd.* (1993), 65 B.L.R. 87 (Eng. Q.B. Div.), at 99-102.
[9] [1999] O.J. No. 3250 (Ont. Gen. Div. [Commercial List]).

This clause ensures that *any* dispute concerning these parties and the agreement in issue will go to arbitration. Ironically, there is still one issue that would not go to arbitration, (i.e., whether an arbitration agreement exists).

Lord MacMillan sets out this principle in *Heyman v. Darwins Ltd.*:

> If it appears that the dispute is whether there has ever been a binding contract between the parties, such a dispute cannot be covered by an arbitration clause in the challenged contract. If there has never been a contract at all, there has never been as part of it an agreement to arbitrate. The greater includes the less.[10]

If the subject matter of the action covers matters for which no arbitration agreement is in existence, then the court must turn to section 7(5) and decide whether that matter should proceed by way of arbitration while others are decided in the court action. In *Angelo Breda*, the Court found that a major dispute was not covered by an arbitration clause and refused to stay the Court proceedings.

An arbitration agreement may be uniquely structured to the specific circumstances of the parties. The parties may incorporate the arbitration clause of an Institute such as the International Chamber of Commerce (ICC) International Court of Arbitration or may devise their own clause. In all cases consideration should be given to the following in drafting the arbitration agreement:

- whether the parties should negotiate and then mediate in an attempt to settle their dispute prior to arbitration, and a time limit for doing so;
- the number of arbitrators and method of choosing them;
- the time frame, including the time for rendering the award;
- the taking of evidence, procedural matters such as agreement with respect to the discoveries and the production of documents;
- whether or not the arbitrator(s) will render reasons;[11]
- whether or not testimony will be transcribed by a court reporter;

---

[10] [1942] A.C. 356 (U.K. H.L.) at 370-371.
[11] Section 38 of the *Arbitration Act, 1991* provides an award shall be made in writing and, except in the case of an award being made on consent, shall state the reasons on which it is based.

- whether or not witnesses will be sworn;[12]
- whether the arbitration will be considered final and binding or whether there will be provisions for appeal;[13]
- costs and arbitrators' fees;
- where the arbitration should take place; and
- the law governing the contract and the arbitral process itself.

The courts have held that an arbitration agreement must be interpreted according to its language and in light of the circumstances in which it is made.[14] The arbitration clause will be interpreted as of the date of its execution and not when the dispute arises.[15] The Act is also retrospective in nature in that it will apply to an arbitration conducted under an arbitration agreement made before the day the Act came into force, if the arbitration is commenced after that day.[16]

You may well be asked to conduct an arbitration on the basis of an arbitration clause that was executed many years ago. In most cases, at the outset of an arbitration, counsel will often file with the arbitral tribunal a new arbitration agreement which usually incorporates the existing arbitration clause and other relevant clauses. The Act defines all agreements whether they consist of a single clause or comprehensive agreement as to procedure and issues as an "arbitration agreement".[17] I will refer to the original arbitration agreement as the "arbitration clause" and the agreement between the arbitrants filed at the outset of the arbitration as the "arbitration agreement".

The parties are free in the arbitration agreement filed at the outset of the arbitration to vary, modify or contradict the original arbitration clause. The Act provides in section 5(2) that the arbitration agreement shall be deemed to form part of the arbitration clause as originally executed. Should an issue of interpretation arise, the arbitral tribunal or the court will interpret the arbitration agreement filed at the outset together with the arbitration clause as originally executed. It is not necessary to file a second arbitration agreement at the outset of the hearing. The original agreement to submit a

---

[12] Under s. 29 of the Act the arbitral tribunal has the power to require a witness to testify under oath.

[13] If an appeal is contemplated, then it is advisable to have the evidence of witnesses recorded.

[14] *Heyman v. Darwins, supra,* note 10.

[15] *Scotia Realty v. Olympia & York SP Corp.* (1992), 9 O.R. (3d) 414 (Gen. Div.).

[16] See s. 2(2) of the Act.

[17] The arbitration clause could even be implicit, as considered in *Breukelman v. Heida,* [1992] O.J. No. 2604 (Ont. Gen. Div.).

matter to arbitration is sufficient to create obligations forcing the parties to proceed to arbitration. A party may define the issues in its statement, which is equivalent to a statement of claim in litigation.

## 3.  RELEVANT LEGISLATIVE PROVISIONS OF THE ARBITRATION ACT OF ONTARIO TO BE CONSIDERED PRIOR TO DRAFTING THE ARBITRATION AGREEMENT

### (a)  Section 3 — Contracting Out

Section 3 of the *Arbitration Act, 1991* applies to all arbitration agreements. This section permits arbitrants flexibility in setting the course of the arbitration subject to certain mandatory sections which cannot be waived. Under the Act, arbitrants are prohibited from breaching the following provisions in conducting their arbitration.

### (b)  Clauses which cannot be Waived

(i)  *Section 5(4) — Stay of Proceedings ("Scott v. Avery" Clauses)*

The court will stay an action to permit previously agreed upon arbitration. Section 7(1) states:

> 7. (1) If a party to an arbitration agreement commences a proceeding in respect of a matter to be submitted to arbitration under the agreement, the Court in which the proceeding is commenced shall, on the motion of another party to the arbitration agreement, stay the proceeding.

The key point to consider is that the court has no jurisdiction to order an arbitration unless the parties to the action have consented to the arbitration. In other words, an agreement amongst parties to submit their dispute(s) to arbitration provides the court with jurisdiction to stay the action. It is critical therefore that only parties to the arbitration agreement can be forced to arbitration. A non-party to the arbitration agreement can commence a court action without concern that the court will order it to arbitrate its dispute.[18] However, section 7(2) of the *Arbitration Act, 1991* continues to

---

[18] See *Serm Investments Ltd. v. Deer Run Shopping Centre Ltd.*, [1998] O.J. No. 108, 1998 CarswellOnt 42 (C.A.).

list cases in which the court has the liberty of refusing to stay the court proceeding even where there is an arbitration agreement between the parties. This arises where (1) a party has entered into an arbitration agreement while under legal incapacity; (2) the arbitration agreement is invalid; (3) the subject-matter of the dispute is not capable of being the subject of arbitration under Ontario law; (4) the motion was brought with undue delay and (5) the matter is a proper one for default or summary judgment.

In *Deuterium of Canada Ltd. v. Burns & Roe of Canada Ltd.*,[19] where the arbitration agreement contained a "*Scott v. Avery*" clause,[20] Laskin J. said that *Scott v. Avery*

> . . . has been taken in a succession of later cases, including cases in this Court, as enabling parties to a contract validly to make a reference to arbitration of all disputes thereunder, whether involving questions of law or not, and an award thereon a condition precedent to resort to the courts . . .[21]

A critical decision for any party involved in a dispute is to choose the appropriate forum. Should the dispute be resolved in the court or should it proceed by way of arbitration? Therefore, depending on the particular case, the court may be asked to stay court proceedings to permit the arbitration to proceed, or to stay the arbitration to permit the court proceedings to proceed. *The key issue is whether the parties' "arbitration clause" covers the present dispute.*[22] If it does, the arbitration will not be stayed. However, it is not necessary for the court to determine that the exact subject-matter

---

[19] (1974), [1975] 2 S.C.R. 124.

[20] Section 5(4) ("*Scott v. Avery*" clauses):

> 5. (4) An agreement requiring or having the effect of requiring that a matter be adjudicated by arbitration before it may be dealt with by a Court has the same effect as an arbitration agreement.

In *Scott v. Avery* (1856), 5 H.L. Cas. 811, [1843-1860] All E.R. Rep. 1, the Court held that while it is against public policy for parties to seek to oust the jurisdiction of the Court totally, parties may agree privately to proceed by means of arbitration prior to submitting their dispute to Court. The Court will enforce this covenant by staying Court proceedings if a *Scott v. Avery* clause exists, until the arbitration is complete. Of course, since the Courts will generally enforce the arbitration award, the Court's recognition of *Scott v. Avery* clauses, generally reduces the Court's role to that of considering an appeal of the award.

[21] *Supra*, note 19, at 147.

[22] In *Breukelman v. Heida*, [1992] O.J. No. 2604 (Ont. Gen. Div.), Mr. Justice Philip held that the application for an Order for arbitration must be dismissed since no agreement, implied or actual, between the parties to enter into arbitration proceedings has ever been made.

of the dispute falls within the arbitration agreement in order to stay the proceeding. If it is *arguable* that the agreement is broad enough to encompass the dispute, the court should stay the proceeding and defer to the arbitrator the task of interpreting the arbitration clause.[23]

In *Ontario Hydro v. Denison Mines Ltd.*,[24] Justice Blair held that a claim for rectification is a dispute arising in connection with the agreement. In another case, *Onex Corp. v. Ball Corp.*,[25] an Ontario court considered the terms "arising under" the agreement "or in relation to the construction of the agreement" in the context of an arbitration clause. As explained by Elderkin and Shin Doi:[26]

> The issue before the court was whether a claim for rectification of a provision in a contract was a dispute "arising under" or "in relation to the construction" of the contract. The parties had entered into an agreement establishing a joint venture for the purpose of operating a metal container packaging business in Canada and creating a corporate structure to do so, as well as other activities. The agreement contained an arbitration clause which read,
>
>> If any question, difference or dispute arises between the parties hereto in respect of any matter arising under this Agreement or in relation to the construction hereof, the parties shall use their best efforts to reach an amiable settlement of such question, difference or dispute. If the parties are not able to reach a settlement within a period of thirty (30) days then, upon notice by any party to the others, the question, difference or dispute shall, unless otherwise expressly provided in this Agreement, be finally settled by arbitration to be held in Chicago, Illinois under the Rules of Conciliation and Arbitrating of the International Chamber of Commerce by three arbitrators appointed in accordance with the Rules . . .
>
> Onex Corp. assented that there was a drafting mistake in a particular provision in the agreement which did not accurately reflect the agreement reached by the parties, and must be rectified. The court considered the language of the arbitration clause. The court held: [at 158]
>
>> On one line of reasoning, the language of Article 21.1 of the agreement — "under" the contract, and "in relation to the construction" of the

[23] See *NetSys Technology Group AB v. Open Text Corp.*, [1999] O.J. No. 3134, citing and adopting the conclusion of the British Columbia Court of Appeal on this issue, in the case of *Gulf Canada Resources Ltd. v. Arochem International Ltd.* (1992), 66 B.C.L.R. (2d) 113 (C.A.).

[24] [1992] O.J. No. 2948 (Gen. Div.).

[25] (1994), 12 B.L.R. (2d) 151 (Ont. Gen. Div.).

[26] Elderkin, C.L. and Shin Doi, J.S., *Behind and Beyond Boilerplate: Drafting Commercial Agreements*, Toronto: Carswell, 1998.

contract — while broad, is arguably not as broad as that of other arbitration agreements which the courts have held to embrace rectification. In *Ontario Hydro*, supra, for example, "all disputes arising in connection with" the agreement in question were to be settled by arbitration. The submission in *MacDonald*, supra, concerned disputes "with respect to [the] contract . . . or with respect to the terms [thereof]."

In *Ashville Investments*, supra, the English Court of Appeal was persuaded that a claim for rectification was caught by an arbitration clause which swept in disputes "in connection with" the contract. In fact, the court declined to hold that additional language referring to disputes "under" the contract was wide enough to catch the rectification remedy.

The court concluded (at 159) that the language of the agreement was "broad enough to encompass the arbitration of a claim respecting rectification". The court further noted that the thrust of the agreement was that the parties would try to settle all of their disputes and that courts should not try to put "too fine a distinction on the nuances between words or phrases such as 'under' or 'in relation to' or 'in connection with' the contract, in such a context". The court held, "At the very least, where the language of an arbitration clause is capable of bearing two interpretations, and on one of those interpretations fairly provides for arbitration, the courts should lean towards honouring that option." The court maintained that the construction of the agreement involved a search for the "true intentions of the parties whose document it is".[27]

The courts therefore will enforce the broad language of the parties' agreement to submit disputes to arbitration. The Ontario Superior Court of Justice has specified in *Cityscape Richmond Corp. v. Vanbots Construction Corp.* that "arbitration clauses are to be given a large, liberal and remedial interpretation to effectuate the dispute resolution goals of the parties".[28] The court should interpret the arbitration agreement in a way that does not overly distort the ordinary meaning of the words used and simultaneously avoids practical, legal and jurisdictional problems.[29] However, if the dispute is outside the terms of the arbitration clause, the arbitration will be stayed. In *Fitz-Andrews v. Meisner*, Morrisey J. held that:

> The onus, is upon the person opposing the stay of proceedings to satisfy the Court that, on the whole, the Court proceeding is a better course than arbitration.[30]

---

[27] *Ibid.*, pp. 120-121.
[28] [2001] O.J. No. 638, 2001 CarswellOnt 517 (S.C.J.) at para 19.
[29] *Islamic Foundation of Toronto Trust (Trustees of) v. Islamic Foundation of Toronto*, [1997] O.J. No. 2787, 1997 CarswellOnt 3060 (Gen. Div.).
[30] [1993] O.J. No. 191, 1993 CarswellOnt 3649 (Gen. Div.), at para 4.

In *Deluce Holdings Inc., v. Air Canada,*[31] Mr. Justice Blair said:

> *The Arbitration Act,* 1991 imposes what is tantamount to a mandatory stay of court proceedings, with certain limited exceptions, in circumstances where the parties have agreed to submit their dispute to arbitration. This legislation represents a shift in policy towards the resolution of arbitrable disputes outside of court proceedings. Whereas prior to the enactment of this legislation the courts in Ontario had a broad discretion whether or not to stay a court action, the focus has now been reversed: the court *must stay* the court proceeding and allow the arbitration to go ahead *unless* the matter either falls within one of the limited exceptions or is not a matter which the parties have agreed to submit to arbitration.

> The Act is based upon an international commercial arbitration model in wide-spread use around the world, including Ontario and other Canadian provinces, respecting international arbitrations. Its clear direction is to compel parties who have agreed to arbitrate disputes to do exactly that, and to discourage them from running to the courts after the agreement has been made if they think there is some particular tactical or strategic advantage in doing so.[32]

In any event, Mr. Justice Blair refused to stay the Court proceedings where "oppressive conduct" may have triggered the arbitration obligation. Justice Blair stated:

> Having regard to those principles, therefore, I see no difficulty in concluding that if the "oppressive" acts of the majority are what are relied upon to trigger the arbitrable mechanism in the agreement, to the advantage of the majority and to the disadvantage of the minority, the majority ought not to be entitled to rely upon that mechanism to effect its wrongful objective. The real subject matter of the dispute, in such circumstances, is not a matter which the parties have agreed to submit to arbitration, but rather one which strikes at the very underpinning of the contractual mechanism itself. It therefore lies beyond the scope of s. 7 of the *Arbitration Act,* 1991, and brings into play the customary principles respecting the stay of arbitration proceedings. [p. 150]

> . . .

> For these reasons, the competing stay motions before me must be resolved through resort to the traditional principles which have been applied to stays in arbitration situations. Courts have long exercised an equitable jurisdiction to restrain the continuation of an arbitration proceeding in circumstances where

---

[31] (1992), 12 O.R. (3d) 131 (Gen. Div. [Commercial List]). See also *Geraghty v. Halcyon Waterspring Inc.,* [1998] O.J. No. 585, 1998 CarswellOnt 82 (Master).

[32] *Deluce Holdings, ibid.,* at 148.

the foundation of the arbitration agreement is under attack. There must be some *prima facie* evidence — I would say, a strong *prima facie* case — that resort to the arbitration mechanism by the party seeking to rely upon it may be impeached. The stay must not cause an injustice to that party. The applicant for the stay must persuade the court that the continuance of the arbitration would be oppressive or vexatious or an abuse of the process of the court: see *Kitts v. Moore*, [1985] 1 Q.B. 253 (C.A.); *The "Oranie" and The "Tunisie"*, [1966] 1 Lloyd's L. Rep. 477 (C.A.), *per Sellers* L.J., at pp. 486-88. [p. 151]

In *Hyundai Auto Canada Inc. v. Dayhu Investments Ltd.,*[33] the Court stayed the arbitration until preliminary matters had been determined, particularly the question of whether or not the severance had been obtained prior to August 1, 1993.[34] In a more recent case, the Ontario Court of Appeal refused to stay the Court proceedings, because the dispute did not fall within the scope of the arbitration clause.[35] The Court stated that an arbitration clause is but a part of a contract and must therefore be interpreted in light

---

[33] (May 21, 1993), Doc. RE2655/93, (1993), 4 W.D.C.P. (2d) 334 (Ont. Gen. Div.), Rosenberg J.

[34] See also:

*Campbell v. Murphy* (1993), 15 O.R. (3d) 444 (Gen. Div.) (referred to arbitration).

*Benner & Associates Ltd. v. Northern Lights Distribution Inc.* (1995), 22 B.L.R. (2d) 79 (Ont. Gen. Div.) (Motion to stay Court action dismissal). In this case, the Court found that the language requiring the parties to arbitrate is vague and must fail for uncertainty.

*Ottawa Rough Riders Inc. v. Ottawa (City)*, [1995] O.J. No. 3797, 1995 CarswellOnt 1329 (Gen. Div.). The Court found that the arbitration provision of the lease agreement was intended by the parties to survive its termination in order to determine disputes as to the financial obligations of the parties under the lease agreement. The action was stayed.

*Botsis v. Unifund Assurance Co.*, [1998] O.J. No. 2346, 1998 CarswellOnt 2238 (Master). The defendants sought an order staying the plaintiff's action of an issue which was also the subject of current arbitration. The Court held that a plaintiff has a one time choice of forums for their dispute and after that choice is made they are barred from bringing an action in another forum. Therefore the Court stayed that portion of the action which was the subject of arbitration proceedings.

*Heyman v. Darwins Ltd.*, [1942] All E.R. 337 (H.L.), and *Campbell v. Murphy* (1993), 15 O.R. (3d) 444 (Gen. Div.) are persuasive as to the circumstances in which arbitration provisions survive the termination of an agreement.

[35] *Huras v. Primerica Financial Services Ltd.* (2001), 55 O.R. (3d) 449 (Ont. C.A.).

of that contract and the relationships which it creates. In this case, the Court found that the defendant's failure to pay a minimum wage to the plaintiff during her mandatory training program was a dispute that arose in the trainer-trainee relationship, prior to the plaintiff becoming a hired employee of the defendant. The agreement containing the arbitration clause was however entered into by the parties after the training program had ended. The Court found that this new contract clearly referred to the "new relationship" and that the parties only intended those disputes arising from this new contractual relationship to be resolved by arbitration.

In *Angelo Breda Ltd. v. Guizzetti*,[36] the Court refused to stay the Court proceeding, but did order that a commitment to attempt a mediated solution must be honoured. The parties were to proceed to mediation before any timetable is set to deal with this matter on the commercial list.

### (ii) *Section 19 — Equality and Fairness*

Section 19 of the *Arbitration Act, 1991* states:

19. (1) In an arbitration, the parties shall be treated equally and fairly.

    (2) Each party shall be given an opportunity to present a case and to respond to the other parties' case.

See *Ontario v. Mitchnick*, in which McCombs J. remarked:

[para 11] Although a high degree of curial deference must be accorded to the decisions of administrative tribunals, the doctrine of curial deference has no application where there has been a denial of natural justice: *Branch Affiliates of the Federation of Women Teachers' Associations of Ontario and the Ontario Public School Teachers Federation v. Board of Education for the City of London*, (unreported July 31, 1995) per, Saunders J., at 4-5 (Ont. Div. Ct.); *Timpaur v. Air Canada et al* (1986), 18 Admin. L.R. 192 (F.C.A.); *Provincial Airways Ltd. v. Canada Labour Relations Board et al.*, (1983), 6 Admin. L.R. 139 (F.C.A.); *Vye v. Vye*, [1969] 2 All E.R. 29 (D.C.).[37]

Under section 19 of the Act, arbitrators have the duty of listening fairly to both sides, giving parties an opportunity to contradict or respond to the other party's evidence and ensuring that the parties know the case they have to meet. However, as was noted by Templeton J. in *Hercus v. Hercus*:

---

[36] *Supra*, note 9.
[37] [1995] O.J. No. 3369, 1995 CarswellOnt 3178 (Ont. Gen. Div.).

The Act does not equate treating the parties 'equally and fairly' with 'the opportunity to present a case and respond to the other parties' cases'. In fact, these elements of the arbitral process are listed as two distinct and separate requirements and are contained in different subsections of the Act. To provide an opportunity to present a case and respond to the other's case does not, therefore, satisfy the requirement that the parties be treated equally and fairly. Both requirements must be met by the arbitrator.[38]

In a situation where the arbitrator has dealt with the substantive merits of the dispute without giving one party an opportunity to fully present its case, a denial of natural justice will have occurred. The court will set aside the award in such circumstances.

(iii) *Section 39 — Extension of Time Limits*

Section 39 of the Act states:

39. The Court may extend the time within which the arbitral tribunal is required to make an award, even if the time has expired.

(iv) *Section 46 — Setting Aside Award*

Section 46(1) of the Act states:

46. (1) On a party's application, the Court may set aside an award on any of the following grounds:

1.  A party entered into the arbitration agreement while under a legal incapacity.

2.  The arbitration agreement is invalid or ceased to exist.

3.  The award deals with a dispute that the arbitration agreement does not cover or contains a decision on a matter that is beyond the scope of the agreement.[39]

4.  The composition of the tribunal was not in accordance with the arbitration agreement or, if the agreement did not deal with that matter, was not in accordance with this Act.

---

[38] [2001] O.J. No. 534, 2001 CarswellOnt 452 (S.C.J.).
[39] See *Deluce Holdings Inc. v. Air Canada, supra*, note 31.

5.    The subject matter of the dispute is not capable of being the subject of arbitration under Ontario law.

6.    The applicant was not treated equally and fairly, was not given an opportunity to present a case or to respond to another party's case, or was not given proper notice of the arbitration or of the appointment of an arbitrator.

7.    The procedures followed in the arbitration did not comply with this Act.

8.    An arbitrator has committed a corrupt or fraudulent act or there is a reasonable apprehension of bias.

9.    The award was obtained by fraud.

(v)  *Section 48 — Declaration of Invalidity of Arbitration*

Section 48(1) of the Act states:

48. (1) At any stage during or after an arbitration, on the application of a party who has not participated in the arbitration, the Court may grant a declaration that the arbitration is invalid because,

(a)    a party entered into the arbitration agreement while under a legal incapacity;

(b)    the arbitration agreement is invalid or has ceased to exist;

(c)    the subject-matter of the dispute is not capable of being the subject of arbitration under Ontario law; or

(d)    the arbitration agreement does not apply to the dispute.

Section 17(2) of the Act specifically states that if the arbitration agreement forms part of another agreement, it is to be considered separate and may survive even if the principal agreement is found to be invalid. Therefore, in order for a court to stay the arbitration under grounds of invalidity, it must be established that the arbitration agreement itself is invalid.

In the *Ontario Federation of Labour v. Ontario (Minister of Economic Development, Trade & Tourism)*[40] decision, it was decided that an arbitration agreement was invalid on the basis that it was entered into by individuals without the power to do so and because the contract containing the arbitration clause had been properly cancelled, hence there was no issue to arbitrate.

---

[40] (1996), 31 O.R. (3d) 302 (Gen. Div.).

An arbitration agreement can also be considered invalid and fail if it is too vague and unclear in its wording.[41] The parties should therefore use clear and simple language when drafting an arbitration agreement.

It is to be noted that an order declaring the arbitration agreement inapplicable and invalid is a final order and not an interlocutory order. When a judge declares that an arbitration agreement is invalid and inapplicable, he or she affects the party's right to submit disputes to arbitration which is a substantive right, thereby making an order that is final.[42]

(vi)  *Section 50 — Enforcement of Award*

Section 50(1) states:

50. (1)  A person who is entitled to enforcement of an award made in Ontario or elsewhere in Canada may make an application to the Court to that effect.

In preparing an arbitration agreement, provisions inconsistent with the mandatory provisions mentioned above must be avoided. Under section 46(1)7, the court may set aside an arbitration award if the procedures followed in the arbitration itself do not comply with the Act. Notwithstanding the apparent freedom and flexibility given to arbitrants in creating their own arbitration agreement, the parties are restricted by the procedural requirements of the Act and must be cognizant of those restrictions when drafting the arbitration agreement. Of course, it would be unlikely that the court would seriously consider an application by one party to set aside an award pursuant to section 46(1)7 for failure to follow the Act's statutory procedural requirements, when the original procedure was defined in the arbitration agreement mutually agreed to by the arbitrants.

It is recommended that the best way to address procedural matters is to provide in either the original arbitration clause or in the arbitration agreement filed at the outset of the arbitration that the arbitrator shall have full authority to determine the procedure of the arbitration. Another option is for the parties to adopt, in whole or in part, a complete code of procedure from the Rules of the ICC International Court of Arbitration or the American Arbitration Association or one's local Construction Association, for example.

---

[41]  See *Benner & Associates Ltd. v. Northern Lights Distribution Inc.*, *supra*, note 34.
[42]  *Huras v. Primerica Financial Services Ltd.*, *supra*, note 35.

The arbitration agreement, once drafted and agreed upon, is somewhat more permanent than pleadings which may be amended by leave of the court. The arbitration agreement is governed by the ordinary rules of contract law[43] and, thus, cannot be amended or revoked without mutual consent or by rescission.

### (c)  Section 31 — Application of Law and Equity

Under section 31, an arbitral tribunal shall decide a dispute in accordance with law, including equity, and may order specific performance, injunctions or other equitable remedies. The arbitral tribunal is required to apply the *law*, which includes rules of equity and specified equitable remedies. Mr. Justice Laidlaw of the Court of Appeal held in *Faubert v. Temagami Mining Co.*[44] that an arbitrator is strictly bound by accepted legal principles and must not make an award based on its own notions of fairness. Hence, the word equity in section 31 does not mean *equitable* as in "fair", it means legal principles flowing from the rules of equity and more specifically equitable remedies such as specific performance and injunctions. The arbitrants can opt out of this section to allow the arbitrator to decide the arbitration on the basis of what the arbitrator considers to be fair in the circumstances and not necessarily in accordance with the principles of law and the rules of equity. *This is always a critical decision.* In drafting the arbitration agreement, the arbitrants must ask: Should the arbitrator have the power to make a "fair" award as opposed to one strictly in accord with legal principles? Should the arbitrator be permitted to effect a compromise between the arbitrants' position?[45]

The power to give an arbitrator the right to compromise should not be confused with the result which may flow from mediation (non-binding ADR) or other dispute resolution mechanisms.

---

[43] See s. 5(5) of the Act.

[44] (1959), 17 D.L.R. (2d) 246 (Ont. C.A.) at 257, affirmed [1960] S.C.R. 235.

[45] The parties might consider an arbitration clause which gives the arbitrator the power to modify or vary the actual agreement itself. It is also suggested that the parties to a long-term commercial contract appoint an arbitrator who could be called upon, in predetermined circumstances, to suspend, modify, vary or rewrite the agreement. In this way, the contract would survive and continue to be capable of *bona fide* performance by the arbitrants. There does not appear to be any prohibition in Canadian law against such powers to be given to an arbitrator.

The arbitrator's decisions will bind the arbitrants even if the arbitral decision is a compromise, while mediation is only effective if the arbitrants, themselves, agree. In this regard, section 35 of the Act states that members of an arbitral tribunal shall not conduct any part of the arbitration as a mediation or conciliation process or other similar process that might compromise or appear to compromise the arbitral tribunal's ability to decide the dispute impartially. Section 35 is a section that arbitrants may agree, expressly or by implication, to vary or exclude.

## (d) Section 33 — Application of Arbitration Agreement, Contract and Usages of Trade

Section 33 states:

33. The arbitral tribunal shall decide the dispute in accordance with the arbitration agreement and the contract, if any, under which the dispute arose, and may also take into account any applicable usages of trade.

In order to better appreciate this section, the House of Lords' decision in *Produce Brokers Co. v. Olympia Oil & Cake Company Ltd.*[46] is helpful. In that case, the House of Lords held that it was properly within the jurisdiction of the arbitrator to decide the existence of a trade, usage or custom affecting obligations under the commercial contract. Lord Atkinson discussed the use of technical terms in a commercial contract and the arbitrator's jurisdiction to interpret those terms:

If, for instance, in a contract relating to any art or trade or business, the parties use terms having technical meanings in that art, trade or business, then those terms should prima facie have the meaning attributed to them, simply because the parties to the contract presumably used those terms in their technical sense. In such a case it would appear to me that arbitrators or an umpire would, under such a submission as exists in this case, necessarily have authority to determine what was the technical meaning of those technical terms.

Now, is there any essential difference between such a case as that and a case where it is sought to construe the language of a contract in relation to, and through the medium of, a trade usage or custom? In my opinion there is not. The language expressing a trade custom is taken to be imported into the language used by the contracting parties, whether written or verbal, because

[46] [1916] 1 A.C. 314 (U.K. H.L.).

it is presumed that they had the usage in their minds when they made their contract, made it in reference to that usage, and intended that the usage or custom should form part of it. If they have used language in their contract inconsistent with the custom, that is one of the most effectual ways of negativing this presumption, excluding the custom, and declaring that their contract is unaffected by it.[47]

### (e)  Section 45 — Appeal on a Question of Law

The arbitrants in entering the arbitration process must determine from the outset whether or not the arbitration will be considered final and binding. If the arbitration agreement fails to address the potential of appeal on a question of law, no such appeal will be allowed without the leave of the court. If the arbitration agreement is silent with respect to the potential for appeal on a question of fact, then no appeal will be entertained. One must be cognizant, however, that the courts have been reticent in overturning consensual arbitration awards.

### (f)  Sections 54 and 57 — Costs and Interest

The arbitration agreement should also address issues relative to interest and costs. Section 57 of the Act provides that the arbitrator may award pre- and post-judgment interest on the award. When the arbitrator is given the authority to deal with costs, including the costs of the arbitration and the counsel fees, he or she is entitled to make an award of costs on the basis of full indemnification of the successful party. In making the award, the arbitrator is entitled to take into consideration the party's conduct during the arbitration as well as prior to the arbitration.[48]

## 4.  ANALYSIS OF DISPUTE RESOLUTION CLAUSES

An arbitration clause is a very important aspect of any commercial agreement. This clause could prove to be crucial in resolving disputes in an amicable and timely fashion. However, the parties and their counsel often

---

[47] *Ibid.*, at 324.
[48] *Rosenfeld v. Iamgold International African Mining Gold Corp.*, [1997] O.J. No. 3770, 1997 CarswellOnt 3676 (Gen. Div.).

take on the drafting of such clauses with much less attention than should be dedicated to it. Thorough preparation and analysis of the situation can prove to be essential in making the arbitral process a quick and effective one. It has also been argued by Stephen R. Bond, former Secretary General of the ICC International Court of Arbitration from 1985 to 1991 that:

> ... the more effective the arbitral clause that is negotiated, the less likely it is that it will ever be used. This is because an ineffective dispute resolution clause will be less of a deterrent to a party that is considering a breach of contract . . . [A]rbitration is a procedure that has too few lawyers in the beginning (when the clause is drafted) and too many lawyers in the end (when an arbitration is actually under way).[49]

### (a)  Pathological Clauses

Frédéric Eisemann, former Secretary-General of the ICC International Court of Arbitration, established four essential functions of an arbitration clause.[50] They are:

1.  An arbitration clause must produce mandatory consequences for the parties;
2.  It must exclude the intervention of state courts in the settlement of the conflict, at least before an award is issued;
3.  It must empower the arbitrator to settle the dispute likely to arise between the parties;
4.  It must allow for the most efficient and rapid procedure leading to an award that is judicially enforceable.

Eisemann referred to those clauses that did not respect these four essential functions as "pathological clauses".

Unclear, ambiguous or conflicting clauses can be the cause of delays and additional expenses through litigation of the interpretation of such clauses. It is to be noted that using such "pathological clauses" does not necessarily mean that they will be invalidated for being too vague or ambiguous, but that the intervention of the court will most likely be needed in

---

[49] "How to Draft an Arbitration Clause (Revisited)", *International Court of Arbitration Bulletin*, 1990, Vol. 1, No. 2, p. 14.

[50] "La clause d'arbitrage pathologique", *Commercial Arbitration Essays in Memoriam Eugenio Minoli*, U.T.E.T., 1974, p. 130.

order to interpret the intention of the parties, hence increasing the cost and time of a procedure that was meant to be short and effective.

It is not imperative that an arbitration clause be lengthy or complicated, but it is critical that the clause be clear if it is to be effective. Therefore the parties should ensure that the clause is tailored to the specific circumstances of the transaction rather than being vaguely worded.

Drafters of arbitration clauses must consider a number of factors in order to avoid many complications that can arise from a "pathological clause". The following is a list of some of the most crucial mistakes that must be avoided.

### (i) *Misnaming an Institute*

When referring to an institute, such as the ICC, either to adopt its Rules or to have its tribunal administer the proceedings, the parties should ensure that their clause refers to the official name of the chosen institute. Otherwise, a party who is reluctant to resolve the dispute could argue that the clause refers to another institute rather than the one intended, hence initiating a court proceeding and lengthening the process.

The International Chamber of Commerce, for example, is often mistakenly referred to as "The International Chamber of Commerce in Geneva" or "in Zurich".[51] In such a case, the ICC has a practice of interpreting the clause as meaning that the parties intended the place of arbitration to be Zurich or Geneva, pursuant to the Rules of the ICC. Another clause referring to the ICC stated that the arbitration was to be held before the "official Chamber of Commerce in Paris, France".[52] In this case such a mistake could prove to be very costly. There is no official Chamber of Commerce in Paris so one party could argue that what was intended was the ICC while another could just as appropriately claim that the "Chambre Arbitrale de Paris" was the intended Institute.

### (ii) *Use of "may" vs. "shall"*

For example, an arbitration clause that has been referred to the ICC provided:

---

[51] Davis, B.G., "Pathological Clauses: Frédéric Eisemann's Still Vital Criteria", *Arbitration International*, 1991, Vol. 7, No. 4, p. 368. See also *supra*, note 35.

[52] *Ibid.*, p. 369.

Any dispute of whatever nature arising out of or in any way relating to the Agreement or to its construction or fulfilment *may* be referred to arbitration.[53] [emphasis added]

The problem with this clause is that it is not clear whether the arbitration is mandatory or whether there is another possible method for resolving the dispute. Furthermore, the clause is not clear as to who can decide whether or not to refer the dispute to arbitration. This clause does not respect the first of Eisemann's essential functions, which is to produce mandatory consequences for the parties. Also, since this provision is not clearly worded, the courts are likely to be asked to intervene in the interpretation of the clause, which in turn would cause further delays.

### (iii) *Failing to Name Place of Arbitration*

According to most institutional rules, the parties are free to designate the place of arbitration. However if the parties fail to specify the place of arbitration, then the arbitral tribunal will choose one for them. The choice of the situs is crucial as it will determine the conduct of the arbitration proceedings and the eventual outcome. Parties have to be very careful when choosing the place of their arbitration because its legislation will determine the extent of involvement of the courts in the arbitration proceedings and the likelihood that the arbitral award will be enforced (depending on whether the State is a signatory to the *New York Convention*, for example). Also, unless the parties have agreed otherwise, the law of the place of arbitration determines the procedural law to be applied to arbitration or, if the parties have agreed on another system of procedural law, they will have to follow the mandatory procedural rules of the situs during the arbitration.

In determining the place of arbitration, the drafter of the clause must ensure that the particular issues that can arise from the agreement between the parties are matters proper to arbitration in terms of the law of the seat. Furthermore, one should also take into consideration that being a considerable distance away from the witnesses, the evidence, the parties and their counsel can significantly increase the overall cost of the arbitration.

---

[53]   *Ibid.*, p. 367.

(iv) *Adopting the Rules of an Institute without a Clear Understanding of those Rules*

As has been said before, arbitration agreements are often drafted quite hastily after the main contract has been agreed to, without devoting much effort. Therefore, sometimes the parties will agree to adopt the rules of an institute without having an in-depth knowledge of those rules. For instance, drafters might be inclined to adopt the Rules of the ICC because of its widespread use and recognition although these rules might not be completely appropriate for the kind of dispute that can arise between the parties to the agreement.

Most institutional rules will allow parties to modify or adapt certain aspects of the rules. For example, parties can agree to use the rules of the ICC but provide certain modifications specific to the disputes relative to their agreement. Finally, if the parties choose the rules of an institution, they should also clarify whether the rules are those in force at the time of signing the agreement or those in force at the time of the arbitration since most institutional rules are subject to frequent changes.

(v) *Using Vague and Unclear Terminology*

Once again if the clause is not clear and precise, court intervention will be necessary in order to interpret the wording, hence causing more delays and increasing the overall cost of the procedure.

A clause that was presented to the ICC stated:

> Any disputes arising from the interpretation of the present contract will be settled by an arbitral tribunal sitting in a country other than that of each of the parties.[54]

This clause lacks in two main areas. First, there is nothing indicating what is meant by "arbitral tribunal". One could argue that it refers to a tribunal of three arbitrators while another party could claim that it means a single arbitrator appointed by both parties. Secondly, there is no established place of arbitration. Presuming there was no specification as to the procedural law that applied, what procedure would be followed if the parties cannot agree on an arbitrator? Usually, that question is determined by the specified procedural law or, if none has been defined, by the procedural law of the place of arbitration.

---

[54] *Ibid.*, p. 385.

### (vi)  *Combining ad hoc Arbitration with Institutional Arbitration*

Although parties are allowed to modify the rules of procedure even if they are abiding to a system of institutional rules, they must be very careful when doing so. The parties must be aware that most institutional rules have certain provisions which are mandatory and cannot be averted or modified. Also, when combining *ad hoc* elements with institutional arbitration there can arise a tension between the clause and the institutional rules.

In the case of *Spectra Innovations Inc. v. Mitel,*[55] the parties had a clause stipulating:

> In case such a dispute is not settled amicably by senior management within (30) days of escalation to senior management, such dispute shall be resolved and determined by an arbitration board acting in accordance with the Rules of Conciliation and Arbitration of the International Chamber of Commerce (I.C.C.), whose decision shall be final and binding upon the parties.

The applicants were arguing that this clause should be interpreted as meaning that the appointed arbitration board would only have recourse to the ICC Rules for procedural guidance whereas the respondents wanted to follow all the ICC Rules. The Court concluded that strict adherence to the ICC model clause was not mandatory in order to provide for arbitration pursuant to the ICC Rules. Therefore, if parties wish to adopt the rules of an institution with certain *ad hoc* provisions, they must make it clear in the clause and they must ensure that there is no incompatibility with mandatory terms of the institutional rules.

### (vii)  *Too Narrowly Defining the Scope of the Arbitration Clause*

Again, when drafting the arbitration clause, the parties should be very careful in choosing the terminology, in order to avoid inadvertently restraining the scope of the clause. For example, in *Huras v. Primerica Financial Services Ltd.,*[56] the Ontario Court of Appeal refused to stay the Court proceedings, because the dispute did not fall within the scope of the arbitration clause. In this case, the Court found that the defendant's failure to pay a minimum wage to the plaintiff during her mandatory training program was a dispute that arose in the trainer-trainee relationship, prior to the plaintiff becoming a hired employee of the defendant. However, the agreement

---

[55]  [1999] O.J. No. 1870 (Ont. S.C.J.).

[56]  *Supra*, note 35.

containing the arbitration clause was entered into by the parties after the training program had ended. The Court found that a proper construction of the clause revealed that the parties had intended those disputes arising from the contractual relationship be resolved by arbitration and not the disputes arising from the prior trainer-trainee relationship. The parties could not present their dispute to an arbitration panel since the clause was not construed broadly enough to encompass the dispute raised in this action.

Further, in the U.S. decision of *Mediterranean Enterprises, Inc. v. Sangyong Corp.*,[57] the Court held that the expression *"arising hereunder"* was somewhat limited in relation to an arbitration clause in that it was considered to be restricted to "disputes and controversies relating to the interpretation of the contract and matters of performance". However, in another U.S. case, the Court of Appeals concluded that the ICC's recommended clause, which uses the expression *"arising in connection with* the present contract", was to be "construed to encompass a broad scope of arbitration issues" and should embrace "every dispute between the parties having a significant relationship to the contract regardless of the label attached to the dispute".[58]

Therefore, although these two phrases seem alike at first glance, the parties should be careful when choosing the wording of a clause since it can have a serious repercussion on the arbitrability of the disputes that may arise.

### (viii)  *No Clear Divisions between Dispute Resolution Methods*

A dispute resolution clause can provide for various methods of resolution. For example, an agreement can expressly state that when a dispute arises, the parties are to attempt to negotiate in good faith, then mediate and finally submit the dispute to arbitration. However, if the clause does not specify on how to go from one method to the next, it could provide an excellent opportunity for a recalcitrant party to further delay the proceedings.

If, for example, a clause provides for mediation before turning to arbitration, without specifying a time frame for the mediation process, a reluctant party could try to delay the settlement of the dispute by arguing that mediation is still a realistic solution and should be continued as the

---

[57] 708 F.2d 1458 (Cal. C.A., 1983).
[58] *J.J. Ryan & Sons, Inc. v. Rhône Poulenc Textile, S.A.*, 863 F.2d 315 (4th Cir. S.C., 1988).

clause provides for it. This idea of setting a clear time frame for any ADR process prior to litigation or arbitration is discussed further by Earle:

> In setting a time frame, it is important that a clear beginning and end be specified. The event which starts the clock running should be one which is in the power of either party to bring about, such as delivery of a notice of appointment of mediator. Care should be taken that one party is not left to the mercy of the co-operation of the other party or some uncontrollable event before the start of the time frame. Otherwise, one party can refuse co-operation in order to gain additional bargaining power or to delay or prevent the process from getting off the ground.[59]

Although other methods of dispute resolution can be very beneficial, the parties should provide for relatively short time periods within which they must be used in order to restrain the duration of the process. The setting of a time period in which to conduct the various steps of ADR is very important since the courts will enforce an agreement to negotiate or mediate a dispute before pursuing arbitration or mediation. In *Angelo Breda Ltd. v. Guizzetti*,[60] the Court refused the application for a stay of court proceedings in order to continue with arbitration. However, Feldman J. ordered that the parties proceed to mediation as stipulated in their agreement before the matter would be referred to the Commercial List.

## (ix)  *Did Not Specify Applicable Law*

The choice of applicable law is not a necessary aspect which, if not specified, would render the arbitration clause invalid. However, if the parties specify the applicable law in the agreement, it could save them a considerable amount of time and costs. If the parties do not specify the law that applies to the contract, it is an issue that is to be decided by the arbitrators, and this decision could bring an unfortunate surprise to the parties. One imperative consideration is that the parties chose a legal system in which the subject matter of the contract is arbitrable. Intellectual property issues, for example, are often not permitted to be arbitrated. Also, it is favourable that the parties chose a legal system that is developed in regard to the issues addressed in their contract.

---

[59] Earle, W.J., *Drafting ADR and Arbitration Clauses for Commercial Contracts*, Toronto: Carswell, 2001, p. 3-12.

[60] [1995] O.J. No. 3250 (Ont. Gen. Div. [Commercial List]).

(x)  *Naming Two Authorities*

The parties should also ensure that they clearly define the arbitral tribunal or the appointing authority in order to avoid further disputes. Again if the institution is not specifically identified or if the clause seems to name more than one, a lengthy and costly confrontation can arise as to who is the intended authority. The following is an example of an agreement that seems to combine two arbitral institutions in the same clause:

> Any controversy or claim arising out of or relating to this Agreement or the breach hereof shall be settled by arbitration in Seoul, Republic of Korea, before the Korean Commercial Arbitration Tribunal by a single arbitrator in accordance with the Rules of Conciliation and Arbitration of the International Chamber of Commerce.[61]

The parties to this arrangement were not capable of agreeing on which arbitral institution was intended and had to engage in several court actions to settle this conflict.[62] This clause could have been interpreted as selecting the Korean Commercial Arbitration tribunal as the appointing authority for the nomination of the arbitrator under the Rules of the ICC or again as designating the Korean Commercial Arbitration Tribunal as the arbitral tribunal, adhering to the Rules of the ICC. Furthermore, a party could also argue that the clause referred to an ICC arbitration and that the reference to the Korean Commercial Arbitration Tribunal was merely for specifying the place of arbitration.[63] When referring to an institution, the parties should clearly indicate whether they intend to have the institution administer the proceedings or simply to incorporate its rules of procedure.

Here is another example of a defective clause:

> Attribution of jurisdiction: in case of contestation, the parties agree to seek recourse to the arbitration of the French Advertising Federation. In case of disputes, only the Seine Court will have jurisdiction.[64]

This clause is extremely problematic. Firstly, there is no specification as to what is the difference between a "contestation" and a "dispute". Therefore a court would have to intervene in order to determine whether a

---

[61]  See Davis, *supra*, note 51, p. 377.
[62]  See Bond, *supra*, note 49, p. 15.
[63]  See Davis, *supra*, note 51, pp. 377-378, discussing the complications of this particular clause.
[64]  *Ibid.*, p. 384.

particular disagreement is a contestation or a dispute and such a decision could be very difficult to reach. Secondly, because of the ambiguous wording, this clause is very far from being clear as to who is the deciding authority.

## (b)  The Sophisticated Clause

A standard dispute resolution clause contains many elements. The clauses below set out various combinations from real situations. The opportunities and problems inherent in these approaches are described.

### Negotiation to Arbitration

### Section 1

### Standard Clause — The Jurisdiction Clause

a.    In the event a dispute or disagreement (hereinafter called "Dispute") arises between the parties in connection with the interpretation of any provision of this Agreement or the compliance or noncompliance therewith, or the validity or enforceability thereof, or the performance or nonperformance of either party to the Agreement, the following dispute resolution process shall be followed by the parties.

b.    If the parties have not been able to resolve the Dispute in a prompt and expeditious manner after delivery of written request from one party to the other to resolve the Dispute, either party may at any time thereafter (until the earlier of resolution or escalation to Senior Management as provided below) request by written notice to the other party that the Dispute be escalated to Senior Management.

c.    In the event such a request with written notice is made, each party shall make available the senior executives specified in the following subparagraph ("Senior Management") who shall meet within fifteen (15) business days after such request is made at the offices of the party which received the request to attempt to resolve the Dispute.

d.    In case such Dispute is not settled amicably by Senior Management within thirty (30) days of escalation to Senior Management, such Dispute shall be resolved and determined by an Arbitration Board acting in accordance with the rules of conciliation and arbitration of the International Chamber of Commerce, whose decision shall be final and binding upon the parties. The Arbitration Board shall consist of the person or persons that the parties may agree on and in default of agreement within twenty (20) days following the expiration of the above-mentioned thirty (30) day period, each of the parties in dispute shall nominate one member to serve on the Arbitration Board and shall give notice to the other party of the name of its nominee. If one party fails to give this notice within fifteen (15) days after the other party has done so, then the member nominated by the other party shall constitute the Arbitration Board. If each party gives this notice then the two members so nominated by agreement shall select a third member who shall be Chairman. If the original two members are unable to agree upon a third member within thirty (30) days after the second notice has been given, then either party may apply to a judge of an appropriate court of the jurisdiction in which the arbitration will take place to appoint the third member who shall be unconditionally accepted by both parties. The place of arbitration for disputes for which arbitration is initiated by DISTRIBUTOR shall be Ottawa, Canada and the place of arbitration for disputes for which arbitration is initiated by [Party A] shall be Singapore. Each member shall have knowledge of and experience in the semiconductor industry. The language of any arbitration will be English.

e.   The arbitration hearing shall commence within sixty (60) days after appointment of the member(s) of the Arbitration Board and shall be completed and a binding award rendered in writing within sixty (60) days after commencement of the hearing unless exceptional circumstances warrant delay. The decision of the Arbitration Board may be entered in any court of competent jurisdiction and execution entered thereupon forthwith. The law specified in paragraph (b) above shall apply.

f.   Each party shall bear the cost of preparing its own case. The Arbitration Board shall have the right to include in the award the prevailing party's costs of arbitration and reasonable fees of attorneys, accountants, engineers and other professionals in connection with the arbitration.[65]

Section 1(a) is a key clause. It sets out the essence of the arbitral procedure. Each lawyer must be concerned that this key clause — the clause that defines the jurisdiction of the arbitration — sets out clearly the intent of the parties. This clause is key for the following reasons:

•   It defines the scope of the court's and the arbitrator's jurisdictions. If the matter in issue falls outside this clause, the courts will issue a stay

---

[65] *Pleadings and Proceedings* IN THE MATTER OF an arbitration to be conducted in Accordance with Article 25 of the Mitel Semiconductor Distributor Agreement dated January 19, 1995 and the Rules of Conciliation and Arbitration of the International Chamber of Commerce.

of the arbitration. The concept of court ordered stays is more fully described in Section 3 of this chapter. The courts will honour the parties' agreement that matters in issue, falling within this clause, are to be dealt with pursuant to the dispute resolution clause.

• Conversely, the second key component of this clause is that it defines the jurisdiction of the arbitrator if the clause calls for arbitration (as this clause does). Ironically, this jurisdiction clause does not prevent a negotiated settlement either directly or through a mediator with terms that fall outside the terms of the jurisdiction clause.

• The final key point is that the courts will force the parties to follow the procedure set out in the clause. As a result it is important that the parties carefully define actions that can be taken outside this clause. For example, the parties might wish to add the following:

The parties, however, will not be required to arbitrate and this Paragraph will not apply to any Dispute relating to:

A.  actual or threatened unauthorized use or disclosure of their respective confidential information; or

B.  payment for projects supplied by [Party A] to distributor hereunder.[66]

There is a tension in every sophisticated dispute resolution clause between the desire to effect a speedy negotiated settlement and the need for a binding resolution if the negotiations fail. The problem with clauses "b" and "c" is that they do not provide that all action taken pursuant to those clauses shall be confidential and without prejudice. Legal counsel must mark all material produced for the negotiation (or mediation) as privileged. Further, it should be ensured that all verbal discussions are privileged.

## (c)  Other Model Clauses

An arbitration clause should always be comprehensive and not leave any important issues to be dealt with at a later time when a dispute arises. This is not recommended since arriving at an agreement when the parties are already in the midst of a conflict can prove to be very difficult. Below are a few samples of effective arbitration clauses.

---

[66] *Pleadings and Proceedings, ibid.*

(i) *Standard ICC Clause*

> All disputes arising out of or in connection with the present contract shall be finally settled under the Rules of Arbitration of the International Chamber of Commerce by one or more arbitrators appointed in accordance with the said Rules.

Note that this sample is the standard recommended provision by the ICC which provides the key elements to an effective arbitration clause: "All disputes", "in connection with" and "finally settled".[67] Parties will often add elements such as the applicable law, the place of arbitration and the number of arbitrators to this clause.

(ii) *Standard AAA (American Arbitration Association) Clause*

> Any controversy or claim arising out of or relating to this contract, or the breach thereof, shall be settled by arbitration administered by the American Arbitration Association in accordance with its Commercial [or other] Arbitration Rules [including the Emergency Interim Relief Procedures], and judgment on the award rendered by the arbitrator(s) may be entered in any court having jurisdiction thereof.

(iii) *Other Model Clause*

1.  Should any dispute or disagreement of any kind, arise with respect to this Agreement, the parties agree that the dispute or disagreement shall be resolved by Arbitration. There shall be a single Arbitrator. The place of Arbitration shall be the province of Ontario. The applicable law is the Arbitration Act of Ontario. The Arbitration shall be governed by the Rules for the Conduct of Commercial Arbitrations (the "Rules") of the Arbitration and Mediation Institute of Canada, with the modifications described below. The Rules are attached as Schedule "A". The provisions of these Rules, as modified by this clause, shall predominate except for mandatory provisions of the Arbitration Act of Ontario. The Arbitration award is final and binding upon the parties who hereby waive all rights of Appeal therefrom.

2.  In the notice commencing the Arbitration, as contemplated by Article 19 of the Rules, the party delivering the notice shall propose three (3)

---

[67] Craig, Park and Paulson, *International Chamber of Commerce Arbitration*, 2nd ed., 1990, p. 111.

Arbitrators. Upon receipt of the notice, the other party(ies) agree to immediately commence good faith negotiations for the purpose of selecting an Arbitrator. If the parties are unable to agree on an Arbitrator within ten (10) days of the delivery of the notice required under Article 19, the Arbitrator shall be selected pursuant to Article 10 of the Rules.

3.　　It is a fundamental aim of the parties to this Agreement that disputes be resolved quickly. Unless the parties otherwise agree, the Arbitrator shall hold the preliminary meeting contemplated by Article 27 of the Rules within 15 days of his or her appointment. At the preliminary meeting, unless the parties otherwise agree, the Arbitrator shall fix the date of the hearing, which hearing shall commence within 90 days of the preliminary meeting.

4.　　The parties agree that good faith negotiation or mediation may occur at any time to attempt to resolve any dispute or disagreement. Such negotiations or mediation shall take place only if all parties agree. Such negotiations or mediation shall, in no way, derogate from the rights of a party to seek to have the dispute/disagreement resolved by binding Arbitration.

## 5. ARBITRAL ISSUES

As set out in the description of the *Breda* case, the key issue is whether or not the dispute is covered by an arbitration agreement. Occasionally, the counsel may confuse the issue to go to arbitration with specific questions to be resolved by the arbitrator in the arbitration. The parties to an agreement do not have to agree on the precise "issue" to be resolved by the arbitrator. Of course, if there is *no pre-existing arbitration clause*, and the parties wish to resolve a precise issue, then an arbitration agreement with a specific issue, i.e., dispute, will occur. In normal situations the parties will simply notify the other side of the dispute according to the terms of the clause. If the clause is silent, section 23(1)3 of the Ontario *Arbitration Act, 1991* provides for a notice demanding arbitration under the agreement. The arbitrator, as selected, will order the parties to submit their statements. These statements (section 25(2)) shall indicate "the facts supporting their positions, *the points at issue* and the relief sought . . .". [emphasis added]

## 6. SELECTING THE ARBITRATORS

One of the delays in establishing an arbitration may be the subtle manoeuvring between the arbitrants in the appointment of the arbitrators. Under sections 11, 12 and 13 of the *Arbitration Act, 1991*, an arbitrant can successfully challenge an arbitrator (which would include, of course, a nominee) if there are circumstances that may give rise to a reasonable apprehension of bias. In other words, the arbitrator must be strictly free, independent and impartial unless the arbitrants, expressly or by implication, agree otherwise. I would, therefore, suggest that the arbitrants attach a list of arbitrators, to the arbitration clause, who may be appropriate in the eyes of the arbitrants to hear the arbitration.

The first matter the arbitrants should decide on is the number of arbitrators. The usual course is to have either a single arbitrator or a three-person board of arbitration.

There are various methods of choosing the arbitrator(s):

- The parties can name a mutually agreed upon person in the arbitration agreement filed at the outset of the hearing.
- The parties can each nominate a party. Those two parties can then name a single arbitrator or name a third party to join the nominees on a three-person arbitration board.
- A party can be named ahead of time who will then appoint an arbitrator when disputes arise.

*A notable advantage of arbitration is that the parties may choose, as arbitrators, specialists in the field in question.* The freedom of the arbitrants to choose an arbitration panel clothed with expertise in the subject matter is a feature that the arbitrants cannot find in court. A judge is often unaware of the technical intricacies or jargon of the subject matter and must be educated in this regard. This can be an expensive process. Keep in mind, however, that the arbitrator who was selected for his or her "specialized knowledge" may turn out to be biased and intolerant, filled to the brim with his or her own "pet theories".

The arbitrants may also want to consider the advantages and disadvantages of having lawyers acting as arbitrators. Martin Teplitsky in *Commercial Arbitration* comments:

> I favour a chairperson who is a lawyer and who has had experience conducting hearings either directly or as a counsel. It is difficult for a lay person to conduct

a hearing with expedition and in accordance both with the principles of natural justice and the adversary system. In my experience, a lay chairperson often creates problems at the hearing. In a three-person board, the nominees may be either lay persons (usually experts in the field) or lawyers . . . In a technical case, a nominee expert may appear to provide an advantage over a legally trained nominee. The vice, of course is versa. Try to arrange when arbitration is invoked, for the sake of all parties, a board of arbitration with a parallel nominee structure. You may also want to consider that the adversary system probably operates more smoothly if the adjudicators are not experts capable of giving expert evidence.

Where the arbitration agreement provides no procedure in appointing the arbitral tribunal or a person with power to appoint the arbitral tribunal, the court may do so.[68]

The method of selecting the arbitrator is now critical in the context of sections 11, 12 and 13 of the Act. Essentially, these provisions require arbitrators to disclose possible biases and allow arbitrants to challenge the appointment of an arbitrator on the basis of bias or lack of qualification.

Section 11 of the Act requires an arbitrator to disclose any circumstances which may give rise to a reasonable apprehension of bias. In the past, some legal counsel have sought to 'educate' their nominee privately on the merits of their client's case. Such an action could now result in the award being set aside.[69]

The Supreme Court of Canada in the 1954 decision of *Szilard v. Szasz*[70] and more recently in *Newfoundland Telephone Co. v. Newfoundland (Commissioners of Public Utilities)*[71] has commented on the necessity of impartiality in any decision making process. In *Szilard*, the Court held that from its inception, arbitration has been in the nature of judicial intervention and captures notions and principles inherent to the process of judicial determination. The arbitrators must exercise their discretion, not as the advocate of the arbitrant nominating them, but instead in a free, independent and impartial manner. Most importantly, their consideration of the case must be untrammelled by such influences as to a fair minded person would raise a reasonable doubt as to their impartiality.[72]

In *Newfoundland Telephone Co. v. Newfoundland (Commissioners of Public Utilities)*, the Court struggled with the issue as to whether or not an

---

[68]  See s. 10 of the Ontario *Arbitration Act, 1991.*

[69]  *Ibid.*, s. 46(1)8.

[70]  [1955] 1 D.L.R. 370 (S.C.C.).

[71]  [1992] 1 S.C.R. 623.

[72]  *Supra*, note 70, at 371 (Rand J.).

individual appointed to the Power Commission in Newfoundland had become biased by statements made by that individual during the course of the hearing themselves.

Cory J. stated that:

> The duty to act fairly includes the duty to provide procedural fairness to the parties. That simply cannot exist if an adjudicator is biased. It is, of course, impossible to determine the precise state of mind of an adjudicator who has made an administrative board decision. As a result, the courts have taken the position that an unbiased appearance is, in itself, an essential component of procedural fairness. To ensure fairness the conduct of members of administrative tribunals has been measured against a standard of reasonable apprehension of bias. The test is whether a reasonably informed bystander could reasonably perceive bias on the part of an adjudicator.[73]

Normally, a reasonable apprehension of bias renders the proceedings void and not just voidable; however, the legislature in Ontario has modified that common law rule so that awards in arbitrations tainted with a reasonable apprehension of bias are not set aside by the courts if the party seeking to do so had the opportunity to challenge the arbitration on the ground complained of and did not do so (section 46(4) of the Act).

It is clear that the combined effect of *Szilard* and the *Newfoundland* decisions is that arbitrants must now be vigilant so as not to appoint arbitrators whom others may reasonably perceive as being biased. The arbitration agreement should carefully provide for the method of selecting the arbitrators or, in the alternative, the arbitrants should expressly agree to contract out of sections 11, 12 and 13. Upon contracting out, the arbitrants would be free to select partisan nominees.

## 7.  MODEL OF ARBITRATOR COMPETENCE — A SKILLS ANALYSIS

### (a)  Case Management Skills

General Definition: The ability to organize and prepare for the arbitration in an efficient and effective manner.

- Ability to design and maintain office systems

---

[73]  *Supra*, note 71, at 636.

- maintains a recording system
- sets up a correspondence system
- regularly reviews and controls diary entries
- maintains a case file monitoring system
- maintains full and up to date costing files
- maintains full and up to date accounting files

- Ability to allocate time, effort and other resources effectively
  - reviews documents received from parties
  - develops an overall perspective of the case
  - draws up a timetable for preparation and conduct of the arbitration

- Ability to work according to systems or rules governing the handling of cases
  - records details of the appointment (e.g., terms, conditions and fee)
  - confirms the appointment in writing with both parties
  - ensures all correspondence is provided to both parties
  - ensures all correspondence received has been provided to the other party
  - draws up a timetable

- Ability to bring the file to completion
  - quickly drafts award
  - if on a panel, works co-operatively to draft the decision
  - promptly notifies the parties on completion of the award

## (b)  Procedural Skills

General Definition: The ability to conduct matters that are referred to arbitration using fair, flexible and effective procedures.

- Ability to determine if appointment is legitimate (jurisdiction)
  - checks contract between the parties and in particular the arbitration clause
  - checks to ensure agreement is effective or in existence
  - ensures that issues in dispute are covered by the terms of the arbitration clause
  - ensures there is no reason for parties to challenge the appointment (e.g., independence and impartiality)
  - ensures appointment is not inconsistent with local laws or institutional rules

- Ability to deal with preliminary matters
  - calls preliminary meeting if requested or required, in consultation with the parties
  - gives directions to parties on pleadings and disclosure of evidence
  - requests that parties disclose all relevant information at the earliest opportunity (to arbitrator and parties)
  - encourages parties to come to an agreement on as many facts as possible prior to the arbitration
  - ensures all procedural steps have been exhausted as required

- Ability to supervise preliminary meetings or pre-trials
  - supervises conduct of the meeting
  - explains in advance the procedure of the meeting or pre-trial and particularly that which might cause surprise
  - intervenes when necessary
  - persuades parties to come to agreement on as many procedural aspects of the case as possible

- Ability to handle interlocutory matters
  - hears the parties' arguments on the matter
  - characterizes and decides the points at issue
  - defines and supervises a fair interlocutory procedure

- Ability to conduct a fair hearing

#### (c) **Introductory**

- clearly explains the role of the arbitrator
- clearly defines ground rules and procedure
- clearly explains procedure to parties
- invites parties to estimate time necessary for the hearing

#### (d) **Hearing**

- affords each party full and proper opportunity to present its case
- allows each party the opportunity to examine the other party's witnesses
- allows parties to make and respond fully to objections
- allows parties adequate time to respond to surprises
- decides quickly on procedural objections
- keeps interruptions to a minimum

- narrows issues (by clarification without unnecessarily adding or inter-jecting)
- maintains order

- Ability to handle witnesses
  - explains procedure to witnesses where necessary
  - for expert witnesses, considers legitimacy of expertise
  - encourages expert witnesses to make use of lay language

- Ability to keep a record of the evidence
  - ensures a proper record is kept of submissions and evidence
  - subjects record to review and organization frequently
  - analyzes record periodically during the hearing
  - limits evidence to relevant topics

- Weighs the evidence, and if necessary, decides upon admissibility

## (e) Decision Making Skills

General Definition: The ability to reach a principled decision deter-mining the rights and liabilities of the parties in the dispute and to expound that conclusion in the form of a reasoned award.

- Ability to understand the factual issues
  - separates the parties' claims and issues
  - identifies the real issues between the parties
  - reconstructs the issues in terms which will facilitate a solution
  - evaluates the strengths of arguments and counter-arguments
  - evaluates the submissions and the relevant evidence
  - acknowledges those issues that are of no or little relevance

- Ability to define the legal issues and apply them to the facts
  - determines the relevant principles of law
  - applies the relevant law to the specific facts of the case
  - distinguishes between different sources of law (i.e., the contract between the parties, the local law, or the law of an institution)
  - uses deduction to determine the application of relevant principles of law

- Ability to come to a decision
  - reaches an independent and impartial decision after careful analysis of all the relevant data

- Ability to articulate the decision
    - articulates succinctly the reasons and the terms of the award as well as the evidence considered and the weight given to the evidence
    - uses terminology appropriate to the audience to which it is directed

## (f)  Award Writing Skills

General Definition: The ability to effectively convey a decision in writing.

- Ability to address formalities
    - cites parties' names, dates, etc.
    - knows requirements of formalities

- Ability to summarize briefly facts and issues
    - briefly describes the nature of the dispute and how it arose
    - summarizes evidence and submissions
    - identifies undisputed facts and law agreed upon
    - distinguishes parties' claims and issues
    - reconstructs issues in terms which facilitate a solution
    - separates relevant and irrelevant facts

- Ability to reference the law relied on

- Ability to substantiate the decision
    - correlates findings with relevant evidence
    - explains chosen weighting of evidence
    - shows inconsistencies in the evidence

- Ability to convey the decision clearly to the parties
    - writes clearly and concisely
    - logically proceeds with thoughts (e.g., connected paragraphs)
    - uses appropriate language for the audience
    - presents decisions in an impartial manner
    - articulates succinctly the reasons for reaching the decision

## (g)  Interpersonal Skills

General Definition: The ability to control the arbitration process in a manner which engenders mutual respect between all those involved in an arbitration, to communicate effectively and facilitate others in doing so and to demonstrate commitment to resolving satisfactorily the dispute entrusted.

- Ability to maintain a good relationship with the parties
  - acts with courtesy, respect and patience
  - indicates interest in the issues and the parties
  - does not pre-judge the parties or the issues
  - is modest in attitudes held towards others and in self regard
  - devotes such care and attention to the case as the parties might reasonably require

- Ability to remain impartial and independent
  - does not send unilateral correspondence
  - discloses all facts which may give rise to doubts about potential impartiality
  - allows equal opportunities to both parties to correspond with arbitrator
  - remains detached but not unfriendly
  - avoids relationships which might expose pressure or coercion
  - controls emotion
  - never discusses the merits of the case with one party in the absence of the other
  - ensures each party has all documents

- Ability to maintain legitimacy
  - personal appearance commands respect
  - is punctual
  - has a quietly assured manner
  - maintains consistent behaviour
  - if uses own expertise, gives parties a chance to comment
  - is discreet and diligent
  - keeps all information confidential
  - acts with self confidence and authority
  - demands respect for the office of arbitrator

- Ability to listen actively
  - remains visibly alert at all times
  - does nor interrupt
  - intervenes selectively

- Ability to speak effectively
  - uses clear diction
  - clarifies or paraphrases where necessary

- asks succinct questions if necessary
- is direct but not intimidating
- adopts a moderate volume and pace of speaking
- uses an unemotional detached tone of voice
- uses simple language
- uses terminology of the parties' profession

- Ability to maintain a civil atmosphere at the hearing
  - uses civil language
  - uses some humour
  - displays understanding of evidence and submission
  - puts parties and witnesses at ease
  - does not use distracting body movements
  - discourages an excessively adversarial climate

# 10

# Arbitration Hearings and Reviews

## 1. JURISDICTION OF THE ARBITRATORS

Section 17(1) of the Ontario *Arbitration Act, 1991* provides that an arbitral tribunal may rule on its jurisdiction to conduct the arbitration and may also rule on objections with respect to the existence or validity of the arbitration agreement.[1]

In *Christopher Brown Ltd. v. Genossenschaft Oesterreichischer Waldbesitzer*,[2] Lord Devlin held the following with respect to an arbitrator's right to adjudicate upon his or her jurisdiction:

> It is not the law that arbitrators, if their jurisdiction is challenged or questioned, are bound immediately to cease to act, and to refuse to act, until their jurisdiction has been determined by some Court which has power to determine it finally. Nor is the law that they are bound to go on without investigating the merits of the challenge and determine the matter in dispute leaving the question of their jurisdiction to be held over until it is determined by some Court which had power to determine it. They might then be merely wasting their time and everybody else's. They are not obliged to take either of those courses. They are entitled to inquire into the merits of the issue whether they have jurisdiction or not, not for the purpose of reaching any conclusion which will be binding on the parties, because that they cannot do, but for the purpose of satisfying themselves, as preliminary matter, whether they ought to go on with the arbitration or not. If it became abundantly clear to them that they had no jurisdiction as, for example, it would be if the submission which was produced was not signed, or not properly executed, or something of that sort, then they might well decide not to proceed with the hearing. They are entitled, in short,

---

[1] S.O. 1991, c. 17 (hereinafter "*Arbitration Act*").
[2] [1953] 2 All E.R. 1039 (Q.B.).

to make their own inquiries in order to determine their own course of action, but the result of that inquiry has no effect whatsoever on the rights of the parties. That is plain.[3]

Questions of jurisdiction are fundamental to the power of the arbitrator. Under section 46 of the *Arbitration Act*, the court may set aside an award if the award deals with the dispute beyond the scope of the arbitration agreement. If the arbitrant believes the arbitration tribunal has exceeded its jurisdiction, the arbitrant is statutorily required under section 17(5) to immediately object. Whether an arbitrator has jurisdiction to deal with the particular issue will be a matter of interpretation of the arbitration agreement. Once the arbitrator has determined that he or she has jurisdiction to hear the arbitration, then he or she may proceed.

In interpreting the powers granted to the arbitrator pursuant to an arbitration agreement, it is appropriate to give a liberal interpretation to the wording in favour of determining arbitrability. For example, in the *Anchor Marine Insurance Co. v. Corbett*,[4] the agreement allowed submissions on "all matters relating to insurance". Under the agreement, the broad issue of damages arising out of an accident and the question of the payment of premiums was considered arbitrable within the terms of the submission.

Generally, arbitrators should establish that they possess the requisite jurisdiction before receiving any evidence from the arbitrants. In some cases, however, the arbitrator can and should defer the determination of jurisdiction until after the hearing of the evidence. For example, in *Toronto (Metropolitan) Commissioners of Police v. Police Assn. (Metropolitan Toronto)*,[5] where the issues between the arbitrants were not agreed upon prior to the arbitration, the Divisional Court held that the arbitrator possessed the discretion to hear evidence first before outlining the issues to be determined, thereby, defining her jurisdiction. In that case, the arbitrator was extended absolute discretion to define the scope of her authority.

There are some limitations on the types of decisions that an arbitrator may make with respect to determining jurisdiction. It would appear that

---

[3] *Ibid.*, at 1042. See also *Hyundai Auto Canada Inc. v. Dayhu Investments Ltd.* (May 21, 1993), Doc. RE2655/93 (Ont. Gen. Div.); *Deluce Holdings Inc. v. Air Canada* (1992), 12 O.R. (3d) 131 (Gen. Div. [Commercial List]); *Campbell v. Murphy* (1993), 15 O.R. (3d) 444 (Gen. Div.); *Buck Brothers Ltd. v. Frontenac Builders Ltd.* (1994), 19 O.R. (3d) 97 (C.A.); *Bab Systems Inc. v. McLurg*, [1994] O.J. No. 3029; *Ontario v. Mitchnick*, [1995] O.J. No. 3369 (Ont. Gen. Div.) (You will find different examples of jurisdiction).

[4] (1882), 9 S.C.R. 73.

[5] (1976), 14 O.R. (2d) 612 (Div. Ct.).

although arbitrators have the power to determine their own jurisdiction, they do not have the power to determine whether the case was a proper one for arbitration or whether they, as a particular arbitrator, in fact, should have been appointed.[6]

## 2. EVIDENCE AND PROCEDURE AT THE ARBITRATION

Like any civil proceeding, the arbitrants exchange pleading-like documents prior to the commencement of the hearing. Under the *Arbitration Act*, these "pleadings" are called statements and must indicate the facts supporting an arbitrant's position, the points at issue and the relief sought. Under section 25, time requirements are imposed with respect to submitting these statements.

While an arbitration agreement may only be amended through the consent of the arbitrants, section 25(4) of the *Arbitration Act* allows the arbitrants to amend or supplement their statements during the course of the arbitration. The arbitration agreement remains fixed as the permanent foundation of the arbitration while one's statement can be amended at will to meet the various exigencies of the arbitration.

The arbitrants must also be vigilant while the arbitration is being conducted. Section 4 of the *Arbitration Act* states:

> A party who participates in an arbitration despite being aware of non-compliance with a provision of this Act, except one mentioned in section 3, or with the arbitration agreement, and does not object to the non-compliance within the time limit provided or, if none is provided, within a reasonable time, shall be deemed to have waived the right to object.

Under this section, one must object *promptly* to non-compliance with the Act or the arbitration agreement. Section 4 is clear that one cannot *sleep on* procedural or other irregularities and then seek to use such irregularities at a later time to set aside the award. It must be noted, of course, that one need not object promptly to the fundamental procedural safeguards outlined in the mandatory provisions of section 3.

---

[6] *Ibid.*

## 3.  SUMMONS TO WITNESS

The *Arbitration Act* gives the arbitrator certain powers, including powers of compelling the attendance of witnesses and the production of documents. The Act gives the arbitral tribunal power to effect the compulsory attendance of witnesses by the issuance of a subpoena pursuant to section 29. There is no reason, however, that a motion to an arbitrator for a subpoena cannot be made *ex parte*. Moreover, there is no reason that the arbitrator cannot issue a number of notices to witnesses pursuant to section 29.

The arbitrator has power to proceed and issue an award in the deliberate absence of a party. In *1018092 Ontario Inc. v. 833749 Ontario Inc.*,[7] the appellant sought to appeal the decision of the General Division which dismissed its appeal from a decision of the arbitrator. The Court of Appeal noted that the appeal arises because the appellant deliberately thwarted the arbitration process and failed to attend two arbitration hearings following the appellant's wrongful termination of a management contract despite ample notice and warning. The Court noted:

> In our view, there is an onus on the appellant to explain its failure to appear before the arbitrator. In the absence of an explanation that the failure to attend was otherwise than a deliberate tactical ploy, we are not prepared to give effect to the arguments of mixed fact and law that are raised on this appeal, particularly in the absence of a proper record.[8]

As with other procedural matters, if the arbitrants wish to formulate their own rules with respect to evidentiary matters, this must be incorporated into the arbitration agreement.

## 4.  THE ARBITRATION PROCESS

The most critical aspect of a successful arbitration is the selection of an experienced arbitrator. Upon appointment of an arbitrator, the counsel will schedule a preliminary motion to set out the timetable. The timetable is the key to a successful arbitration. This preliminary motion can be done by telephone. The purpose of the timetable is to schedule the exchange of pleadings, the delivery of documents, the examinations for discovery and

---

[7] [1998] O.J. No. 553 (Ont. C.A.).
[8] *Ibid.*

the date of the hearing itself. There may well be critical preliminary motions with respect to the jurisdiction of the arbitrator. As a general rule, the courts will encourage the arbitrator to make a preliminary ruling on his or her jurisdiction even if the making of this ruling determines key issues not yet presented fully into evidence.

The arbitrator's jurisdiction is defined by the arbitration agreement. The arbitrator's procedural authority is set out in the rules governing the arbitration. If the rules are silent, the mandatory provisions of the governing law would apply. If there are no mandatory provisions in the governing law, the arbitrator has his or her own discretion.

The demands of complex commercial arbitration require the arbitrator to control the process. As a general principle, arbitrators enjoy great authority over the proceedings and should govern proceedings with a firm but fair hand. Many key issues will be considered by the arbitrator prior to the hearing itself.

Experienced counsel will be continually re-evaluating their case in the light of the productions and discoveries ordered pursuant to the timetable. A propitious time for further negotiations or mediation may arise. Further, modern arbitrators are aware of the dynamic aspect of mediation and may seek to encourage the parties to schedule a mediated session which may lead to a settlement.

With respect to the timetable, the arbitrator must exercise strict authority over the timetable. For example, if the arbitration is to be run effectively and efficiently counsel cannot have unlimited time for examinations for discovery as in standard litigation. One approach is to clearly delineate the amount of time proposed for examinations for discovery or depositions to direct counsel to complete their discoveries within the period fixed. Further complex or unnecessary motions related to the production of documents on discovery or questions flowing from the examination for discovery can be resolved speedily by telephone motions. Short of settlement, the arbitrator must insist that the parties comply with the timetable.

Another critical component of the timetable is the motion to determine the actual hearing itself. There are a number of matters which must be resolved. Unlike a normal case, the arbitrator must govern the arbitration process, at all times of course, by being sensitive to the need to treat each party fairly and equally. The matters to be resolved by the arbitrator include:

- The preparation of a common document brief.
- The exchange of expert reports.
- Witness statements in the place of live witnesses.
- Evidence by video technology to save travel expense.

The standard by which the evidence is judged is similar to the powers of a judge.

> The role of the arbitrator in apportioning disputed property rather than deciding rights strictly was recognised, though only to be condemned, by the writer to *The Times* on 11 August 1892, who, though anonymous, is believed to be Lord Justice Bowen, later a Law Lord:
>
> > The mercantile public is not fond of law, if law can be avoided. They prefer even the hazardous and mysterious changes of arbitration, in which some arbitrator who knows as much of the law as he does of theology, by the application of a rough and ready moral consciousness, or upon the affable principle of dividing the victory equally between both sides, decides intricate questions of law and fact with equal ease.
>
> Ours may be the first age which has expected arbitrators to behave like judges, making all-or-nothing awards which leave one party with no more than would have been gained by the loser in litigation. Yet experience suggests that, even today, there are arbitrators whom not sharing Lord Bowen's confidence that litigation is an end in itself, occasionally find it impossible to resist the temptation to impose a wiser apportionment, rather than make an award in punctilious conformity with the law. There is no trace in Ancient Greece of antipathy to apportionment in principle (though, of course, there are many objection to its results) from arbitrators, or the authorities, or from the parties themselves, even those who might have expected to gain the whole if the decision had been made by applying the strict law to determine their rights.[9]

The arbitrator must decide the issue pursuant to precise principles of law to enable the arbitrator to apportion property or to make decisions based on what is "fair" in the circumstances. This express power must be provided in the arbitration agreement. The arbitrator would make a clear error in law if he or she were to assume the power of making a "fair" decision without such authority in the arbitration agreement.

The arbitrator must also demand the respect of the parties and prevent bad behaviour from counsel or witnesses. Most arbitrators have little difficulty maintaining civility in the hearing room. The same principles which must govern civil relations between counsel must also govern the arbitration process. It must be emphasized that arbitration is not a court trial, and assumptions and expectations brought from the courtroom may be misplaced in arbitration. Further, the arbitrator, pursuant to section 21 of the *Arbitration Act* (which incorporates sections 14, 15 and 16 of the *Statutory*

---

[9] Roebuck, D., *Ancient Greek Arbitration*, Holo Books - The Arbitration Press, Oxford, 2001, p. 25.

*Powers Procedure Act*), may therefore legitimately entertain hearsay evidence. On the other hand, it must be emphasized that the streamline provisions of an effective arbitration hearing require counsel to be thoroughly prepared in the same manner as at a court trial.

Section 21 of the *Arbitration Act* provides that sections 14, 15 and 16 of the *Statutory Powers Procedure Act*[10] apply to the arbitration with necessary modifications. Hence, an arbitral tribunal is statutorily mandated to accept, as evidence, any oral testimony, documents or other things as provided in the *Statutory Powers Procedure Act*.[11] This, of course, allows the arbitral tribunal to legitimately entertain hearsay evidence.

---

[10] R.S.O. 1990, c. S.22.

[11] Sections 14, 15 and 16 of the *Statutory Powers Procedure Act* are set out below:

14. (1) A witness at a oral or electronic hearing shall be deemed to have objected to answer any question asked him or her upon the ground that the answer may tend to criminate him or her or may tend to establish his or her liability to civil proceedings at the instance of the Crown, or of any person, and no answer given by a witness at a hearing shall be used or be receivable in evidence against the witness in any trial or other proceeding against him or her thereafter taking place, other than a prosecution for perjury in giving such evidence.

(2) A witness shall be informed by the tribunal of the right to object to answer any question under section 5 of the *Canada Evidence Act*.

15. (1) Subject to subsections (2) and (3), a tribunal may admit as evidence at a hearing, whether or not given or proven under oath or affirmation or admissible as evidence in a Court,

    (a) any oral testimony; and
    (b) any document or other thing,

relevant to the subject-matter of the proceeding and may act on such evidence, but the tribunal may exclude anything unduly repetitious.

(2) Nothing is admissible in evidence at a hearing,

    (a) that would be inadmissible in a Court by reason of any privilege under the law of evidence; or
    (b) that is inadmissible by the statute under which the proceeding arises or any other statute.

(3) Nothing in subsection (1) overrides the provisions of any Act expressly limiting the extent to or purposes for which any oral testimony, documents or things may be admitted or used in evidence in any proceeding.

(4) Where a tribunal is satisfied as to its authenticity, a copy of a document or other thing may be admitted as evidence at a hearing.

## 5.  POWER OF THE ARBITRAL TRIBUNAL TO GRANT INJUNCTIONS

An arbitral tribunal may order specific performance, injunctions and other equitable remedies by virtue of section 31 of the *Arbitration Act*. An arbitral tribunal can issue an interim or interlocutory injunction or other interlocutory equitable remedies.

Under section 41, the arbitral tribunal is empowered to make one or more interim awards. In addition, section 42 empowers the tribunal to make one or more final awards.

Essentially, this allows the arbitrator to make his or her award in stages, depending upon the particular issues being considered. For example, the arbitrator could award an interlocutory injunction and then go on to address other issues in a final award. To eliminate contentious argument on the power of the arbitrator to grant remedies such as injunctions, it is best to allow for such authority in the arbitration agreement.

In asking an arbitrator to grant an interlocutory injunction, the adverse arbitrant may argue that such a remedy can only be granted when the dispute is decided (e.g., in the context of the final award). This argument is buttressed by section 8(1) of the *Arbitration Act* which seemingly gives the court the ultimate power to grant an interim injunction, thereby excluding the power of the arbitrator to do so.

---

(5) Where a document has been filed in evidence at a hearing, the tribunal may, or the person producing it or entitled to it may with the leave of the tribunal, cause the document to be photocopied and the tribunal may authorize the photocopy to be filed in evidence in the place of the document filed and release the document filed, or may furnish to the person producing it or the person entitled to it a photocopy of the document filed certified by a member of the tribunal.

(6) A document purporting to be a copy of a document filed in evidence at a hearing, certified to be a copy thereof by a member of the tribunal, is admissible in evidence in proceedings in which the document is admissible as evidence of the document.

16. A tribunal may, in making its decision in any proceeding,

    (a) take notice of facts that may be judicially noticed; and

    (b) take notice of any generally recognized scientific or technical facts, information or opinions within its scientific or specialized knowledge.

In the recent case of *National Ballet of Canada v. Glasco*,[12] the arbitrator made an interlocutory order suspending the non-renewal of the employment contract and ordering interim specific performance such that the dancer in this case would be assigned regular roles and performances with the ballet. The ballet appealed this order, arguing that the arbitrator did not have jurisdiction to grant the interim relief. However, it was held that the arbitrator was sitting as an arbitrator under the *Arbitration Act* and that under sections 31 and 41 had the express power to grant the interim injunction.

The parties in this case had chosen to arbitrate their dispute under the *Arbitration Act* and not to proceed through the labour board or grievance arbitration, where there are some limitations on interim reinstatement, as per the *Labour Relations Act, 1995*.[13] Justice O'Leary concluded that the arbitrator was right when he acknowledged that he had all the powers granted to an arbitrator under the *Arbitration Act*, and that included the power of granting an interlocutory injunction. It is apparent from the judgment that the arbitrator was aware that an order of specific performance of an employment contract is very rare. However, there is no absolute rule against such an order. The arbitrator did not err only because a judge could have exercised his or her discretion differently.

The court has the power to substitute its own remedy for that of an arbitrator under section 50(7) of the *Arbitration Act*. This power is triggered upon the application of the arbitrant to enforce the award. The court will only substitute its own remedy where it lacks jurisdiction to grant the arbitrator's remedy or where it would not have granted that remedy in similar circumstances.[14] While section 50(7) is of general application, an unsuccessful arbitrant who had sought a permanent injunction before an arbitrator may ask the court to impose injunctive relief where the arbitrator had not.

---

[12] (2000), 49 O.R. (3d) 223 (Div. Ct.), affirmed (2000), 49 O.R. (3d) 230 (S.C.J.).

[13] S.O. 1995, c. 1, Sched. 1.

[14] See section 50(7) of the Act:

> 50. (7) If the award gives a *remedy* that the Court does not have jurisdiction to grant or would not grant in a proceeding based on similar circumstances, the Court may,
>
> (a) grant a different remedy requested by the applicant; or
> (b) in the case of an award made in Ontario, remit it to the arbitral tribunal with the Court's opinion, in which case the arbitral tribunal may award a different remedy. [emphasis added]

## 6. THE ROLE OF THE COURT IN THE COURSE OF THE ARBITRATION

Generally, the court's role[15] in the course of the arbitration is limited.[16] The court can, however, uphold an important function in determining questions of law as they arise. Before such a question can be referred to a court, all arbitrants, as well as the arbitrator, must agree that the matter should be referred to the court. This eliminates the former practice in Ontario where one arbitrant could unilaterally make application to the court on a question of law, thereby delaying the arbitration process and in some cases causing unnecessary expenses.

The court also has the power to order the consolidation of arbitrations, provided the arbitrants consent. In other words, the court has no inherent or statutory jurisdiction to force similar arbitrations to be heard together. The essential tenet of arbitration is that it is consensual, and the court's power with respect to consolidation recognizes this point.

The court under section 13(1) of the *Arbitration Act* is also empowered to remove an arbitrator upon the application of an arbitrant, on one of the following grounds:

1. Circumstances exist that may give rise to a reasonable apprehension of bias.

2. The arbitrator does not possess qualifications that the parties have agreed are necessary.

In addition, an arbitrant may make an application to remove the arbitrator pursuant to section 15(1) if the arbitrator becomes unable to perform his or her functions, permits a corrupt or fraudulent act, causes undue delays

---

[15] See section 6 of the Act:

> 6. No Court shall intervene in matters governed by this Act, except for the following purposes, in accordance with this Act:
>
> 1. To assist the conducting of arbitrations.
> 2. To ensure that arbitrations are conducted in accordance with arbitration agreements.
> 3. To prevent unequal or unfair treatment of parties to arbitration agreements.
> 4. To enforce awards.

[16] See *Hyundai Auto Canada* and *Deluce Holdings*, *supra*, note 3.

in conducting the arbitration or does not conduct it in accordance with section 19 (equality and fairness).

If an arbitral tribunal has ruled on an objection to its jurisdiction, an arbitrant may, within thirty days after notice of the ruling, make an application to the court to determine the matter (section 17(8)). Section 45 provides for further court intervention through the appeal process on questions of law or questions of fact. On an appeal, the court may confirm, vary or set aside the award or may remit the award to the arbitral tribunal with the court's opinion on the question of law.

Section 48 allows parties not participating in the arbitration to make application to the court to challenge the arbitration process. Section 48(1) provides that at any stage during or after an arbitration the court may grant a declaration that the arbitration is invalid for any of the following reasons:

(a)  a party entered into the arbitration agreement while under a legal incapacity;

(b)  the arbitration agreement is invalid or ceased to exist;

(c)  the subject matter of the dispute is not capable of being the subject of arbitration under an Ontario law; or

(d)  the arbitration agreement does not apply to the dispute.

## 7.  SETTING ASIDE AND APPEALING ARBITRATION AWARDS

Does your client have a right to either appeal, apply to set aside, or move for judicial review of an arbitration award? Generally, a decision of an administrative tribunal is subject to these three distinct remedies, although it depends on the statute under which the tribunal is created. The specific provisions of the *Arbitration Act* limit the scope of these remedies and in the case of common law judicial review prohibit it altogether (note that section 46 of the Act provides the court with discretion to set aside an award under certain circumstances). Generally, it is the arbitration agreement itself which determines the party's remedies on appeal.

## 8. COMMON LAW JUDICIAL REVIEW NO LONGER AVAILABLE

Historically, a court would not review the result of a consensual arbitration, with the exception of an error of law on the face of the record.[17] Gradually, the inherent jurisdiction of the court to review such awards has expanded so that arbitration awards became subject to judicial review. The courts, although with jurisdiction, were hesitant to review such awards, believing that the parties had entered into the process consensually, and as a general rule must live with the outcome of the arbitrator's decision. Mr. Justice Mocatta in *Gunter Henck*[18] discusses the reason for the court's reticence:

> It is well established on the authorities that although the Courts are entitled to ... set aside awards ... this jurisdiction is not likely to be exercised. If parties choose to have their disputes settled by arbitrators, then, subject to certain limited exceptions the attitude of the Courts has been that the party should take arbitration for better or for worst ...[19]

The *Arbitration Act* clearly establishes that the common law right to judicial review is no longer available. Instead, section 46 (discussed subsequently) provides for certain grounds upon which a court may set aside an award. Section 6 provides:

> 6. No court shall intervene in matters governed by this Act, except for the following purposes, in accordance with this Act:
>
> 1. To assist the conducting of arbitrations.
>
> 2. To ensure that arbitrations are conducted in accordance with arbitration agreements.
>
> 3. To prevent unequal or unfair treatment of parties to arbitration agreements.
>
> 4. To enforce awards.

---

[17] See *Hodgkinson v. Fernie* (1857), 140 E.R. 712 (C.P.).
[18] *Gunter Henck v. Andre & Cie S.A.*, [1970] Lloyd's Rep. 235 (Q.B. Com. Ct.).
[19] *Ibid.*, at 238.

In *VAV Holdings Ltd. v. 720153 Ontario Ltd.*,[20] the judge asserted that section 6 specifically provides that a court cannot intervene in the procedure, unless it is in accordance with the Act. In other words, unless the remedy is specifically provided for by the Act, the court will not have the jurisdiction to review a binding arbitral decision. In *Superior Propane Inc. v. Valley Propane (Ottawa) Ltd.*,[21] the Court held that there is no judicial review of an arbitral tribunal's decision. In this case, the parties agreed that the arbitration would be "final and binding" but a motion was brought for leave to appeal from the arbitration decision. The Court dismissed the motion and the applicant appealed. The respondent brought a cross-motion to strike the application for judicial review.[22] Dismissing the application for judicial review, Justice Chadwick stated:

> Where the parties agree in advance that the decision of the arbitrator will be final and binding then it should not be open to judicial review unless the arbitrator has acted improperly. To allow judicial review because the procedure is conducted under the provisions of the *Arbitration Act, 1991* would defeat the whole purpose and value of consensual arbitration.[23]

The *Arbitration Act* provides a comprehensive and exhaustive procedure for dealing with domestic arbitrations and accordingly no other procedures can be used.[24] In *Hillmond Investments Ltd. v. Canadian Imperial Bank of Commerce*, the Ontario Court of Appeal held:

> . . . it is clear on authority that when a statute such as the *Arbitration Act*, 1991 provides a mechanism for appealing an arbitral award, that mechanism must be complied with. The appellate method of judicial review is entirely the creation of the legislature and where, as here, leave is required to appeal the award to an appellate court, there can be no appeal without that leave. At this moment, the court is without jurisdiction to hear this matter.[25]

---

[20] [1996] O.J. No. 1027, 1996 CarswellOnt 5554 (Ont. Gen. Div.). This decision was reversed on appeal but the above principle was not disputed.

[21] [1993] O.J. No. 442 (Ont. Gen. Div.).

[22] *Ibid.*

[23] *Ibid.*

[24] See John J. Chapman "Judicial Scrutiny of Domestic Commercial Arbitral Awards", 74 C.B.R. 402; *C.U.P.E., Local 963 v. New Brunswick Liquor Corp.*, [1979] 2 S.C.R. 227.

[25] (1996), 29 O.R. (3d) 612 (C.A.) at 616.

Although common law judicial review is no longer available, the principles found in those cases are of value in assisting arbitrants and the court in determining what constitutes a question of law, fact or misconduct.


## 9. APPEALS

Section 45 of the *Arbitration Act* provides the statutory scheme for appealing an arbitral award. The specific remedies available on appeal are: a confirmation of the arbitrator's award; a variance or setting aside of the award; or a remittance of the award to the arbitral tribunal with the court's opinion on the question of law.[26] As a procedural point, the proper court in which to seek a remedy under section 45 is the Ontario Superior Court of Justice, and not the Divisional Court.[27]

It is important to recognize that an appeal lies only from a final *award* of an arbitral tribunal. If the tribunal's decision relates to a procedural matter, the statutory scheme under sections 45 and 46 of the *Arbitration Act* does not apply. In *Environmental Export International of Canada Inc. v. Success International Inc.*,[28] the Court was asked to decide whether a decision respecting the admissibility of evidence could be set aside under section 46(1) on grounds that the applicant was not treated equally and fairly. The Court dismissed the application stating, in effect, that it does not have the jurisdiction to review a procedural decision of an arbitral tribunal. MacPherson J. stated:

> There is nothing in the Arbitration Act providing for appeals from, or applications to set aside, decisions of arbitrators on procedural points. It would be wrong, in my view, for the courts to invent such a remedy and inject it into the arbitration process.[29]

The difference between a procedural decision and an arbitral award has been clearly described by J. Brian Casey:

---

[26] *Arbitration Act, 1991*, s. 45(5).
[27] *Metropolitan Separate School Board v. Daniel Lakeshore Corp.*, [1993] O.J. No. 2375 (Ont. Gen. Div). See also, Norman M. Fera, "The Procedural Map From the Arbitration Table to the Court Room Door; The Road Away from ADR in Family Law", (1995-96), 13 *Canadian Family Law Quarterly* 314.
[28] [1995] O.J. No. 453, 1995 CarswellOnt 2485 (Ont. Gen. Div.), affirmed [1995] O.J. No. 3357, 1995 CarswellOnt 4168 (Ont. C.A.).
[29] *Ibid.*

A judgment or order of the arbitral tribunal is commonly referred to as an "award". An award may be interim or final, but, in either case, disposes of part or all of the dispute between the parties. It is important to recognize a distinction between a direction or order of the arbitral tribunal which deals with matters of procedure, and an award which deals with matters of substance.[30]

An award may be set aside under section 46(1) if the procedure followed by the arbitral tribunal did not comply with the Act, but the procedural matter itself cannot be appealed or reviewed prior to the determination of the substantive issues before the tribunal. Furthermore, one should not seek to appeal an interim award, but should wait and seek to appeal the final award.[31]

## (a)  Agreement Dealing with Appeals

Section 45 of the *Arbitration Act* permits a party to appeal an award to a court on a question of law, or fact, or mixed law and fact in the appropriate circumstances. If the arbitration agreement specifically states that a party may appeal an award on a question of law, then an appeal is as of right.[32] Similarly, if the arbitration agreement provides that there may be an appeal on a question of fact or on a question of mixed fact and law then such an appeal exists as of right.[33]

## Question of Fact

It is very difficult to convince a court to overturn a finding of fact when appealing an arbitral award. The decision in *Canadian Northern Railway Co. v. Billings*,[34] is helpful to determine when a question of fact will be overturned in the context of an arbitration. In that case, Fitzpatrick C.J. held:

> There is no doubt that upon the hearing of the appeal below it was competent for the Court to decide any question of fact upon the evidence taken before

---

[30] *International and Domestic Commercial Arbitration*, Toronto: Carswell, 1993, p. 8-1.
[31] *Hillmond Investments Ltd. v. Canadian Imperial Bank of Commerce* (1996), 29 O.R. (3d) 615 (C.A.).
[32] *Arbitration Act, 1991*, s. 45(2).
[33] *Ibid.*, s. 45(3).
[34] (1916), 31 D.L.R. 687 (S.C.C.).

the arbitrators, as in a case of original jurisdiction, sec. 209 *Railway Act*. But I submit with all deference that on such appeals certain rules have been laid down by which we are bound: First, an appeal from a decision of arbitrators upon a question which is merely one of value should be discouraged. Sir Richard (Lord) Couch in *Musson v. C.A. Rly.*, in the Privy Council, 17 L.N. 179, at 181; second, in cases of this nature the *Courts, as in reviewing the verdict of a jury, or a report of referees, upon questions of fact, cannot reserve unless there is a plain and decided preponderance of evidence against the finding of the arbitrators or commissioners as to border strongly on the conclusive. And that rule should, perhaps, be still more strictly adhered to on an arbitrator's award than on a verdict of a jury, as the arbitrators are generally chosen not only because of their well-known integrity, but also because of their experience in such matters and previous local knowledge.* They also view and review the premises as often as they may think it necessary to enable them to form a correct estimate, and must surely be in a better position to determine the exact amount than any Court can be, and than were any of the witnesses who gave their opinions in this case.[35] [emphasis added]

### Question of Law

A court considering an appeal on a question of law will not substitute its opinion for that of the arbitrator if the question of law is the specific question referred to the arbitrator and forms the fundamental basis of the arbitrator's decision. This view is captured in *Kelantan (Government) v. Duff Development Co.*,[36] where Viscount Cave held:

If this be so, I think it follows that, unless it appears on the face of the award that the arbitrator has proceeded on principles which were wrong in law, his conclusions as to the construction of the deed must be accepted. No doubt an award may be set aside for an error of law appearing on the face of it; and no doubt a question of construction is (generally speaking) a question of law. But where a question of construction is the very thing referred for arbitration, then the decision of the arbitrator upon that point cannot be set aside by the Court only because the Court would itself have come to a different conclusion. If it appears by the award that the arbitrator has proceeded illegally — for instance, that he has decided on evidence which in law was not admissible or on principles of construction which the law does not countenance, then there is error in law which may be ground for setting aside the award; but the mere dissent of the Court from the arbitrator's conclusion on construction is not enough for that purpose.[37]

---

[35] *Ibid.*, at 693-694.
[36] [1923] A.C. 395 (H.L.).
[37] *Ibid.*, at 409.

The reasoning of Viscount Cave is mirrored in *Canadian National Railway v. Canadian Pacific Ltd.*,[38] where the Supreme Court of Canada endorsed the reasoning of the British Columbia Court of Appeal:

> If an allegation of error is to form a basis for setting an award aside or remitting it to the arbitrators, it must be established that the arbitrators made an error; that the error was on a point of law; that the face of the record shows that the error was made; that the decision on the point of law formed a part of the reasoning leading to the answer to the question submitted (*Re Bailey Construction Co. and Etobicoke*, [1949] 3 D.L.R. 68 at p. 73, [1949] O.R. 352); and that the point of law was not the very question referred to arbitration (*Government of Kelantan v. Duff Development Co. Ltd.,* [1923] A.C. 395; *Faubert and Watts v. Temagami Mining Co. Ltd.* (1960), 22 D.L.R. (2d) 220, [1960] S.C.R. 235; and *A.B.C. Sheet Metal & Plumbing Ltd. v. United Ass'n of Journeymen, etc. Local 170* (1961), 31 D.L.R. (2d) 147).[39]

To establish that an error appears on the face of the record, the award or a document incorporated in the award must contain "some legal proposition which is the basis of the award and which you can say is erroneous".[40]

## (b) Agreement Not Dealing with Appeals

The statutory scheme applies very differently to an arbitration agreement which does not address the issue of an appeal. In these circumstances, a party will not have a right to appeal a question of fact or mixed fact and law.[41] With respect to appealing a question of law, a party may only do so with leave of the court. Section 45(1) of the *Arbitration Act* states that leave shall only be granted if it is satisfied that:

> (a) the importance to the parties of the matters at stake in the arbitration justifies an appeal; and

---

[38] (1978), 95 D.L.R. (3d) 242 (B.C. C.A.), reversing (1978), 83 D.L.R. (3d) 86 (B.C. S.C.), affirmed without written reasons [1979] 2 S.C.R. 668.

[39] *Ibid.*, 95 D.L.R. (3d) 242 at 257.

[40] See *Champsey Bhara & Co. v. Jivraj Balloo Spinning & Weaving Co.*, [1923] A.C. 480 (P.C.), per Lord Dunedin; *Fort McMurray School District No. 2833 v. Fort McMurray Roman Catholic Separate School District No. 32* (1984), 9 D.L.R. (4th) 224 (Alta. Q.B.) at 230-231.

[41] *Pachanga Energy Inc. v. Mobil Investments Canada Inc.* (1993), 8 Alta. L.R. (3d) 284 (Q.B), affirmed (1993), 15 Alta. L.R. (3d) 1 (C.A.).

(b) determination of the question of law at issue will *significantly affect* the rights of the parties. [emphasis added]

When determining whether the court will grant leave, the court may consider the decision of Lord Denning in *Pioneer Shipping v. B.T.P. Tioxide.*[42] This case considered a similar section of the U.K. *Arbitration Act, 1979*[43] which read:

(4) The High Court shall not grant leave under subsection (3)(b) above unless it considers that, having regard to all the circumstances, the determination of the question of law concerned could *substantially affect* the rights of one or more of the parties to the arbitration agreement; and the Court may make any leave which it gives conditional upon the applicant complying with such conditions as it considers appropriate. [emphasis added]

Lord Denning held the following with respect to the question of leave:

Leave is not to be given unless the point of law could substantially affect the rights of one or both of the parties. In short, it must be a point of practical importance not an academic point, nor a minor point.

The decision of the arbitrator is final unless the judge gives leave. Once he gives leave, the judge is to hear the appeal. His decision is final unless he certifies that the question is one of general importance, or is one which for some other special reason should be considered by the Court of Appeal. This finality gives rise to these reflections.

## (c)  Agreement Prohibits Appeals

Section 45(1) of the *Arbitration Act* states that leave of the court is required if the arbitration agreement is silent on the issue of an appeal. What happens if the agreement specifically prohibits it? In circumstances when the arbitral award is intended to be conclusive, it would seem to be difficult to accept that at the same time the parties have retained their appeal rights. Under section 3 of the Act, the parties to an arbitration may agree, expressly or by implication, to exclude all but a few provisions of the Act. Section 45(1) may be excluded. A rational interpretation of this provision suggests that an agreement which states that the arbitrator's decision is to be "final and binding" is not appealable. The case law, however, has not formulated

---

[42] [1980] 3 All E.R. 117 (C.A.), appeal dismissed (1981), [1982] A.C. 724 (H.L.).
[43] *Arbitration Act, 1979* (U.K.), s. 1.

such a consistent rule. In *L.I.U.N.A., Local 183 v. Carpenters and Allied Workers, Local 27*,[44] the Court granted leave to appeal an arbitrator's award even though the arbitration agreement provided that the decision was to be "final and binding". Dealing with the issue of whether such awards should be afforded deference, Matlow J. stated:

> In my view, the agreement to treat the arbitration award as "final and binding" should not be interpreted as the removal of any right of appeal. Rather, it should be interpreted as an agreement to be bound by any arbitration award so long as it stands and nothing more. It does not, either expressly or by implication, mean that the parties have excluded the application of the appeal rights set out in section 45 of the Act.[45]

However, this decision was reversed on appeal. Finlayson J.A. of the Court of Appeal for Ontario noted that since the agreement between the parties was drafted under the old *Arbitration Act*, which provided no right of appeal without the express agreement of the parties, the terms "final and binding" in this case were sufficient to demonstrate the intention of the parties to exclude any appeal of the arbitration award. Dealing with this issue, he stated:

> Looking at the agreement in appeal from this perspective, it is apparent that the parties intended to exclude, to the fullest extent possible under the law, any review of the resolution of their dispute. At the time of the making of the agreement, it was not necessary to exclude a right of appeal expressly, because there was no right of appeal without their express agreement under the former Arbitration Act.[46]

Yet, it is important to note that this decision was rendered according to the former *Arbitration Act*. The current *Arbitration Act, 1991* provides expressly that if the agreement does not deal with appeals, a party may appeal an award to the court on a question of law with leave. Therefore, under the new *Arbitration Act*, appeals are allowed unless expressly excluded by the parties. The decision could therefore have been very different if rendered under the new Act.

A similar conclusion concerning the new *Arbitration Act* was reached in *Bramalea Ltd. v. T. Eaton Co.*,[47] in which the issue was whether a party

---

[44] [1994] O.J. No. 274, 1994 CarswellOnt 2392 (Gen. Div.).
[45] *Ibid.*
[46] (1997), 34 O.R. (3d) 472 (C.A.) at 479.
[47] [1994] O.J. No. 38 (Ont. Gen. Div.).

had a right to seek leave to appeal on a question of law where the agreement stated that the award was to be "final and binding". Refusing to grant leave, Lane J. reasoned:

> Is there then jurisdiction in the court to give leave to appeal under s. 45(1)? In my view, there is not. The opening words of s. 45(1) provide, "If the arbitration agreement does not deal with appeals on questions of law," and this arbitration agreement does deal with such appeals. It prohibits them.[48]

Unfortunately this issue has not been resolved by the Court of Appeal and there remains no definitive answer. It is unlikely that an answer will be forthcoming in the near future since, as will be discussed later, a General Division's decision to deny leave to appeal cannot be appealed.[49]

### (d)  Standard of Review on Appeals

The appropriate standard of review on appeal differs depending on whether the arbitration agreement provides for an appeal. If the arbitration agreement expressly states that the parties may appeal the arbitrator's decision, the appropriate standard for review is one of *correctness*. In *Petro-Lon Canada Ltd. v. Petrolon Distribution Inc.*,[50] the Court stated:

> On the basis of these comments, I conclude that the standard of review is correctness in reviewing decision of an arbitrator on an appeal brought in the circumstances of this appeal. In the submission to arbitration, an appeal is specifically provided for. There is no private clause or any qualifying language of any kind. In the very recently released judgment of MacPherson J. in *887574 Ontario Inc. v. Pizza Pizza Ltd.,* April 7, 1995, the standard of review of an arbitrator's decision was discussed at pp. 7-12. MacPherson J. concluded, in very similar circumstances, that the appropriate standard of review was correctness. He referred to the *Pezim* decision and also the recent decision of the Court of Appeal in *Ontario (Director of Income Maintenance, Ministry of Community & Social Services) v. Wedekind* (1994), (sub nom *Wedekind v. Ontario (Ministry of Community & Social Services)*) 21 O.R. (3d) 289, where Griffiths J.A. stated at p. 296:
>
>> . . . the jurisdiction of a court of appeal is much broader than the jurisdiction of a court on judicial review. Where there is a statutory right of

---

[48] *Ibid.*
[49] *Hillmond Investments Ltd. v. Canadian Imperial Bank of Commerce, supra,* note 31.
[50] (1995), 19 B.L.R. (2d) 123 (Ont. Gen. Div.), MacDonald J.

appeal which allows the appellate court to substitute its opinion for that of the tribunal on questions of law or mixed questions of law and fact, and where the tribunal has no greater expertise than the court on the issue, then the standard of review is one of correctness.

MacPherson J. went on to say at p. 10 of the judgment:

> And, given that the essence of the arbitrator's decision was his interpretation of various provisions of a contractual document, the Franchise Agreement, in light of the relevant principles of contract law, it would appear that he would not have any greater expertise than a court interpreting the same document.

I agree with the interpretation of MacPherson J. with respect to the appropriate standard of review. I conclude, therefore, that the concept of correctness, as set out above, is the appropriate standard to be applied in this case.[51]

If the arbitration agreement is silent on the issue of an appeal, and if leave to appeal a question of law is granted, the courts will impose a higher standard of review; one of *unreasonableness*. Therefore a court will not grant a remedy against an arbitral award unless the arbitrator's decision was unreasonable. In *Dascon Investments Ltd. v. 558167 Ontario Ltd.*,[52] the Court, after granting leave, stated:

> I am not persuaded that the arbitrator was wrong in her interpretation and in the result at which she had arrived. In any event, I am satisfied that the interpretation of the lease which is implicit in her findings is one that is not unreasonable and can rationally be supported.[53]

If, however, the agreement states that the award shall be "final and binding", and assuming the court applies Matlow J.'s reasoning in *L.I.U.N.A.* and grants leave to appeal, then the appropriate standard of review is one of *patent unreasonableness*. In *VAV Holdings Ltd. v. 720153 Ontario Ltd.*,[54] the Court explained why the standard is much higher than that of correctness:

> While I have no difficulty in finding that the Arbitrator proceeded on a wrong principle of law, the issue as to whether the award is "patently unreasonable" is more difficult. Although the case law supports the respondent's assertion

---

[51] *Ibid.*, at 134-135.
[52] [1993] O.J. No. 731, 1993 CarswellOnt 3659 (Ont. Gen. Div.).
[53] *Ibid.*, at para 13.
[54] [1996] O.J. No. 1027, 1996 CarswellOnt 5554 (Ont. Gen. Div.), reversed (1996), 1996 CarswellOnt 4233 (C.A.).

that "where the parties refer a specific question of law to a consensual arbitra-tion, they oust the jurisdiction of the courts", I do not accept the contention that the question put to this Arbitrator was a question of law. If parties provide an agreed statement of facts of a motor vehicle accident, for example, and ask an arbitrator to determine which of the parties was negligent, that in my respectful opinion, would be a case of referring a specific question of law to an arbitrator, the answer to which would bind the parties to a consensual arbitration, even if the arbitrator's decision differed from what a court would have found. The rationale for that principle, although not articulated in the cases, in my view, is that legal reasoning is not the only form of rational thinking.[55]

## (e)  Appeal from Refusal to Grant Leave to Appeal

A recent decision of the Ontario Court of Appeal clearly establishes that in Ontario, there is no appeal from a refusal to grant leave to appeal.

Modern systems of alternative dispute resolution, commonly referred to as A.D.R., are designed to help parties solve disputes efficiently without resort to formal litigation and with a minimum of judicial interference. Allowing an appeal from a refusal to grant leave to appeal defeats the object of arbitration by frustrating the legislated impediment to appeals as of right. The purpose of s. 45 of the *Arbitration Act, 1991* is to stop an appeal unless the Ontario Court (General Division) grants one.[56]

The function of the Superior Court of Justice as a check on unnecessary or frivolous appeals is defeated if the Court of Appeal may hear an appeal from the Superior Court's refusal to grant leave. The Court of Appeal could then hear every case.

Arbitration is meant to be a summary procedure, exhibiting the advan-tages of speed and finality. Thus, there are good policy reasons for limiting the availability of appeals in an arbitration context.[57]

However, there is an exception to the general rule that no appeal lies from an order granting or refusing leave to appeal. The exception applies where it is argued that the judge refusing leave to appeal mistakenly declined

---

[55]  *Ibid.*
[56]  *Hillmond Investments Ltd. v. Canadian Imperial Bank of Commerce, supra,* note 31, at 618.
[57]  Casey, *supra,* note 30, p. 9-12.

jurisdiction.[58] In *Denison Mines Ltd. v. Ontario Hydro*,[59] the Ontario Court of Appeal dismissed a motion to quash an appeal of a judge's refusal to grant leave to appeal an arbitration award because the appeal fell within the exception. The Court confirmed the general rule of non-appealability of decisions refusing or granting leave to appeal and that it should be applicable to appeals from orders made under section 45 of the *Arbitration Act*. Nonetheless, in this case, the Court held that the issue fell within the exception as the appellant argued that the application judge erred in concluding that the parties had contracted out of a right of appeal, and mistakenly declined jurisdiction.

## 10. SETTING ASIDE AWARD — SECTION 46

A second and very distinct appeal remedy is the power of a court to set aside an award. This remedy is likened to a judicial review, however the grounds are limited to those set out in section 46(1) of the *Arbitration Act*. Note that these provisions cannot be contracted out of using an arbitration agreement since section 3 of the Act provides that a party cannot limit the court's jurisdiction to set aside an award.

The Compendium to the *Arbitration Act* describes the court's power to set aside an arbitral award:

Section 46: Setting Aside Award

The *Arbitration Act* sets out all the grounds for what is in effect a judicial review of the application, to replace the present vague term "misconduct". The list of grounds is intended to give those involved in arbitration advance notice of things to be avoided. The grounds, stated broadly, include a fundamental flaw in the arbitration or in the composition of the tribunal and a fundamental departure from equal treatment or fair opportunity to put or meet a case.

The rights to have an award set aside are limited. If the party seeking to set the award aside has waived the objection under the provisions of the Act, or has raised a challenge earlier on the same ground and has failed, or has the opportunity to raise the point and has not done so, then the award shall not be set aside.

---

[58] *Canadian Utilities Ltd. v. Deputy Minister of National Revenue* (1963), [1964] S.C.R. 57.

[59] (2001), 56 O.R. (3d) 181 (C.A.).

The Act specifies the power of the Court when an award is set aside and allows the Court to remit the award to the tribunal rather than setting it aside.[60]

The specific grounds upon which a court may set aside an award are:[61]

1.  A party entered into the arbitration agreement while under a legal incapacity.

2.  The arbitration agreement is invalid or has ceased to exist.

3.  The award deals with a dispute that the arbitration agreement does not cover or contains a decision on a matter that is beyond the scope of the agreement.

4.  The composition of the tribunal was not in accordance with the arbitration agreement or, if the agreement did not deal with that matter, was not in accordance with this Act.

5.  The subject-matter of the dispute is not capable of being the subject of arbitration under Ontario Law.

6.  The applicant was not treated equally and fairly, was not given an opportunity to present a case or to respond to another party's case, or was not given proper notice of the arbitration or of the appointment of an arbitrator.

7.  The procedures followed in the arbitration did not comply with this Act.

8.  An arbitrator has committed a corrupt or fraudulent act or there is a reasonable apprehension of bias.

9.  The award was obtained by fraud.

These grounds can be grouped into three categories, each of which justifies the setting aside of an award. The first is where the arbitral tribunal *does not have the jurisdiction* to resolve the dispute. If it can be established that the agreement is invalid, either because a party does not have the legal capacity or because the arbitration agreement has ceased to exist, then there is no consensual basis for the arbitration and the award should be set aside.[62]

If the arbitration deals with a dispute which the agreement was not intended to resolve, the court has *exceeded its jurisdiction*. In these circumstances, the court may sever that part of the award which the arbitrator was

---

[60] *Compendium to the Arbitration Act, 1991,* Ministry of the Attorney General, Province of Ontario, 1991 [unpublished].

[61] *Arbitration Act, 1991,* S.O. 1991, c. 17, s. 46(1).

[62] Casey, *supra,* note 30, p. 9-12.2.

not authorized by the agreement to order, or the court may remit the matter back to the tribunal with directions.[63]

The final group of grounds for setting aside an award are circumstances where the arbitral tribunal has *failed to follow proper procedures.* If an award is attacked on any of these grounds it will be up to the court to determine whether the conduct complained of is of sufficient character to warrant setting aside the award.[64]

Given the purpose of the arbitration process, which is to avoid the expense and delay of court proceedings, these grounds of review should be applied strictly. Loose standards of jurisdictional review will obviously defeat the purpose of arbitration. According to the decision in *Turgeon v. Turgeon*, a court should refrain from interfering with an arbitrator's award unless it is convinced that the arbitrator acted on a wrong principle, over-looked essential evidence or misapprehended the evidence.[65] In *Marriott Corp. of Canada Ltd. v. C.U.P.E.*, the Court concluded:

> Although the reasons given for the award, measured against a formal judicial standard, manifest some deficiencies, these, in the circumstances, do not result in a loss of jurisdiction. . . . it cannot be said that the award, which did not tie sick leave to monthly work performance, was patently unreasonable.[66]

## 11. ENFORCEMENT OF THE AWARD[67]

### (a) Introduction

Most parties who are unsuccessful in arbitral proceedings will volun-tarily perform the award. Inevitably, however, there will be cases where the losing party will fail to carry out the award and the successful party will have to take steps to enforce performance of it.[68] The objective of this chapter is therefore to review the statutory framework which provides for the en-forcement of both domestic and foreign arbitral awards. Procedures which

---

[63] *Arbitration Act*, s. 46(8).

[64] Casey, *supra*, note 30, p. 9-16.

[65] [1997] O.J. No. 4269, 1997 CarswellOnt 5575 (Gen. Div.).

[66] (1995), 80 O.A.C. 389 (Div. Ct.) at 389.

[67] Section written by Andre Ducasse, Gowlings Lafleur Henderson, LLP.

[68] For a brief discussion of some of the available statistics on this point, see Redfern, A. and Hunter, M., *Law and Practice of International Commercial Arbitration*, 3rd ed., London: Sweet & Maxwell, 1999, pp. 443-445.

need to be followed in the Province of Ontario to seek enforcement of domestic and foreign arbitral awards will also be reviewed.

## (b)  Recognition and Enforcement

From the outset, a distinction must be drawn between the recognition of an arbitral award and its enforcement. Recognition is essentially a defensive process. For example, "a defendant in an action may raise as a defence the fact that an arbitration has taken place and he or she was found not liable for the claim now being advanced by the plaintiff."[69] If the arbitral proceedings disposed of all the issues raised in the new court proceedings, the defendant will adduce the arbitral award before the court and ask the court to recognise the award in order to put an end to the court proceedings as *res judicata*.

Enforcement however goes beyond recognition. When a court is asked to enforce an award it is asked to ensure that the award is respected and carried out, failing which the court can impose legal sanctions on the defaulting party. Enforcement therefore invokes the power of the state and compels a party to carry out the award.

## (c)  Enforcement of Domestic Arbitral Awards

### (i)  *Application for Enforcement*

An arbitral award made in Ontario or elsewhere in Canada may be enforced pursuant to the *Arbitration Act, 1991*.[70] The *Arbitration Act* applies to an arbitration conducted under an arbitration agreement, unless the application of the Act is excluded by law or the *International Commercial Arbitration Act* applies to the arbitration.[71] The *Arbitration Act* applies, with necessary modifications, to an arbitration conducted in accordance with another Act, unless that Act provides otherwise. However, in the event of a conflict between the *Arbitration Act* and another Act, or regulations made under the other Act, the other Act or regulations prevail.[72]

The *Arbitration Act* in and of itself does not permit enforcement. To enforce in Ontario an arbitral award made in Ontario or elsewhere in Canada,

---

[69] Casey, *supra,* note 30, p. 10-1. See also Redfern and Hunter, *supra*, note 68, pp. 448-449.

[70] S.O. 1991, c. 17.

[71] *Ibid.*, s. 2(1).

[72] *Ibid.*, s. 2(3).

an application must be brought before a judge of the Ontario Superior Court of Justice (the "Court").[73] The Court held in *Schreter v. Gasmac Inc.*[74] that an application for the enforcement of an arbitral award is made by notice of application pursuant to Rule 14 of the Ontario *Rules of Civil Procedure.*[75] The application must be made on notice to the other party in accordance with the Court Rules and must be supported by the original award or a certified copy thereof.[76] A "certified copy" means a copy authenticated as a true copy by the arbitral tribunal.[77] The Court in *Kanto Yakin Kogyo Kabushiki-Kaisha v. Can-Eng Manufacturing Ltd.* was of the opinion that an affidavit of a party stating that the attached copy of an arbitral award is a true copy is likely not sufficient.[78]

### (ii) *Duties and Powers of the Court*

The *Arbitration Act* grants various powers to, and imposes numerous duties on, the Ontario Superior Court of Justice with respect to an application for the enforcement of a domestic arbitral award.

Pursuant to section 50(3), the court is to grant judgment with respect to an arbitral award made in Ontario unless:

(a) the thirty-day period for commencing an appeal or an application to set aside the arbitral award has not yet elapsed;

(b) there is a pending appeal, application to set the award aside or application for a declaration of invalidity; or

(c) the award has been set aside or the arbitration is the subject of a declaration of invalidity.

It must be noted that this list is exhaustive. There are no other grounds for refusing to grant judgment under the *Arbitration Act.*

Slightly different considerations apply with respect to arbitral awards made elsewhere in Canada (section 50(4)). Under these circumstances the court is to grant judgment unless:

[73] *Ibid.*, s. 50(1).
[74] (1992), 7 O.R. (3d) 608 (Gen. Div.), additional reasons at (1992), 1992 CarswellOnt 326 (Gen. Div.).
[75] R.R.O. 1990, Reg. 194 (hereinafter the "Court Rules").
[76] *Arbitration Act*, s. 50(2).
[77] Casey, *supra*, note 30.
[78] (1992), 7 O.R. (3d) 779 (Gen. Div.), affirmed (1995), 22 O.R. (3d) 576 (C.A.).

(a) the period for commencing an appeal or an application to set aside the award provided by the laws of the province or territory where the award was made has not yet elapsed;

(b) there is a pending appeal, application to set the award aside or application for a declaration of invalidity in the province or territory where the award was made;

(c) the award has been set aside in the province or territory where it was made or the arbitration is the subject of a declaration of invalidity granted there; or

(d) the subject-matter of the award is not capable of being the subject of arbitration under Ontario law.

If the period for commencing an appeal or an application to set aside the award or an application for a declaration of invalidity has not yet elapsed, the court may nonetheless enforce the award or order, on such conditions as are just, that enforcement of the award be stayed until the relevant period has elapsed.[79] If the court stays the enforcement of an arbitral award made in Ontario until a pending proceeding is finally disposed of, it may give directions for the speedy disposition of the proceeding.[80]

Pursuant to section 50(8) of the *Arbitration Act*, once a judgment has been entered the Ontario Superior Court of Justice has the same powers with respect to the enforcement of an arbitral award as with respect to the enforcement of one of its own judgments. Accordingly, a party who refuses to carry out a judgment obtained pursuant to the provisions of the Act is exposing itself to the court's censure, up to and including contempt proceedings.

The *Arbitration Act*, at section 50(7), sets out some "unusual remedies". In essence, this provision grants a certain margin of discretion to the court. It provides that if the arbitral award gives a remedy that the court does not have jurisdiction to grant or would not have granted in a proceeding based on similar circumstances, the court may grant a different remedy requested by the applicant or, in the case of an award made in Ontario, remit it to the arbitral tribunal with the court's opinion, in which case the arbitral tribunal may award a different remedy.

---

[79] *Arbitration Act*, s. 50(5).
[80] *Ibid.*, s. 50(6).

(iii) *Miscellaneous*

The *Arbitration Act* also contains other provisions which are relevant to the enforcement of arbitral awards. The Act sets out a limitation period within which a party must bring an application before the court to seek enforcement of an arbitral award. An application for the enforcement of an arbitral award must be commenced within two years after the day on which the applicant received the award.[81] Further, if the arbitral award is a money award, the Act provides for prejudgment and postjudgment interest. Section 57 of the Act stipulates that the provisions of the Ontario *Courts of Justice Act* pertaining to prejudgment and postjudgment interest apply to an arbitration, with necessary modifications. Postjudgment interest runs from the date of the award and not from the date of the judgment enforcing the award.[82] Accordingly, to avoid any confusion, good advocacy requires having the judge specifically state in his or her endorsement that postjudgment interest is to be calculated from the date of the arbitral award at the appropriate rate.

---

[81] *Ibid.*, s. 52(3).
[82] Casey, *supra*, note 30, p. 10-4.

# 11

# International Dispute Resolution

## 1. INTRODUCTION

Today, international commercial transactions are very common and can likely involve some type of disagreement. However, in most of these instances, the parties wish to solve their differences in a timely fashion in order to return to their commercial activities.

Also, in international business, parties desire an international forum to avoid the necessity of one party going before the national court of the other party to resolve such disputes. International commercial arbitration is this forum:

> ... commercial arbitration is valuable in international transactions because it permits opportunities for flexibility in procedure, for specialized knowledge of arbitrators which may not be available in national courts, and for disputes to be resolved in privacy and in a relatively informal, friendly atmosphere. For these reasons, arbitration is being increasingly used, not only in connection with contracts between parties from countries which have traditional patterns of trade; it has also become the preferred method for resolving disputes between parties from countries where major trading is relatively recent, such as between capitalist and socialist countries, and between industrialized and developing economies. Indeed, arbitration clauses are now the almost universal practice in commercial contracts between parties from different social, economic, and legal systems, because arbitration is seen to be the best available bridge between those who approach contract disputes from divergent cultural perspectives.[1]

---

[1] Holtzman, H.M., "The Importance of Choosing the Right Place to Arbitrate an International Case", Private Investors Abroad — Problems and Solutions in International Business: Symposium of the Southwestern Legal Foundation, 1977, p. 184 [unpublished].

Well respected international institutions with specific rules have been established for decades in order to facilitate international arbitration. The London Chamber of Arbitration was inaugurated in 1892 (in 1903 the name of the tribunal was changed to the London Court of Arbitration) while the Court of Arbitration of the International Chamber of Commerce ("ICC") was founded in 1922. The ICC International Court of Arbitration (the "Court") has administered nearly 10,000 international arbitration cases since its founding and has been widely acknowledged as the leading institution for the arbitration of international disputes.[2] The Court and its Secretariat are headquartered in Paris in the ICC offices.

## 2. INTERNATIONAL BACKGROUND TO CANADA'S INVOLVEMENT IN ENFORCEMENT OF FOREIGN ARBITRAL AWARDS AND THE ADOPTION OF THE *MODEL LAW*

An essential purpose of international arbitration is the resolution of disputes between parties of different States. This is often achieved through the agreement of the parties to submit their disputes to a third party (an arbitrator) with a goal of arriving at a final and binding decision in the form of an award. The losing party may seek to challenge the validity of an award or may resist any attempts by a winning party to obtain recognition or enforcement of an award. Therefore, one of the fundamental concerns of both parties involved in international arbitration is whether an arbitral award can be enforced in the place where it matters most, namely, where the losing party has a place of residence or has assets which could be used to satisfy the arbitral award.

In 1959, the global community moved to remedy the inherent difficulties in enforcement of international awards when the *United Nations Convention on the Recognition and Enforcement of Foreign Arbitral Awards* ("New York Convention") was signed.[3] The States ratifying the New York Convention agreed to recognize and enforce foreign arbitral awards. A State ratifying the Convention had the option to restrict recognition of foreign arbitral awards to only those awards from States that had ratified the Convention, or the ratifying State could recognize all foreign

---

[2] Derains, Y. and Schwartz, A., *A Guide to the New ICC Rules of Arbitration*, Cambridge: Kluwer Law International, 1998, p. 1.

[3] (1958-1959) 330 U.N.T.S. 38.

arbitral awards.[4] After the Convention, foreign arbitral awards became easier to enforce than foreign court awards. The Convention set out very limited grounds whereby a State could refuse to recognize and enforce a foreign arbitral award.[5]

Canada did not ratify the New York Convention until 1986, and therefore until the mid-1980s it was a difficult process to enforce arbitral awards in Canada in view of the right of States under the Convention to restrict recognition of arbitral awards to States that had signed the Convention. Since Canada was not a party to the New York Convention, an arbitration held in Canada before 1986 would solve the problem of enforcement of the award in Canada but would not solve the problem of enforcement of the arbitral award in the jurisdiction in which the assets of the other party might be located.[6]

Finally, in 1986, Canada approved and declared the New York Convention to have the force of law in Canada. In Canada, the Convention applies only to differences arising out of a commercial legal relationship, whether contractual or not.[7] Canada agreed to recognize and enforce all foreign commercial arbitral awards whether or not the awards emanated from a State which had approved the New York Convention.

The Parliament of Canada also passed the *Commercial Arbitration Act*,[8] which implemented the newly drafted *UNCITRAL Model Law*.[9] UNCITRAL is the acronym for the United Nations Commission on International Trade Regulation.

The *UNCITRAL Model Law* differs from the New York Convention in that it was not drafted as a treaty, but rather as the UNCITRAL's attempt *to harmonize the global practice of international arbitration.*

A complete framework for the arbitration process is provided by the *Model Law*. The *Model Law* provides the definition of what is meant by an arbitration agreement, and provides a set of provisions for the regulation of arbitral proceedings, i.e., proceedings for the recognition, enforcement and

---

[4] *Ibid.*, Article I.
[5] *Ibid.*, Article V.
[6] Thompson, B.J., "Commercial Arbitration — A New Look at a New Era", *The Advocate* at 186.
[7] *United Nations Foreign Arbitral Awards Convention Act*, R.S.C. 1985, c. 16 (2nd Supp.).
[8] R.S.C. 1985, c. 17 (2nd Supp.); amended R.S.C. 1985, c. 1 (4th Supp.); amended S.C. 1993, c. 44, s. 50.
[9] *United Nations Commission on International Trade Law* (UNCITRAL) *Model Law on International CommercialArbitration* (1985), adopted in June 1985, 24 I.L.M. 1302 (hereinafter the "*Model Law*").

refusal of awards.[10] Additionally, the law strives to ensure equality among the parties and to prevent one party from taking undue advantage of the other. *Finally, the law is intended to be lex specialis, i.e., to be a special regime of law, which prevails over any contradictory domestic law that deals with the same subject.* The domestic statutes dealing with subject matter not covered by the *Model Law* remain applicable.[11] Also, the *Model Law* does not prevail over treaties in effect in the adopting country.[12]

In 1986, Ontario passed the *Foreign Arbitral Awards Act*[13] which implemented the New York Convention. In 1988, this Act was subsequently repealed and replaced by the *International Commercial Arbitration Act*[14] (the "*ICAA*") which essentially combined the New York Convention and the *Model Law*. Other Canadian provinces enacted similar statutes. By these steps, Canada and its provinces incorporated international arbitration procedures and standards directly into federal and provincial laws.

One cannot study international forms of dispute resolution without an awareness of the subtle tensions between civil law "regimes" and common law jurisdiction. For example, civil law does not contemplate juridical review of administrative tribunals (e.g., an arbitrator) while common law courts have historically reviewed the decisions of arbitrators (at the same time bowing before the Doctrine of Curial Deference). In fact, Judge Wilkey, an American jurist, in his dissent in the *Softwood Lumber* Extraordinary Challenge Committee decision expressed serious concerns about Mexican panellists being able to understand American administrative law because they are trained in a civil law system rather than a common law system.[15]

R.K. Paterson has written:

> Anglo-Canadian law differs substantially from other legal systems in that it has not treated the arbitration of commercial and other types of disputes separately. Civil law countries have long encouraged arbitration for commercial disputes, securing them more effectively from Court intervention than under English law . . .

---

[10] Dore, I.I., *Arbitration and Conciliation Under the UNCITRAL Rules: A Textual Analysis*, Martinus Nijhoff Publishers, 1986, pp. 89-90.
[11] For example, statutes governing the capacity to conclude an arbitration agreement, statutes governing the non-arbitrability of certain disputes and statutes defining periods of time for the enforcement of arbitral awards.
[12] *Model Law, supra*, note 9, Article 1(1).
[13] S.O. 1986, c. 25 (assented July 7, 1986).
[14] S.O. 1988, c. 30 (assented June 8, 1988).
[15] *Softwood Lumber Products from Canada ECC*, ECC-94-1904-01-USA (August 3, 1994), pp. 62-63 of the dissenting reasons.

In the past, Canadian trade and economic relations have been mainly with other Commonwealth countries and the United States. The unavailability of alternative dispute settlement mechanisms to litigation was less significant for parties with similar levels of developments, the same language and similar legal systems. As Canadian trade with the rest of the world (particularly east Asia) expands, however, Canadians will be less able to predict the outcome of any disputes arising from such trade. Parties with different languages and from different legal systems are naturally less confident that disputes can be satisfactorily resolved in the Courts of either side. Trade with Asian and eastern bloc countries will often be pursuant to long-term arrangements (such as those for the supply of natural resources), and resort to litigation to settle differences may be inappropriate and unappealing to both sides.

In this changing Canadian international trade environment arbitration becomes more appealing as a tool of dispute resolution. In courageously enacting the UNCITRAL Model Law, almost without amendment, British Columbia [and the rest of Canada] has sent a signal to its trading partners that in British Columbia [and the rest of Canada] they can take the advantage of a set of non-partisan principles of autonomous dispute resolution. The Act [of British Columbia and of other Canadian provinces] establishes a system of arbitration rules that upholds the freedom of the parties to depart from the rules of law that might otherwise govern their dispute and modifies the application of the provisions of the Act[s] itself in accordance with their particular needs. In limiting the adoption of the Model Law to international commercial disputes, the province has preserved scope for the play of different policy considerations in disputes that are domestic in character.[16]

As a result, Ontario has two separate arbitration schemes: the *Arbitration Act, 1991*[17] (for domestic arbitrations) and the *ICAA* (for international arbitrations) based on the *UNCITRAL Model Law*. The *ICAA* applies to arbitrations in which at least one of the parties are non-Canadians. Article 1(3) and (4) of the Schedule to the *ICAA* defines an international arbitration.

(3) An arbitration is international if:

(a)    the parties to an arbitration agreement have, at the time of the conclusion of that agreement, their places of business in different States, or

---

[16] "International Commercial Arbitration Act: an Overview", in Paterson, R.K. and Thompson, B.J., Q.C. (ed.), *UNCITRAL Arbitration Model in Canada*, Carswell, 1987, p. 123.

[17] *Arbitration Act, 1991*, S.O. 1991, c. 17, repealing and replacing *Arbitrations Act*, R.S.O. 1990, c. A.24.

(b)    one of the following places is situated outside the State in which the parties have their places of business:

    (i)    the place of arbitration if determined in, or pursuant to, the arbitration agreement,

    (ii)    any place where a substantial part of the obligations of the commercial relationship is to be performed or the place with which the subject-matter of the dispute is most closely connected; or

(c)    the parties have expressly agreed that the subject-matter of the arbitration agreement relates to more than one country.

(4)    For the purposes of paragraph (3) of this article:

(a)    if a party has more than one place of business, the place of business is that which has the closest relationship to the arbitration agreement;

(b)    if a party does not have a place of business, reference is to be made to his habitual residence.

Section 1(7) of the *ICAA* is clear that different States referred to in Article 1 of the Schedule mean different countries.

The *Model Law* is bound to have *considerable influence* on the further worldwide development of international commercial arbitration. As stated in *ABN Amro Bank Canada v. Krupp MaK Maschinenbau GmbH*:

> Since the enactment of the ICAA in Ontario and of similar provisions in other provinces in Canada the courts have been quick to recognize the importance of this legislation as a public policy statement showing the importance of encouraging agreement for dispute resolution adopted by the parties themselves and of the need for the predictability, certainty and uniformity in the international comity.

> The importance of these goals was confirmed by the Ontario Court of Appeal in *Automatic Systems Inc. v. Bracknell Corp.* (1994), 18 O.R. (3d) 257, 12 B.L.R. (2d) 132 (C.A.). Austin J.A. in delivering the judgment of the court commented at p. 264 O.R., p. 142 B.L.R.:

>> The purpose of the United Nations conventions and the legislation adopting them is to ensure that the method of resolving disputes, in the forum and according to the rules chosen by the parties, is respected. Canadian courts have recognized that predictability in the enforcement of dispute resolution provisions is an indispensable precondition to any interna-

tional business transaction and facilitates and encourages the pursuit of freer trade on an international scale . . .[18]

As a result the Court found that the application of the *ICAA* should be favoured unless there was clear reason why it should not be applied. Austin J.A. said at p. 266 O.R., p. 144 B.L.R.:

> Having regard to international comity, and to the strong commitment made by the legislature of this province to the policy of international commercial arbitration through the adoption of the ICAA and the *Model Law*, it should, in my respectful view, require very clear language indeed to preclude it.[19]

This would be the case even if a contrary result would be achieved if the dispute had occurred within a purely domestic context. As Henry J. stated in *Rio Algom Ltd. v. Sammi Steel Co.*:[20]

> [t]he purpose and spirit of the ICAA in adopting the Model Law, was to make Ontario commercial arbitration law consistent with the laws of other international trading countries so as to enhance and encourage international commerce in Ontario and the resolution of disputes by rules of international commercial arbitration . . .

These cases illustrate the extent to which Canadian courts have embraced the worldwide trend toward restricting judicial control over international commercial arbitration disputes.

## 3. BASIC CONSIDERATIONS RELEVANT TO INTERNATIONAL DISPUTES

The basic feature of international disputes is that they occur between parties from different countries. A dispute is a:

---

[18] (1994), 21 O.R. (3d) 511 (Gen. Div.) at 515.

[19] In *Automatic Systems Inc. v. E.S. Fox Ltd.* (1995), 19 C.L.R. (2d) 35 (Ont. Gen. Div.), Mr. Justice Adams confirmed the modern trend of comity extended by the judiciary to private dispute resolution proceeds adopted by contracting parties. The arbitration obligation survives the completion of the contract as well as its fundamental breach. Similarly, it is to be assumed that the parties intended the arbitration process to have at its disposal a full range of remedies including monetary relief to resolve their claims.

[20] (1991), 47 C.P.C. (2d) 251 (Ont. Gen. Div.) at 257.

conflict [which] arises between two or more individuals, corporations or groups when the fulfilment of the interest, needs or goals of one side are perceived to be incompatible with the fulfilment of the interest, needs or goals of the other side.[21]

An international dispute is consequently a conflict between individuals, corporations or groups from two or more countries. Since an international dispute is complex by definition, the dispute resolution mechanism must be *simple and clear.*

In the preparation of appropriate dispute resolution provisions, it is critical that the parties address the following issues:

- What is to be the proper law of the *contract*?
- Where is the *place* of arbitration?
- What arbitral *procedure* or rules will govern the arbitration?

The parties must select the proper law of contract which may differ from the law governing the arbitration procedure. It is well recognized that the law of one jurisdiction may govern the contract and that of another the arbitration process.[22] However, *until the arbitration actually commences,* the only law governing the situation is the law of the contract.

In the absence of an expressed choice, the arbitral procedural law is *prima facie* the law of the place where the arbitration is held since this is likely the place most closely connected with the proceedings. In *James Miller & Partners Ltd. v. Whitworth Street Estates (Manchester) Ltd.,*[23] Lord Wilberforce, quoting from *Dicey and Morris,* explained the above considerations as follows:

> It cannot however be doubted that the Courts would give effect to the choice of the law [i.e., the law governing the arbitral process] other than the proper law of the contract. Thus, if parties agreed on an arbitration clause expressed to be governed by English law, but providing for arbitration in Switzerland, it may be held that, whereas English law governs the validity, interpretation and effect of the arbitration clause as such (including the scope of the arbitrator's jurisdiction) the proceedings are governed by Swiss law. It is also submitted that where the parties have failed to choose the law governing the arbitration proceedings, the proceedings must be considered, at any rate *prima facie,* as

---

[21] Michael Noone, *Mediation,* London: Cavendish Publishing Ltd., 1996, p. 3.

[22] Anthony Walton, *Russell on the Law of Arbitration,* 19th ed., London: Stevens & Sons, 1979, p. 68.

[23] [1970] A.C. 583 (H.L.).

being governed by the law of the country in which the arbitration is held on the ground that is the country most closely connected with the proceedings.[24]

To avoid any uncertainty, the parties should expressly select the substantiative law applicable (the proper law) as this choice is generally recognized by all national systems of conflict of laws.[25] At the same time, the parties should select the place of arbitration and the arbitral rules which will be applicable.

Where the parties choose a foreign law to govern the arbitral procedure, it may not be open to them to entirely exclude all the provisions of the law applicable to the place of arbitration. Some provisions may in fact be mandatory and may override conflicting procedures in the chosen foreign law.

In this regard, if international commercial arbitration takes place in Ontario, then the *ICAA* would normally apply and govern the procedure. On the other hand, the parties may choose a private set of arbitral rules. If so, then these rules govern unless the mandatory provisions of the underlying arbitral procedural law, in this case those of the *ICAA*, override the rules adopted. The parties may wish to select the arbitration rules of, for example, the Arbitration and Mediation Institute of Canada or the International Chamber of Commerce. These rules have features which may be entirely advantageous to a particular situation, or may conversely prove extremely cumbersome when an actual dispute arises. Whatever procedural rules are chosen, their implications should be carefully considered by all parties when drafting the arbitration clauses.

If the parties wish to conduct the arbitration in Ontario, it is perhaps advisable for the sake of simplicity that the parties choose the law of Ontario as the proper law of the contract, select Ontario as the place of arbitration and stipulate that the *ICAA* will govern the procedure. As will be further discussed, the *ICAA* sets out an arbitral procedure which governs the actual conduct of the arbitration in Ontario.

Despite the parties' best intentions and careful drafting, issues regarding the interpretation of arbitration clauses can arise. In such a case, the arbitration agreement must be interpreted according to its language and in light of the circumstances in which it is made.[26] However, the most important

---

[24] *Ibid.*, at 616.

[25] Castel, J.-G., *Canadian Conflict of Laws*, 3rd ed., Toronto: Butterworths, 1994, p. 306.

[26] *Heyman v. Darwins Ltd.*, [1942] 1 All E.R. 337 (H.L.) at 343.

consideration will not be the specific wording of the clause, but rather the intent of the parties.[27]

## 4.  ICC ARBITRATION[28]

### (a)  Advantages to Arbitration

Among the available dispute resolution alternatives to courts, arbitration is by far the most commonly used internationally. The reasons for this are clear.

#### (i)  *Final, Binding Decisions*

While several mechanisms can help parties reach an amicable settlement — for example through conciliation under the ICC Rules of Conciliation — all of them depend, ultimately, on the goodwill and cooperation of the parties. A final and enforceable decision can generally be obtained only by recourse to courts or by arbitration. Because arbitral awards are not subject to appeal, they are much more likely to be final than the judgements of courts of first instance. Although arbitral awards may be subject to being challenged (usually in either the country where the arbitral award is rendered or where enforcement is sought), the grounds of challenge available against arbitral awards are limited.

#### (ii)  *International Recognition of Arbitral Awards*

Arbitral awards enjoy much greater international recognition than judgements of national courts. More than 120 countries have signed the 1958 United Nations Convention on the Recognition and Enforcement of Foreign Arbitral Awards, known as the "New York Convention". The Convention facilitates enforcement of awards in all contracting States. There are several other multilateral and bilateral arbitration conventions that may also help enforcement.

---

[27] *A Guide to the New ICC Rules of Arbitration, supra*, note 2, p. 90; *Onex Corp. v. Ball Corp.* (1994), 12 B.L.R. (2d) 151 (Ont. Gen. Div.).

[28] Written by Paul-A. Gelinas, Chairman of the ICC Commission on International Arbitration, for presentation at the 1st National ADR Conference of Russia, May 29-30, 2000, ICC Publication No. 800.

(iii) *Neutrality*

In arbitral proceedings, parties can place themselves on an equal footing in five key respects:

1.  Place of arbitration
2.  Language used
3.  Procedures or rules of law applied
4.  Nationality
5.  Legal representation

Arbitration may take place in any country, in any language and with arbitrators of any nationality. With this flexibility, it is generally possible to structure a neutral procedure offering no undue advantage to any party.

(iv) *Specialized Competence of Arbitrators*

Judicial systems do not allow the parties to a dispute to choose their own judges. In contrast, arbitration offers the parties the unique opportunity to designate persons of their choice as arbitrators, provided they are independent. This enables the parties to have their disputes resolved by people who have specialized competence in the relevant field.

(v) *Speed and Economy*

Arbitration is faster and less expensive than litigation in the courts. Although a complex international dispute may sometimes take a great deal of time and money to resolve, even by arbitration, the limited scope for challenge against arbitral awards, as compared with court judgements, offers a clear advantage. Above all, it helps to ensure that the parties will not subsequently be entangled in a prolonged and costly series of appeals. Furthermore, arbitration offers the parties the flexibility to set up proceedings that can be conducted as quickly and economically as the circumstances allow. In this way, a multi-million dollar ICC arbitration was once completed in just over two months.

(vi) *Confidentiality*

Arbitration hearings are not public, and only the parties themselves receive copies of the awards.

## (b) *Ad hoc* or Institutional Arbitration?

Parties using arbitration have a choice between designating an institution such as the ICC to administer it, or proceeding *ad hoc* outside an institutional framework. In *ad hoc* cases, the arbitration will be administered by the arbitrators themselves. However, should problems arise in setting the arbitration in motion or in constituting the arbitral tribunal, the parties may have to require the assistance of a state court, or that of an independent appointing authority such as the ICC. Although institutional arbitration requires payment of a fee to the administering institution, the functions performed by the institution can be critical in ensuring that the arbitration proceeds to a final award with a minimum of disruption and without the need for recourse to the local courts. The services an institution may offer are exemplified by the role of the ICC Court, which provides the most thoroughly supervised form of administered arbitration in the world. Among other things, the ICC Court will, as necessary: (i) determine whether there is a *prima facie* agreement to arbitrate; (ii) decide on the number of arbitrators; (iii) appoint arbitrators; (iv) decide challenges against arbitrators; (v) ensure that arbitrators are conducting the arbitration in accordance with the ICC Rules and replace them if necessary; (vi) determine the place of arbitration; (vii) fix and extend time-limits; (viii) determine the fees and expenses of the arbitrators; and (ix) scrutinize arbitral awards.

## (c) ICC Arbitration: Distinctive Features

### (i) *The ICC International Court of Arbitration*

The ICC International Court of Arbitration is the world's foremost institution in the resolution of international business disputes. While most arbitration institutions are regional or national in scope, the ICC Court is truly international. Composed of members from some 70 countries and every continent, the ICC Court is the world's most widely representative dispute resolution institution.

The ICC Court is not a "court" in the ordinary sense. As the ICC arbitration body, the Court ensures the application of the Rules of Arbitration of the International Chamber of Commerce. Although its members do not decide the matters submitted to ICC arbitration — this is the task of the arbitrators appointed under the ICC Rules — the Court oversees the ICC arbitration process and, among other things, is responsible for: appointing arbitrators; confirming, as the case may be, arbitrators nominated by the parties; deciding upon challenges of arbitrators; scrutinizing and approving all arbitral awards; and fixing the arbitrators' fees. In exercising its functions, the Court is able to draw upon the collective experience of distinguished jurists from a diversity of backgrounds and legal cultures as varied as that of the participants in the arbitral process.

## (ii) *The Secretariat of the ICC Court*

The Court is assisted by a Secretariat located at ICC Headquarters in Paris. The Secretariat currently has a full-time staff of 42 persons, including 23 lawyers of 14 different nationalities. The Secretariat closely follows all ICC cases and is available to provide assistance and information in a dozen different languages. At present, each case is followed by one of six teams headed by a Counsel. The Secretariat has state-of-the-art computerized case management and information retrieval systems which function in four different languages.

## (iii) *Designation of Arbitrators*

It is commonly said that an arbitration is no better than the arbitrators. The selection of the arbitral tribunal is, therefore, one of the most critical steps in arbitration.

Under the ICC Rules, the arbitral tribunal is composed of one or more arbitrators. When only one arbitrator is to be designated, he or she is appointed by the Court, unless the parties agree otherwise. When three arbitrators are to be designated, each party nominates an arbitrator; the third arbitrator, who chairs the tribunal, is appointed either with the agreement of the parties or co-arbitrators, or by the Court. When the parties are unable to agree on the number of arbitrators, the ICC Rules provide that the Court shall appoint a sole arbitrator, "save where it appears to the Court that the dispute is such as to warrant the appointment of three arbitrators."

When it comes to the appointment of arbitrators, the ICC — unlike other arbitral institutions — enjoys the support of national committees in approximately 70 different countries. National committees are able to identify potential arbitrators with appropriate qualifications all over the world. Unlike certain other institutions, the ICC does not require that arbitrators be selected from pre-established lists, thus ensuring the greatest possible freedom of choice and flexibility in the constitution of the arbitral tribunal.

(iv) *Monitoring the Arbitral Process*

Unlike many other institutions, the ICC Court monitors the entire arbitral process, from the initial Request to the final Award. The ICC Rules require that, within two months of receiving the file, the tribunal prepare and submit to the Court a document defining its Terms of Reference. A unique feature of ICC arbitration, the Terms of Reference serve the useful purpose of bringing the arbitrators and parties together at an early stage, to identify the issues they will be required to deal with and the procedural details that need to be addressed. It is also sometimes possible at that stage for the parties to reach agreement on certain outstanding issues, such as the language of the arbitration or the governing substantive law. A fact which users should not overlook is that a significant proportion of the ICC arbitration cases are amicably settled at the stage of the Terms of Reference.

During the proceedings, the Court regularly reviews the progress of all pending cases, and, in the process, considers whether there are any measures that need to be taken in order, for example, to help ensure that the case advances as quickly as reasonably possible and that the proceedings are being conducted in conformity with the Rules. In this connection, the staff of the Court's Secretariat closely follow the case and receive copies of all written communications and pleadings exchanged in the arbitration proceedings.

(v) *Fixing Arbitrator Remuneration*

The rules of many arbitral institutions provide either that the arbitrators fix the amount of their own fees or that the fees be established on the basis of a daily or hourly rate fixed or arranged by the institution.

Under the ICC Rules, however, the arbitrators are not remunerated on the basis of an hourly or daily rate, and the arbitrators play no role in determining their own fees. Rather, their fees are fixed by the Court at the end of the arbitration on the basis of a published scale attached to the ICC Rules. Under that scale, the arbitrators' fees are fixed with reference to the amount in dispute. In fixing the arbitrators' fees, the Court also considers the diligence of the arbitrators, the time spent, the rapidity of the proceedings and the complexity of the dispute. Thus, the Court, rather than the arbitrators, determines the final fees, taking into account the manner in which the arbitration was handled, and, in particular, the arbitrators' efficiency.

The fees and expenses system is therefore intended to encourage the efficient handling of cases within a financial framework that is proportionate to the amount at stake in the arbitration. The fact that the scales are based on the sum in dispute also has the virtue of discouraging the submission of frivolous claims and counter-claims, which could otherwise have an immediate and direct impact on the cost of the arbitration. An arbitration cost calculator is available for helping parties at the outset to form a general idea of the cost of the arbitration.

### (vi) *Scrutinizing Arbitral Awards*

One of the most important functions of the Court is the scrutiny of arbitral awards. The ICC Rules provide that the Court must approve all awards as to their form and that the Court may also, without affecting the arbitrators' liberty of decision, draw their attention to points of substance. In the ICC arbitration, scrutiny is a key element ensuring that arbitral awards are of the highest possible standards and thus less susceptible to annulment in the national courts than they might otherwise be. The scrutiny process provides the parties with an additional layer of protection that would not otherwise be available, since arbitral awards are generally not subject to appeal. This unique quality-control mechanism makes the ICC arbitration the world's most reliable arbitration system.

### (d) Drafting the Arbitration Agreement

The ICC arbitration is possible only if there is an agreement between the parties providing for it. The ICC recommends that all parties wishing to have recourse to the ICC arbitration include the following standard clause in their contracts:

> All disputes arising out of or in connection with the present contract shall be finally settled under the Rules of Arbitration of the International Chamber of Commerce by one or more arbitrators appointed in accordance with the said Rules.

It may also be desirable for the parties to stipulate in the arbitration clause itself:

- the law governing the contract;
- the number of arbitrators;
- the place of arbitration; and

- the language of the arbitration.

Parties should also consider the possible need for special provisions in the event that arbitration is contemplated among more than two parties. In addition, the law in some countries may lay down certain requirements in respect of arbitration clauses.

In principle, parties should also always ensure that the arbitration agreement is:

- **in writing** — the effectiveness of an arbitration clause first of all depends on proof of its existence. It should therefore generally be in writing. The 1958 New York Convention specifically states (Art. II) that Contracting States shall recognize arbitration agreements "in writing".
- **carefully drafted** — time and again, the Court receives requests for arbitration based on ambiguous arbitration clauses. Badly worded clauses, at the very least, cause delay. At worst, they may impede the arbitration process.

### (e)  Existence and Validity of the Arbitration Agreement

Issues concerning the existence and validity of the agreement to arbitrate are dealt with in the following way: If the Respondent does not file an Answer or if any party raises a plea concerning the existence, validity or scope of the arbitration agreement, the Court may decide, without prejudice to the admissibility or merits of the plea, that the arbitration shall proceed if it is *prima facie* satisfied that an arbitration agreement under the Rules may exist. In such a case, any decision as to the arbitral tribunal's jurisdiction is then taken by the arbitral tribunal itself. If the Court decides that the arbitration cannot proceed, the parties retain the right to ask any court having jurisdiction whether or not they are bound by an ICC arbitration agreement.

## 5. OVERVIEW OF THE *INTERNATIONAL COMMERCIAL ARBITRATION ACT* — ONTARIO

By passing the *ICAA*, Ontario (in step with the other Canadian provinces) has incorporated international arbitration standards directly into provincial law. In fact, section 13 of the *ICAA* provides that the Report of the United Nations Commission on International Trade Law on the work of its eighteenth session (June 3-21, 1985) and the Analytical Commentary contained in the Report of the Secretary General to the eighteenth session of the United Nations Commission on International Trade Law are to be used as aids in the interpretation of the *ICAA*.

If the parties have provided for arbitration, the first determination is to establish whether the dispute to be submitted to arbitration is an international arbitration under the *ICAA*, held in Ontario. If the *ICAA* applies then the *Model Law*, with minor Ontario modifications, governs the arbitration, unless the parties have made their own arrangements, provided they do not conflict with the mandatory provisions of the *Model Law*. In other words, the *Model Law* acts as an emergency tool kit.

In enacting *ICAA*, one of the most important issues was to determine whether the Provinces and Territories of Canada should be treated as separate states under the Act. If they were treated as separate states then an arbitration between parties with places of business in different Provinces would be an international arbitration. Ontario decided against such an interpretation. Section 1(7) states that the reference to "different states" in Article 1(3) of the *Model Law* means different countries. Therefore, arbitration between Canadians, no matter where resident, will be determined by the domestic arbitration law of the appropriate Canadian province.

On the other hand, an arbitration is international if it falls within Article 1(3) of the *Model Law*.[29]

The *ICAA* (Article 1(2)) governs international commercial arbitration only if the *place of arbitration* is in Ontario. The choice of the place of arbitration is therefore critical to ensure that an award will be enforceable. The procedural autonomy under the *Model Law* (Article 20) allows the parties to choose the place of arbitration. In the absence of an agreed choice the arbitral tribunal will determine the place of arbitration, having regard to the circumstances of the case. Also, as stated by Isaak I. Dore,[30] the place of arbitration is important for five additional reasons:

> (1) It triggers the application of the model law if it is situated in the territory of a state that has adopted the model law, under article 1(2); (2) the award is made there; (3) it is filed and registered there, if national law so requires; (4) or the place of arbitration is usually the place with reference to which the law of procedure to be applied is determined, if the parties have not agreed oth-

---

[29] *Supra*, note 9.
[30] *Supra*, note 10, p. 117.

erwise; and (5) under both articles 31(3) and 36(1)(a)(v) of the model law and article I(1) of the New York Convention, the place of arbitration determines recognition and enforcement of the award.

## 6. MEANING OF "COMMERCIAL"

The *ICAA* (section 2(2)) only applies to international *commercial* arbitration agreements but the term "commercial" is undefined in the Act itself. In *Carter v. McLaughlin*,[31] the Court considered the definition of commercial as it appears in the analytical commentary contained in the Report of the Secretary General to the Eighteenth Session of the UNCITRAL. Article 1 of the Commentary advises:

> The term "commercial" should be given a wide interpretation so as to cover matters arising from all relationships of a commercial nature. Relationships of a commercial nature include, but are not limited to, the following transactions: any trade transaction for supply or exchange of goods; distribution agreement; commercial representation or agency; factoring; leasing; construction of works; consulting; engineering; licensing; investment; financing; banking; insurance; exploitation agreement or concession; joint venture and other forms of industrial or business co-operation; carriage of goods or passengers by air, sea, rail or road.[32]

The Court found that the term commercial shall be given a broad interpretation so as to embrace all relationships of a commercial nature. In the facts of the case, the Court found that the *ICAA* applied to an arbitration involving the sale of a personal residence.

> The transaction was done in a business-like way, with the assistance of professional realtors and within a legal framework appropriate for a transaction involving a large sum of money. It bears all the earmarks of what goes on in trade and commerce except that the parties were not "commercial persons" or merchants in regards to that transaction. It was not part of their usual business. Nevertheless, the relationship of the parties was commercial in nature. Indeed, they had no other relationship. Their relationship had only one dimension, involving the sale of property.[33]

---

[31] (1996), 27 O.R. (3d) 792 (Gen. Div.), Rutherford J.
[32] *Ibid.*, at 796.
[33] *Ibid.*, at 798.

## 7.  EXTENT OF COURT INTERVENTION

The general theme of the *Model Law* is to provide for effective, high quality, international arbitrations which are relatively free from recourse to the courts of individual states. Article 5 of the *Model Law* provides, "In matters governed by this law, *no court shall intervene except where so provided in this law*". [emphasis added] Therefore, one must find the right to intervene in either the *ICAA* itself, or in the *Model Law*. The *Analytical Commentary on Draft Text of A Model Law on International Commercial Arbitration* states:

> Although the provision, due to its categorical wording may create the impression that court intervention is something negative and to be limited to the utmost, it does not itself take a stand on what is the proper role of courts. It merely requires that any instance of court involvement be listed in the Model Law. *Its effect would, thus, be to exclude any general or residual powers given to the courts in a domestic system which are not listed in the Model Law.* The resulting certainty of the parties and the arbitrators about the instances in which court supervision or assistance is to be expected seems beneficial to international commercial arbitration.[34] [emphasis added]

A limitation on court intervention flows from the civil law roots of the *Model Law* in which arbitration is considered to be an alternative dispute resolution system and not an "inferior court" to be judicially reviewed in common law courts. A quick perusal of Ontario's domestic arbitration law will demonstrate differences between arbitral processes flowing from the common law and arbitral processes flowing from international arbitrations. In appropriate circumstances, a losing party under the *Arbitration Act, 1991*[35] of Ontario may appeal a question of fact or law. In fact, section 50(7) of the Act states:

> (7) If the award gives a remedy that the court does not have jurisdiction to grant or would not grant in a proceeding based on similar circumstances, the court may,
>
> (a)   grant a different remedy requested by the applicant; or
>
> (b)   in the case of an award made in Ontario, remit it to the arbitral tribunal

---

[34] *Analytical Commentary on Draft Text of A Model Law on International Commercial Arbitration*, United Nations Commission on International Trade Law, Eighteenth Session, Vienna, June 3-21, 1985, p. 113.

[35] S.O. 1991, c. 17.

with the court's opinion, in which case the arbitral tribunal may award a different remedy.

Once the parties are engaged in an international commercial arbitration under the *Model Law*, the opportunities to go to court to delay or disrupt the proceeding are sparse. There is no right to appeal or seek judicial review for errors of fact or law. The limited grounds to challenge awards are described subsequently.

## 8.  THE ARBITRATION AGREEMENT

Article 7 of the *Model Law* defines the form and definition of an arbitration agreement. An arbitration agreement may be in the form of an arbitration clause in a contract or in the form of a separate agreement.

If the parties in a contract have provided for arbitration pursuant to the laws of Ontario and one party's place of business is outside Canada, the parties have automatically engaged the *ICAA* and its *Model Law*. It is an error for legal counsel to consider that a second arbitration agreement must be negotiated before the arbitration can commence. The parties may wish to negotiate a second arbitration agreement but this is unnecessary. Often a party seeking to delay or disrupt an arbitration proceeding will seek to engage in protracted negotiations, to appoint the arbitrator and fix the issues.

## 9.  STAY OF PROCEEDINGS

Article 8 of the *Model Law* must be carefully considered. A party seeking to stay court proceedings in the face of an agreement to submit matters in dispute to arbitration must act promptly to seek the court's stay and referral to arbitration. Article 8 states as follows:

(1)  A court before which an action is brought in a matter which is the subject of an arbitration agreement shall, *if a party so requests not later than when submitting his first statement on the substance of the dispute*, refer the parties to arbitration unless it finds that the agreement in null and void, inoperative or incapable of being performed.

(2)  Where an action referred to in paragraph (1) of this article has been brought, arbitral proceedings may nevertheless be commenced or continued,

and an award may be made, while the issue is pending before the court. [emphasis added]

In *ABN Amro Bank Canada v. Krupp MaK Maschinenbau GmbH*,[36] the Divisional Court allowed on appeal from the decision of Madame Justice Haley[37] who had refused to stay court proceedings on the basis that the request for arbitration must be made prior to the filing of any pleading on the substance of the dispute.

The Divisional Court disagreed:

(1) The Model Law is mandatory and there is judicial deference to arbitration agreements.
(2) Article 8 permits a party to raise a demand for arbitration in a statement of defence.
(3) A litigant which is an assignee of rights under an international agreement which contains an arbitration clause is bound by the submission to arbitration.[38]

As a matter of international comity, an Ontario court should refrain from interfering in any way with a foreign international judicial process. It should rather defer to a review being conducted in the foreign country where the process initiated.[39]

## 10. AVAILABILITY OF INTERIM ORDERS

Arbitrations can be conducted expeditiously provided the parties have agreed upon an arbitral mechanism which clearly allows for the prompt appointment of the arbitrator and gives the arbitrator the power to make interim orders. However, the prevailing judicial thinking in Ontario is that

[36] (1996), 135 D.L.R. (4th) 130 (Ont. Div. Ct.).
[37] *Supra*, note 18.
[38] *Supra,* note 36. See also *Fisser v. International Bank*, 282 F.2d 231, 233 n. 6 (2nd Cir., 1960) at 233; *Banque de Paris et des Pays-Bas v. Amoco Oil Co.*, 573 F. Supp. 1464, 1469 (N.Y.D.C. 1983) at 938-939 and 941.
[39] See *Europcar Italia S.p.A. v. Alba Tours International Inc.,* [1997] O.J. No. 133, 1997 CarswellOnt 91 (Gen. Div.) where an application for enforcement of an award was adjourned pending the outcome of an appeal of the award in Italy.

the courts will endeavour to honour whatever dispute resolution mechanism was agreed to by the parties.[40] If the parties have committed themselves to a process of negotiation followed by mediation and then arbitration, a party seeking to delay the adjudication of a pressing issue may consequently be able to persuade the court that the chosen dispute resolution mechanism, albeit lengthy, must nevertheless be followed. Therefore, the parties must consider whether the applicable rules of procedure, be it the rules of a national system or those of an arbitral institution, contemplate and allow for interim relief. Where such powers have been anticipated, they may nonetheless conflict with certain mandatory rules of the place of arbitration or the place where the measures are to be enforced. The power to grant interim relief pursuant to the Ontario *ICAA* will be described subsequently.

When the arbitration concerns a licensing agreement, the arbitrator may be asked to make an interim order containing some of the following provisions, pending the outcome of the arbitration:

The Licensee shall not:

- use the trade-mark or patent or confidential know-how or secret information of the Licensor;
- sell products manufactured under the licence;
- hold itself, or one of its subsidiaries, out as an authorized Licensee of the product;
- grant sub-licences to third parties;
- take any other action that could possibly affect the validity and/or value of the intellectual property rights.

The ability of a party to prolong the dispute resolution process, and in particular the arbitration process, so that parties seeking such an interim order on an emergency basis cannot proceed quickly may be of concern. In this type of situation, the key is whether the arbitration provision or rules incorporated by the parties allow the parties to seek an interim order of a national court, without that action being considered incompatible with the arbitration agreement. In drafting the arbitration provisions, the parties may also be prepared to nominate an individual who is empowered to grant interim emergency relief or provide a mechanism to do so. In all the circumstances, the best approach is to stipulate in the dispute resolution clause that

---

[40] *ABN Amro Bank Canada v. Krupp MaK Maschinenbau GmbH, supra,* note 36; see also *Angelo Breda Ltd. v. Guizzetti,* [1995] O.J. No. 3250 (Ont. Gen. Div. [Commercial List]).

the parties are not precluded from bringing an application to a court for interim or interlocutory equitable relief, including injunctive relief.

The World Intellectual Property Organization (WIPO) has proposed supplementary emergency interim relief rules in order to deal with the critical issue of obtaining interim relief in the face of a dispute resolution clause. Article 10 of the proposed rules states that the emergency arbitrator may make "any award" the emergency arbitrator or arbitral tribunal considers urgently necessary to preserve the rights of the parties, pending the final determination of those rights in a subsequent judicial or arbitral proceeding. In particular, the emergency arbitrator may order one, or all, of the following:

- an interim injunction or restraining order;
- the performance of a legal obligation by a party;
- the payment of an amount by one party to the other, or to a third party;
- any measure necessary to establish or preserve evidence;
- any measure necessary for the conservation of any property; and
- an amount of damages to be paid by a party for the breach of the award.

Under Article 9, the emergency arbitrator is given the power to convene a hearing on the shortest possible notice, provided the arbitrator is satisfied that the other party has been given adequate notice of the time, date and place of hearing to enable it to be present. The emergency arbitrator may also convene *ex parte* hearings and make *ex parte* awards if convinced that these measures are necessary in order to avoid irreparable harm to one of the parties. Of course, these emergency orders operate pending a final determination of the rights following subsequent judicial or arbitral proceedings.

Conceptually, procedures such as those proposed by the WIPO can be useful in jurisdictions where interim relief is not available from a judicial authority in a timely manner. Such procedures also offer a means of obtaining interim relief in several jurisdictions using a single process, provided that the relevant jurisdictions recognize and give effect to the arbitral tribunal's power to grant interim relief.

## 11. INTERIM MEASURES OF PROTECTION — SECTION 9, ARTICLES 9 AND 17

The *ICAA* provides that both the court and the arbitral tribunal have the power to order an interim measure of protection. Section 9, Articles 9 and 17 are as follows:

**9. Interim measures and security** — An order of the arbitral tribunal under article 17 of the Model Law for an interim measure of protection and the provision of security in connection with it is subject to the provisions of the Model Law as if it were an award.

**Article 9. Arbitration agreement and interim measures by court** — It is not incompatible with an arbitration agreement for a party to request, before or during arbitral proceedings, from a court an interim measure of protection and for a court to grant such measure.

**Article 17. Power of arbitral tribunal to order interim measures** — Unless otherwise agreed by the parties, the arbitral tribunal may, at the request of a party, order any party to take such interim measure of protection as the arbitral tribunal may consider necessary in respect of the subject-matter of the dispute. The arbitral tribunal may require any party to provide appropriate security in connection with such measure.

Pursuant to section 9 of the *ICAA*, an order of the arbitral tribunal under Article 17 for an interim measure of protection has the same legal nature as an award of the arbitral tribunal. Article 9 of the *Model Law* provides that it is not incompatible with an arbitration agreement for a party to request, before or during arbitral proceedings, from a court an interim measure of protection and for a court to grant such measure. Article 9 lays down the principle that resort to a court and subsequent court action with respect to interim measures of protection are compatible with an arbitration agreement.

The *Analytical Commentary* on these articles states:

The range of interim measures of protection covered by article 9 is considerably wider than that under article 17, due to the different purposes of these two articles. Article 17 deals with the limited power of the arbitral tribunal to order any party to take an interim measure of protection in respect of the subject matter of the dispute and does not deal with enforcement of such orders. Article 9 deals with the compatibility of the great variety of possible measures by courts available in different legal systems, including not only steps by the parties to conserve the subject matter or to secure evidence but also other measures, possibly required from a third party, and their enforcement. This would, in particular, include pre-award attachments and any similar seizure of assets.[41]

The clear wording of Article 17 authorizes the arbitral tribunal to seize assets which are the subject matter of the dispute. The power given to an arbitral tribunal by Article 17 means that it can order that the subject matter of the dispute be maintained within the jurisdiction. In considering the power of the arbitral tribunal, it must always be remembered that the arbitral tribunal *derives its jurisdiction from the arbitration agreement* which may narrow the scope of its authority. However, Article 17 is not limited to "sales transactions" and would, for example, cover measures designed provisionally to determine and stabilize the relationship of the parties in a long-term project. Examples of such *"modus vivendi"* orders include the use or maintenance of machines or works with a continuation of a certain phase of a construction and, if necessary, to prevent irreparable harm. Finally, an order may serve the purpose of securing evidence which otherwise might be unavailable at a later stage of the proceeding.[42]

Article 17 does not, however, grant power to the tribunal to seize general assets. If a party feared that the assets are being removed from the jurisdiction, the appropriate remedy would be to seek a Mareva Injunction. It is not appropriate to grant a Mareva Injunction to preserve the "very subject matter of the action".[43] On the other hand, the court may grant an Anton Piller Order, allowing the plaintiff access to the defendant's premises for the purposes of inspecting materials or documents. This Order is normally granted *ex parte*. While the arbitral tribunal has the power to make such an Order (see Article 17), the arbitral tribunal cannot act *ex parte*. Since the purpose of an Anton Piller Order is to seize materials or documents before they are destroyed, the only practical recourse would be to seek a court order.

## 12. COMPOSITION OF THE ARBITRAL TRIBUNAL

Article 10 of the *Model Law* gives the parties the liberty to determine the number of arbitrators. Failing such a determination, the number of

---

[41] *Analytical Commentary, supra*, note 34, p. 120.
[42] *Ibid.*, p. 135.
[43] *Picotte Insulation Inc. v. Mansonville Plastics (B.C.) Ltd.* (1985), 48 C.P.C. 169 (Ont. H.C.).

arbitrators shall be three.[44] This "default" number (i.e., three arbitrators) was adopted because it appears to be the most common number in international commercial arbitrations. I would caution any party or legal counsel though that three arbitrators in international commercial arbitration can be very expensive. Moreover, the speed of arbitrations, domestic or international, is accentuated by the ability to conduct motions and other procedural matters by conference telephone call. The ability to enlist three arbitrators in a telephone conference motion is difficult. If the parties wish a single arbitrator, this requirement should either be clearly set out in the dispute resolution clause or in the "Arbitration Rules" adopted in the dispute resolution clause.

If the parties fail to agree on a mechanism for appointing the arbitrator, Article 11(3) provides a clear mechanism where each party must appoint one arbitrator and the two arbitrators thus appointed appoint a third arbitrator. In Article 12, a person approached in connection with his or her possible appointment as an arbitrator shall disclose any circumstances likely to give rise to justifiable doubts as to his or her impartiality or independence. Article 13 provides for a procedure to challenge the arbitrator.

## 13. JURISDICTION OF THE ARBITRAL TRIBUNAL

Article 16(1) of the *Model Law* grants the tribunal the power to rule on its own jurisdiction including any objections with respect to the existence or validity of the arbitration agreement. This power, often referred to as "Kompetenz-Kompetenz", is an essential and widely accepted feature of modern international arbitration. Furthermore, a finding by the tribunal that the contract is null and void does not require the conclusion that the arbitration clause is invalid. The tribunal would, thus, not lack jurisdiction to decide on a nullity of the contract unless it finds the defect which causes the nullity of the contract affects also the arbitration clause itself.

Article 16(2) provides that a plea that the tribunal does not have jurisdiction must be raised not later than at the time of the submission of the statement of defence. However, the arbitral tribunal may permit an objection to be raised at a later time, if it is justified. Any concern that the tribunal does not have jurisdiction should be raised as soon as possible by motion before the tribunal. All objections to the tribunal's jurisdiction go to the

---

[44] Note the difference with the Ontario *Arbitration Act, 1991*, S.O. 1991, c. 17, s. 9 which provides for a single arbitrator unless the parties agreed otherwise.

very foundation of the arbitration. Jurisdictional questions are thus antecedent to matters of substance and usually ruled on first in a separate decision in order to avoid possible waste of time and costs. Within thirty (30) days after receiving notice of the tribunal's ruling on its jurisdiction, a party may request a court to decide on the matter, from which decision there is no appeal.[45]

In *Aoot Kalmneft to Glencore International AG and Andrew Berkeley*,[46] the Commercial Court in England held that an arbitrator may make a ruling on his jurisdiction at the outset if he believes it would be more efficient in cost and time, even if this ruling involves making a conclusion in respect of a major issue on the merits of the underlying claim. The Court goes on to pronounce the following:

> Provided that he has satisfied himself that such a course is time efficient and cost efficient and fair to all parties, the arbitrator should not be deterred from taking that course simply because the issues on jurisdiction and liability are co-extensive.[47]

## 14. CONDUCT OF ARBITRAL PROCEEDINGS

Article 19 of the *Model Law* has been referred to as the "Magna Carta" of arbitral procedure. Article 19 reads as follows:

> (1) Subject to the provisions of this Law, the parties are free to agree on the procedure to be followed by the arbitral tribunal in conducting proceedings.

> (2) Failing such agreement, the arbitral tribunal may, subject to the provisions of this Law, conduct the arbitration in such manner as it considers appropriate. The power conferred upon the arbitral tribunal includes the power to determine the admissibility, relevance, materiality and weight of any evidence.

Subject to the fundamental principles of fairness set out in Article 18 (the parties shall be treated with equality and each party shall be given a full opportunity of presenting its case), Article 19 recognizes the parties' freedom to lay down the rules of procedure.

---

[45] *Model Law*, Article 16(3).
[46] (July 27, 2001), Case No: 2001 Folio 285 (Enf. Comm. Ct.), per Justice Colman [unreported].
[47] *Ibid.*, at para 84.

This flexibility with respect to procedural detail is echoed in the ICC Rules of Arbitration. The Rules have been designed to provide a general framework for the arbitration process, providing relatively little procedural detail. As such, the Rules do not impede the parties or the arbitrators from tailoring the procedures to the unique circumstances of each case, nor do they impose either a common or civil law (or other) procedural bias on the overall process.[48]

Failing agreement of the parties, the arbitral tribunal is given wide discretion to conduct the proceedings. The *Analytical Commentary* is helpful:

> 2. Paragraph (1) guarantees the freedom of the parties to determine the rules on how their chosen method of dispute settlement will be implemented. This allows them to tailor the rules according to their specific needs and wishes. They may do so by preparing their own individual set of rules, or, as clarified in article 2(d), by referring to standard rules for institutional (supervised or administered) arbitration or for pure *ad hoc* arbitration. The parties may, thus, take full advantage of the services of permanent arbitral institutions or of established arbitration practices of trade associations. They may choose those features familiar to them and even opt for a procedure which is anchored in a particular legal system. However, if they refer to a given law on civil procedure, including evidence, such law would be applicable by virtue of their choice and not by virtue of being the national law.[49]
>
> . . .
>
> 6. In practical terms, the arbitrators would be able to adopt the procedural features familiar, or at least acceptable, to the parties (and to them). *For example, where both parties are from a common law system, the arbitral tribunal may rely on affidavits and order pre-hearing discovery to a greater extent than in a case with parties of civil law tradition, where, to mention another example, the mode of proceedings could be more inquisitorial than adversary.* Above all, where the parties are from different legal systems, the arbitral tribunal may use a liberal "mixed" procedure, adopting suitable features from different legal systems and relying on techniques proven in international practice, and, for instance, let parties present their case as they themselves judge best. Such procedural discretion in all these cases seems conducive to facilitating international commercial arbitration, while being forced to apply the "law of the land" where the arbitration happens to take place would present a major disadvantage to any party not used to that partic-

---

[48] *A Guide to the New ICC Rules of Arbitration, supra,* note 2, p. 3.
[49] *Analytical Commentary, supra,* note 34, p. 136.

ular and possibly peculiar system of procedure and evidence.[50] [emphasis added]

The tribunal may conduct the arbitration on the basis of documents only or may order a hearing. If any party requests a hearing, the arbitral tribunal must grant one. As per Article 20(2) of the *Model Law*, the tribunal can meet anywhere it deems appropriate for discussions between the panel members, for hearing witnesses or for inspecting any documents or goods.

## 15. STATEMENTS OF CLAIM AND DEFENCE

Article 23 of the *Model Law* states:

(1) Within the period of time agreed by the parties or *determined by the arbitral tribunal*, the claimant shall state the facts supporting his claim, *the points at issue* and the relief or remedy sought, and the respondent shall state his defence in respect of these particulars, unless the parties have otherwise agreed as to the required elements of such statements. The parties may submit with their statements all documents they consider to be relevant or may add a reference to the documents or other evidence they will submit. [emphasis added]

(2) Unless otherwise agreed by the parties, either party may amend or supplement his claim or defence during the course of the arbitral proceedings, unless the arbitral tribunal considers it inappropriate to allow such amendment having regard to the delay in making it.

Article 23(1) permits the claimant to state the points at issue; too often legal counsel are under the impression that the *points at issue* must be negotiated prior to the appointment of the arbitrator. If this were true, a party seeking to delay or obfuscate the proceedings could use the time to negotiate the issues for such purpose. This is unnecessary. Once there is a dispute covered by an arbitration agreement, the arbitrator can be appointed immediately either by the mechanism agreed to by the parties or by the court. Once the arbitral tribunal has been appointed, the claimant should immediately file the statement of claim within the time defined by the arbitral tribunal.

Article 23(2) permits a party to amend its claim or defence during the proceedings; however, the amendment must not exceed the jurisdiction of the arbitral tribunal as set out in the arbitration agreement. This restriction,

---

[50] *Ibid.*, p. 138.

while not expressed in the Article, seems self-evident in view of the fact that the jurisdiction of the tribunal is based on, and given within, the limits of that agreement. Furthermore, while not expressly stated, counterclaims are permitted within Article 23. Any provision of the *Model Law* referring to the claim would apply *mutatis mutandis* to a counter-claim.[51]

By Article 24, subject to any contrary *agreement* by the parties, the arbitral tribunal shall decide whether to hold oral hearings for the presentation of evidence or for oral argument, or whether the proceedings shall be conducted on the basis of documents and other materials.

## 16.  DEFAULT OF A PARTY

By virtue of Article 25 of the *Model Law*, a defaulting party, particularly a respondent, cannot cripple the proceedings. Article 25 is as follows:

Unless otherwise agreed by the parties, if, without showing sufficient cause,

(a)    the claimant fails to communicate his statement of claim in accordance with article 23(1), the arbitral tribunal shall terminate the proceedings;

(b)    the respondent fails to communicate his statement of defence in accordance with article 23(1), the arbitral tribunal shall continue the proceedings without treating such failure in itself as an admission of the claimant's allegations;

(c)    any party fails to appear at a hearing or to produce documentary evidence, the arbitral tribunal may continue the proceedings and made the award on the evidence before it.

Article 25(b) ensures that the arbitration cannot be frustrated by the respondent's failure to communicate his statement of defence. It obliges the arbitral tribunal to continue the proceedings "without treating such failure as an admission of the claimant's allegations". This rule concerning the assessment of the respondent's failure seems useful in view of the fact that under many national laws on civil procedure, default of the defendant in court proceedings is treated as an admission of the claimant's allegations. However, this does not mean that the arbitral tribunal would have *no* discretion as to how to assess the failure and would be bound to treat it as a full denial of the claim and all supporting facts.[52]

---

[51]  *Ibid.*, p. 131.
[52]  *Ibid.*, p. 147.

## 17. RULES APPLICABLE TO THE SUBSTANCE OF THE DISPUTE

Article 28 of the *Model Law* states:

(1) The arbitral tribunal shall decide the dispute in accordance with *such rules of law as are chosen by the parties* as applicable to the substance of the dispute. Any designation of the law or legal system of a given State shall be construed, unless otherwise expressed, as directly referring to the substantive law of that State and not to its conflict of laws rules. [emphasis added]

(2) Failing any designation by the parties, the arbitral tribunal shall apply the law determined by the conflict of laws rules which it considers applicable.

(3) The arbitral tribunal shall decide *ex aequo et bono* or as *amiable compositeur* only if the parties have expressly authorized it to do so.

(4) In all cases, the arbitral tribunal shall decide in accordance with the terms of the contract and shall take into account the usages of the trade applicable to the transaction.

As with procedural matters, the *Model Law* grants the parties full autonomy to determine which rules of law are applicable and, failing agreement, by entrusting the arbitral tribunal with that determination. The reference to choosing "rules of law" provides the parties with a wide range of options and allows them to designate, as is applicable to their case, rules of more than one legal system. The right of parties to determine which rules of law are applicable provides parties with the necessary flexibility to subject their relationship to those rules of law which they regard as the most suitable ones for their specific case. The doctrine of "amiable composition" and the role of the amiable composition will be discussed subsequently.

## 18. ENFORCEMENT OF FOREIGN ARBITRAL AWARDS[53]

### (a) Introduction

Ontario counsel will, at times, be called upon to seek the enforcement of foreign arbitral awards. A party seeking the enforcement of a foreign

---

[53] Section written by Andre Ducasse, Gowling Lafleur Henderson LLP.

arbitral award must rely on the *International Commercial Arbitration Act.*[54] This statute appends and incorporates as a schedule to the *UNCITRAL Model Law on International Commercial Arbitration.*

### (b) Application of the *Model Law* and the *International Arbitration Act*

Article 1(3) of the *Model Law* provides that an arbitration is "international" if:

(a) the parties to an arbitration agreement have, at the time of the conclusion of that agreement, their places of business in different States; or

(b) one of the following places is situated outside the State in which the parties have their places of business:

    (i)   the place of arbitration if determined in, or pursuant to, the arbitration agreement,

    (ii)  any place where a substantial part of the obligations of the commercial relationship is to be performed or the place with which the subject-matter of the dispute is most closely connected; or

(c) the parties have expressly agreed that the subject-matter of the arbitration agreement relates to more than one country.

For the purposes of Article 1(3) of the *Model Law*, if a party has more than one place of business, the place of business is that which has the closest relationship to the arbitration agreement. If a party does not have a place of business, reference is to be made to the party's habitual place of residence.[55] Despite Article 1(3) of the *Model Law*, the *International Arbitration Act* stipulates that an arbitration conducted in Ontario between parties that all have their places of business in Ontario is not international only because the parties have expressly agreed that the subject-matter of the arbitration agreement relates to more than one country.[56] Furthermore, section 10 of the *International Arbitration Act* stipulates that for the purposes of Article 35 (Recognition and enforcement) and Article 36 (Grounds for refusing recognition and enforcement) of the *Model Law*, an arbitral award includes a commercial arbitral award made outside Canada, even if the arbitration

---

[54] R.S.O. 1990, c. I.9 (hereinafter the "*International Arbitration Act*").

[55] *Ibid.*, Schedule, Article 1(4).

[56] *Ibid.*, s. 2(3).

to which it relates is not international as defined in Article 1(3) of the *Model Law*.

The term "commercial" has been broadly interpreted by the courts in Ontario. The Court held in *Canada Packers Inc. v. Terra Nova Tankers Inc.* that the *International Arbitration Act* applies to all disputes arising out of commercial relationships, whether contractual or not.[57] In addition, it has been held that the term "commercial" includes all commercial relationships regardless of whether the parties were commercial persons.[58]

To summarize, at first glance the terms used in the *International Arbitration Act* seem rather restrictive. However, given the statutory definition of the term "international" and the judicial consideration of the term "commercial", Ontario courts will grant some latitude to an applicant who is seeking to enforce a foreign arbitral award. This purposive approach is reflected in some of the case law. For example, it has been decided that the *Model Law* was enacted specifically to avoid the delays which are dependant upon court proceedings and to provide a more efficient means of dealing with disputes where the parties have agreed that arbitration is the method to be used.[59]

### (c) Recognition of the Arbitral Award and Application for Enforcement

Under the *Model Law*, an arbitral award, irrespective of the country in which it was made may be enforced upon application to the Ontario Superior Court of Justice.[60] An application for the enforcement of an arbitral award is made by notice of application pursuant to Rule 14 of the Rules of Civil Procedure.[61] The party relying on the arbitral award or applying for its enforcement must provide the duly authenticated original award or a duly certified copy thereof, along with the original arbitration agreement or a duly certified copy of the arbitration agreement.[62] Furthermore, if the award or agreement is not made in one of Canada's official languages, the party relying on the award must supply a duly certified translation thereof.[63] An

---

[57] (1992), 11 O.R. (3d) 382 (Gen. Div.), additional reasons at (February 2, 1993), Doc. 92-CQ-22196 (Ont. Gen. Div.).
[58] *Carter v. McLaughlin* (1996), 27 O.R. (3d) 792 (Gen. Div.).
[59] *Fleet v. Bimman Realty Inc.*, [1994] O.J. No. 3018, 1994 CarswellOnt 2370 (Gen. Div.).
[60] *International Arbitration Act, supra*, note 54, Schedule, Article 35(1).
[61] *Schreter v. Gasmac Inc.* (1992), 7 O.R. (3d) 608 (Gen. Div.).
[62] *International Arbitration Act, supra*, note 54, Schedule, Article 35(2).
[63] *Ibid.*

arbitration agreement may be in the form of an arbitration clause in a contract.[64]

When a foreign arbitral award is recognized by the court it will be enforceable by that court in the same manner as a judgment or order of that court.[65] Once recognized by the court, the arbitral award will be binding on the persons between whom it was made and may be relied on by any of those persons in any legal proceedings upon application to the court and upon submission to that court of a certified copy of the arbitration agreement.[66]

### (d)  Grounds for Refusing Recognition or Enforcement

The grounds for refusing recognition of a foreign arbitral award under the *Model Law* are more numerous than those provided for in the *Arbitration Act*. This is likely due to the fact that some parties to a foreign arbitration may not have had the benefit of the same rights of appeal or rights to set aside the award under the laws of the foreign jurisdiction.

Pursuant to Article 36 of the *Model Law*, recognition or enforcement of a foreign arbitral award may be refused only at the request of the party against whom it is invoked by adducing sufficient evidence that:

1.  A party to the arbitration agreement was under some incapacity;

2.  The arbitration agreement is not valid under the law to which the parties have subjected it or, failing any indication thereon, under the law of the country where the award was made;

3.  The party against whom the award is invoked was not given proper notice of the appointment of an arbitrator or of the arbitral proceedings or was otherwise unable to present his or her case;

4.  The award deals with a dispute not contemplated by or not falling within the terms of the submission to arbitration, or it contains decisions on matters beyond the scope of the submission to arbitration. If the decisions on matters submitted to arbitration can be separated from those not so submitted, that part of the award which contains decisions on matters submitted to arbitration may be recognised and enforced;

5.  The composition of the arbitral tribunal or the arbitral procedure was

---

[64] *Ibid.*, Schedule, Article 7.

[65] *Ibid.*, s. 11(1).

[66] *Ibid.*, s. 11(2).

not in accordance with the agreement of the parties or, failing such an agreement, was not in accordance with the law of the country where the arbitration took place; or

6.  The award has not yet become binding on the parties or has been set aside or suspended by a court of the country in which, or under the law of which, that award was made.

As in the case of the *Arbitration Act*, the *Model Law* grants a certain margin of discretion to the court with respect to the recognition or enforcement of a foreign arbitral award which would otherwise be enforceable. The court may refuse to recognize or enforce a foreign arbitral award if:

1.  The subject-matter of the dispute is not capable of settlement by arbitration under the law of Ontario; or

2.  The recognition or enforcement of the award would be contrary to Ontario public policy.[67]

Therefore, by virtue of Article 36 of the *Model Law*, a court may exercise its discretion to refuse recognition and enforcement of a foreign arbitral award only if the responding party can prove one or more of the enumerated grounds. Article 36 of the *Model Law* clearly places the burden upon the respondent to prove the existence of one of the grounds set out in Article 36.[68] Further, even in cases where a respondent successfully demonstrates that one of the Article 36 grounds exists, the court is not obliged to refuse recognition and enforcement of the award. This specific decision is a discretionary one.[69]

It is interesting to note, as the court did in the *Schreter* case, that neither the failure to give reasons for an award nor an error on the face of the record are grounds to refuse recognition or enforcement of an award. Further, an award will not be invalid simply because the arbitral tribunal wrongly decided a point of law.[70] The issue of the validity of the arbitration agreement

---

[67] *Ibid.*, Schedule, Article 36(1)(b).

[68] *Schreter, supra*, note 61, at 618.

[69] *Ibid.*, at 614.

[70] *Standard Life Assurance Co. v. Parc-IX Ltd.* (1991), 3 O.R. (3d) 782 (Gen. Div.). See also *Quintette Coal Ltd. v. Nippon Steel Corp.* (1990), 50 B.C.L.R. (2d) 207 (C.A.); *Middlemiss & Gould v. Hartlepool Corp.*, [1973]1 All E.R. 172 (C.A.).

is to be determined by the laws of the place of arbitration and not domestic provincial law.[71]

## (e) Public Policy

It was stated above that one of the grounds which the Ontario Superior Court of Justice may consider in refusing recognition or enforcement of a foreign arbitral award is that to do so would be contrary to public policy. Although an in-depth discussion of this issue is beyond the scope of this chapter, it would be helpful to consider the circumstances under which a court might conclude that the recognition or enforcement of an arbitral award would be contrary to public policy.

The issue of a foreign arbitral award being contrary to public policy was raised in the *Schreter* case. The Court had to address the issue of determining if a foreign arbitral award which provided for the acceleration of royalty payments was contrary to Ontario public policy. In concluding that the arbitral award was not contrary to Ontario public policy, the Court made the following comments:

> The concept of imposing our public policy on foreign awards is to guard against enforcement of an award which offends our local principles of justice and fairness in a fundamental way, and in a way which the parties could attribute to the fact that the award was made in another jurisdiction where the procedural or substantive rules diverge markedly from our own, or where there was ignorance or corruption on the part of the tribunal which could not be seen to be tolerated or condoned by our courts.

> It is true that arbitral awards have been viewed with less confidence than judgments of a court because the procedures of the courts are more regulated and standardized, and judges are sworn to uphold those procedures and to apply the law, while the qualifications and training of arbitrators may diverge greatly. And it is of concern to a court in this jurisdiction that a party to a foreign arbitration may feel that justice was not done or that the award is perverse in law.

> However, if this court were to endorse the view that it should reopen the merits of an arbitral decision on legal issues decided in accordance with the law of a foreign jurisdiction and where there has been no misconduct, under the guise of ensuring conformity with the public policy of this province, the enforcement procedure of the Model Law could be brought into disrepute.

---

[71] *Kanto Yakin Kogyo Kabushiki-Kaisha v. Can-Eng Manufacturing Ltd.* (1992), 7 O.R. (3d) 779 (Gen. Div.), affirmed (1995), 22 O.R. (3d) 576 (C.A.).

A similar sentiment was expressed by the United States Court of Appeals Second Circuit in the case of *Waterside Ocean Navigation Co. v. International Navigation Ltd.*, 737 F.2d 150 (1984) [at p. 152]:

> This defense must be construed in light of the overriding purpose of the Convention, which is "to encourage the recognition and enforcement of commercial arbitration agreements in international contracts and to unify the standards by which agreements to arbitrate are observed and arbitral awards are enforced in the signatory countries" . . . Thus, this court has unequivocally stated that the public policy defense should be construed narrowly. It should apply only where enforcement would violate our "most basic notions of morality and justice."[72]

Ontario courts have even rejected public policy arguments where a party relied on a foreign law which, although applicable in the foreign jurisdiction, was contrary to public policy in Ontario. This was the case in *Boardwalk Regency Corp. v. Maalouf*.[73] In this case, the Ontario Court of Appeal had to determine whether or not a gambling debt could be enforced in Ontario. The contracting parties had agreed that the law applicable to the transaction was the law of the State of New Jersey. Under that law the debt was legal. In rejecting the respondent's public policy argument Lacourcière J.A. made the following comments:

> In my opinion, the respondent has not satisfied the burden of showing that the enforcement of the contract or of the New Jersey judgment would be contrary to public policy. I agree that the foreign judgment should not be declared unenforceable on grounds of public policy unless its enforcement would violate conceptions of essential justice and morality. I am here referring to domestic public policy as well as national public policy at the international level. Where the foreign law is applicable, Canadian courts will generally apply that law even though the result may be contrary to domestic law.[74]

Although this case addresses the enforceability of a foreign judgment it nonetheless illustrates that Ontario courts will be reticent to set aside judgments or awards on grounds of public policy.

A similarly restrictive approach has been adopted in Great Britain. Although commenting on the *New York Convention*, the predecessor of the

---

[72] *Schreter, supra*, note 61, at 623-624.
[73] (1992), 6 O.R. (3d) 737 (C.A.), additional reasons at (1992), 1992 CarswellOnt 1738 (C.A.).
[74] *Ibid.*, at 748 (O.R.).

*Model Law* in many respects, Redfern and Hunter's following comments are insightful:

> Recognition and enforcement of an arbitral award may also be refused if it is contrary to the public policy of the enforcement state. It is understandable that a state may wish to have the right to refuse to recognise and enforce an arbitration award that in some way offends that state's own notions of public policy. Yet when reference is made to "public policy" it is difficult not to recall the sceptical comment of the English judge who said, more than a century ago, "It is never argued at all but where other points fail."
>
> Certainly, the national courts in England are reluctant to excuse an award from enforcement on grounds of public policy. Indeed, according to one learned commentator: "there is no case in which this exception has been applied by an English court." Indeed, in most countries this "pre-enforcement bias" of the New York Convention has been faithfully observed.[75]

This brief review of some of the authorities reveals that Ontario Courts will be reluctant to excuse a foreign arbitral award from enforcement on grounds of public policy. A party attempting to be excused from the recognition or enforcement of such an award must overcome an onerous burden.

### (f)  Non-merger of the Arbitral Award

Often, a party seeking enforcement of an arbitral award in Ontario will have already obtained judgment in the foreign jurisdiction confirming the award. It is important to note that under such circumstances the arbitral award does not merge in the confirmatory judgment.[76] Under the *Model Law*, the arbitral award can be enforced as an award, and it is not necessary to attempt to enforce it as a foreign judgment. It would be prudent, however, to rely upon the foreign judgment in the Application Record as an alternative argument in case recognition or enforcement of the arbitral award is not granted. Accordingly, in the absence of reciprocal enforcement of judgment legislation, an applicant should rely on the Supreme Court of Canada decision in *Morguard Investments Ltd. v. De Savoye*[77] which provides that a Canadian court is to recognize a foreign judgment where there is a real and

---

[75] Redfern and Hunter, *Law and Practice of International Commercial Arbitration*, 3rd ed., London: Sweet & Maxwell, 1999, pp. 471-472.

[76] *Schreter, supra*, note 61, at 617-620.

[77] [1990] 3 S.C.R. 1077.

substantial connection between the original jurisdiction and the subject-matter of the proceeding or the defendant.

### (g) Recourse against Award Recognition and Enforcement of Awards

Article 34 provides very limited grounds to set aside an international arbitration award. Under this provision, it is the applicant who bears the onus of proving that the award should be set aside. Similarly, Article 36 also provides very limited grounds to refuse to recognize or enforce an award. In fact, the grounds which must be established to set aside an award (see Article 34(2)) are essentially the same grounds which must be established to refuse recognition or enforcement.

These grounds are:

1.  That a party to the arbitration agreement is under some incapacity or the agreement is not valid under the law.
2.  A party was not given proper notice.
3.  The award deals with a dispute not contemplated by or falling within the terms of the submission to arbitration.
4.  The court finds that the composition of the arbitral tribunal was not in accordance with the agreement of the parties.
5.  The court finds that the subject matter of the dispute is not capable of settlement by arbitration.
6.  The award is in conflict with the public policy of this State.

If the applicant fails to satisfy the court that the award falls within one of the grounds enumerated in Article 36, Article 35 expressly requires the court to recognize and enforce the award.

Article 36 adopts almost literally the well known grounds set forth in Article V of the 1958 New York Convention and declares them as applicable to refusal of recognition or enforcement of all awards, irrespective of where they were made. Thus the provision, like Article 35, covers foreign as well as domestic awards, provided they are rendered in "international commercial arbitration" as referred to in Article 1 and, of course, subject to any multilateral or bilateral treaty to which the enforcement State is a party.[78]

It has been stated that where the arbitral tribunal's jurisdiction is called into question, an applicant has to overcome "a powerful presumption" that

---

[78] *Supra*, note 9, at 166.

the tribunal in fact acted within its powers.[79] Similarly, the public policy ground for refusing enforcement of arbitral awards is also narrowly construed. In fact, Lax J. of the Ontario Superior Court of Justice noted in the case of *Corporacion Transnacional de Inversiones, S.A. de C.V. v. STET International, S.p.A.*:

> [T]o succeed on this ground the awards must fundamentally offend the most basic and explicit principles of justice and fairness in Ontario, or evidence intolerable ignorance or corruption on the part of the Arbitral Tribunal. The applicants must establish that the awards are contrary to the essential morality of Ontario.[80]

## 19. ARBITRATOR BIAS

The *Model Law* provides in Article 12 that an arbitrator is responsible for disclosing any circumstances that could lead the parties to doubt his impartiality or independence. The arbitrator can only be challenged and ultimately removed if such circumstances exist that give rise to justifiable doubts as to his impartiality and independence.

In the recent case of *AT&T Corporation v. Saudi Cable Co.*,[81] the English Court of Appeal dealt with the question of arbitrator bias and the appropriate test to apply to such instances. In this case, one of the three arbitrators was a non-executive director of Nortel, a Canadian company which had been a disappointed bidder for the project at issue in the arbitration, having lost its bid to AT&T. When the directorship of the arbitrator came to the attention of AT&T, the arbitration was quite advanced and a number of rulings and awards had already been made. AT&T refused the arbitrator's offer of resolving the matter by resigning from his directorship of Nortel and subsequently challenged his appointment under the ICC Rules.

In citing the appropriate test to apply, the Court concluded that:

> a court should ask itself whether, having regard to those circumstances, there was a *real danger of bias* on the part of the relevant member of the tribunal in question, in the sense that he might unfairly regard (or have unfairly re-

---

[79] See *Corporacion Transnacional de Inversiones, S.A. de C.V. v. STET International, S.p.A.* (1999), 45 O.R. (3d)183 (S.C.J. [Commercial List]), affirmed (2000), 2000 CarswellOnt 3315 (C.A.).

[80] *Ibid.*, at 193 (O.R.).

[81] [2000] E.W.J. No. 2595 (Eng. C.A.).

garded) with favour, or disfavour, the case of a party to the issue under consideration by him . . .[82] [emphasis added]

This test must be applied by considering the matter in the eyes of a reasonable person. In establishing the application of this "real danger" test, the Court rejected the submission of the applicants that the test should be of a lower threshold when the matter concerns arbitrators rather than courts. Lord Woolf for the Court of Appeal contended that a court should apply the same test "irrespective of whether it is a judge or an arbitrator who is the subject of the allegation of bias".

In this case, the English Court of Appeal ruled that there was no real danger of bias on the part of the arbitrator since any benefit that he could receive from Nortel as a result of the arbitration would be so minimal that it would not influence him. He readily offered to resign from his directorship of Nortel, hence he did not attach much importance to his involvement with that company and he conducted himself throughout the arbitration in a way that did not support any allegation that he was prejudiced.

---

[82] *Ibid.*, citing a passage from Lord Goff in *R. v. Gough*, [1993] A.C. 646 (Eng. C.A.).

# 12

## Use of Conciliation, Mediation and Amiable Composition in International ADR

### 1. INTRODUCTION

Whether the parties to an international commercial agreement wish to submit a dispute to arbitration, conciliation, mediation or any other form of alternative dispute resolution, it is imperative that such a clause or section of a contract establishing the desired dispute resolution mechanism be seriously considered and negotiated *before* any dispute arises, i.e., before battle lines become drawn. One of the major problems inherent to cross-cultural business disputes is the diverse and often contradictory legal and commercial "baggage" each party carries into the contract negotiations. The common arbitration clause is one way to resolve future uncertainties. Yet, in situations which involve negotiations between parties of different cultures and legal systems, it may be preferable to leave the third party (or parties) assigned the task of finding a solution(s) to a given business dispute a certain amount of flexibility which an arbitrator, strictly speaking, does not have.

The parties to an international agreement should also consider including a provision requiring the parties to embark on the process of conciliation or mediation prior to resorting to amiable composition.

## 2. AMIABLE COMPOSITION

One such compromise has been developed within the legal tradition of France: "amiable composition". The concept of amiable composition is not "new" to the international legal community. Indeed, this form of dispute resolution is provided for in the *Model Law*:

> . . . The arbitral tribunal shall decide *ex aequo et bono* or as "amiable compositeur" only if the parties have expressly authorized it to do so . . .[1]

As well, the rules of commercial institutions such as the ICC provide for amiable composition:

> The arbitrator shall assume the powers of an amiable compositeur if the parties are agreed to give him such powers.[2]

The amiable compositeur of the "*amicabilis compositor*" was initially a type of mediator. As stated by John E.C. Brierley:

> If one returns to the earliest use of the expression amiable composition "*ex aequo et bono*" in continental European Romanus and canonical, it is clear that this association of ideas did exist. A remarkable survival of the same association was also found, among modern civilian codes, in the case of Québec.

> . . . In any event, Québec law since 1986, like French law (at least since the Napoleonic codification) no longer associates the two ideas, nor does the Model Law itself . . . Mediation and amiable composition are thus distinct functions.[3]

The term "*amicabilis*" is synonymous with the term "*compositor*" and means a friendly compromise solution. Slowly, the amiable compositeur became more than a mediator; in order to facilitate conflict resolution, the amiable compositeur became an "equitable arbitrator". In fact, the amiable composition was defined as the equitable jurisdiction of the arbitrator.[4] The

---

[1] Article 28(3).
[2] Article 13(iv) of the ICC Rules. See also the Rules of the Inter-American Commission and the Centre d'Arbitrage, Euro-arabe.
[3] "Equity and Good Conscience: An Amiable Composition in Canadian Arbitration Law" (1991) 19 *Canadian Business Law Journal* 461 at 472.
[4] *Tuquin v. Poulé*, 9 A. de J. 420.

"equitable arbitrator" was able to rule on a dispute and put aside the rule of law in order to resolve the issues before him or her based on common sense.[5]

Even if there are sometimes important differences, the use by the arbitrator or the arbitration tribunal of the equitable jurisdiction is referred to as "amiable composition", arbitration "*ex aequo bono*", "en conscience" or "selon leur savoir et entendement".

The amiable compositeur is an arbitrator, not a conciliator or mediator per se. A decision is rendered that is binding on the parties. However, amiable composition constitutes a method of dispute resolution where the person chosen or designated by the parties to the contract need not follow the "strict rules of law" but may refashion the rules in the interest of fairness and the continuation of a working relationship between the parties to the commercial contract. He or she may thus be said to have the function of legislator as well as judge.

The power does not mean that strict legal rules will necessarily be disregarded; they may indeed coincide with fairness. What it does mean is that the arbitrator acting as amiable compositeur will not apply the letter of the law unless he is in fact satisfied that it corresponds with fairness. As stated by Redfern and Hunter, the amiable compositeur:

> . . . may take a more flexible approach to the quantification of damages in order to reflect commercial fairness and reality, rather than regarding themselves as bound by the rules of law governing standards of compensation. Nonetheless the powers of amiable compositeur are not unlimited, nor indeed should they be; they must observe due process in giving equality of treatment of the parties, and they are bound by the public policy rules, and any mandatory provisions, of the "*lex arbitri*". [E.g., in France, any award by an amiable compositeur without reasons may be set aside].[6]

The fact that amiable composition is not likely to be well understood nor accepted as "legitimate" by national judges in certain countries, such as England, may prove important; where a commercial agreement involves property in such a jurisdiction, it may be unwise to provide for amiable compositeur arbitration.

---

[5] Loquin, E., *Amiable composition en droit comparé international*, Vol. 7, Paris: Librairies Techniques Paris, 1980.

[6] *International Commercial Arbitration*, London: Sweet & Maxwell, 1986, p. 23.

Most of the countries are ready to give equitable powers to the arbitrators, but the attitudes vis-a-vis the amiable composition are different around the world.[7]

There are some countries that presume that the parties to a conflict will want an arbitration that will follow the rule of law but also give the parties an option for amiable composition arbitration. This is the case in France and in other civil law countries.

Other countries assume that the parties will want an amiable composition arbitration but allow them to choose an arbitration that will follow the rule of law. A number of Latin American countries such as Bolivia, Equator, Uruguay, Peru and Venezuela have adopted such an approach.

Some countries, such as the United States, make no reference in their laws to the concept of amiable composition; the fact that the arbitration will be conducted following equitable principles is, for these countries, self-evident.[8]

Next, there is the approach adopted by the English law and by the common law Canadian provinces which is to follow closely and apply the rule of law to most arbitrations. However, the influence of the Quebec civil law and the international *Model Law* are slowly changing the traditional concept of arbitration in the common law Canada, and provinces are starting to introduce amendments to their statutes to offer solutions which closely resemble the amiable composition.[9]

The arbitrator even in his role of amiable compositeur must follow the rules of natural justice. Even if in a number of countries the arbitrator does not have to motivate his or her decision, it must in any event be based on solid grounds and not be arbitrary.[10] Although the amiable compositeur has to follow the rules of natural justice, he is usually permitted to avoid the procedure's formalities in order to get to the core of the dispute.

One must also ask oneself whether or not the amiable compositeur has the same flexibility with respect to the procedure to be followed when the

---

[7] Antaki, N., *L'amiable composition*, International Arbitration Conference, 1985, p. 151 [unpublished].

[8] Domke, M., *The Law in Practice of Commercial Arbitration*, Mundellien, L. 968 at 256.

[9] *Supra*, note 3, p. 463. For example, the new *Commercial Arbitration Act* of British Columbia has somehow deviated from the traditional principles. It states that the arbitrator shall decide in law (section 23) unless the parties expressly agree with the terms of an Exclusion Agreement contemplated in section 34 to exclude the jurisdiction of the court and provide that the dispute may be decided "on equitable grounds, grounds of conscience or on some other basis".

[10] See David, R., *Le droit du commerce international* (1987), p. 132.

parties have determined, ahead of time by contract or by reference to a particular set of arbitration rules,[11] the procedure to follow in case of a dispute. If the amiable compositeur is able to use his equitable jurisdiction to put aside a contract or certain parts of a contract, one can argue that the amiable compositeur also has the authority to put aside the disposition of a contract with respect to the procedures to be followed if it seems just and fair for him or her to do so.[12] However, in international arbitration the amiable compositeur must respect the rules of procedure established for international arbitration. These few rules of procedure usually coincide with the minimal rules of practice applicable to any hearing.

The equity clause or the amiable composition clause gives a very broad power to the arbitrator; what is then the extent of this power? One must of course examine this question in the common and civil law context. The equity clause in the civilian context should be viewed as "the device whereby the arbitrator is invited to exercise discretion in the selection and application of the rules of positive law. The zone in which the discretion may be exercised lies within the range of those rules that fall short of being characterized as rules of public order at one end of the spectrum but which, at the other end, can go beyond the non-observance of mere 'technicalities' or 'formalities' of the rule of positive law."[13] In the common law context, "the scope of the authority to decide *ex aequo bono* while extending beyond the excusing of mere 'technicalities' and 'strict constructions', will turn, in final analysis, upon the conception of public order or public policy as found to exist by the courts of the jurisdiction in question when examining the content of the award rather than merely the elements of the process that has produced it."[14]

In cross-cultural contracts, if the arbitrator can step outside the law, another important issue is whose ethical or subjective values shall be applied? The choice of the arbitrator, should he or she have amiable compositeur power, becomes crucial. Occasionally, someone may want an arbitral tribunal to undertake the task of amiable composition. The *Model Law* accommodates such a wish by providing as well for arbitral tribunals.[15]

The amiable compositeur remains bound by imperative norms of public policy as well as by the express terms of the clause in the contract which provides his or her mandate. The amiable compositeur is still required to

---

[11] *Supra*, note 7, p. 161.
[12] *Ibid.*, pp. 161-162.
[13] *Supra*, note 3, p. 480.
[14] *Ibid.*, p. 481.
[15] Article 28.

render decisions in accordance with the fundamental principles of natural justice, following the basic rules of procedure established within international arbitration. A contractual provision providing this power is simply a recognition by the parties that the positive law cannot and should not provide the *entire* basis upon which to solve the future disputes. It has been remarked by Craig, Park and Paulson[16] that:

> . . . in the international setting, arbitrators tend to adjust the application of law in favour of giving full effect to the parties' agreement rather than "adjust the parties" agreement in order to give effect to a personal evaluation of what would have been a fair bargain. Indeed, international arbitrators are likely to moderate the application of law in favour of the parties' agreement even if they do not have amiable compositeur authority.

The amiable compositeur may be a person with an expertise in the area or areas covered by the relevant commercial agreement(s). Not being encumbered by the "strict letter of the law", he or she may provide an interpretation of the relationship between the parties which would allow the contract to survive and continue to be capable of *bona fide* performance.

It may be noted that amiable composition may be more suited for long-term commercial arrangements. Indeed a study by Eric Loquin[17] found that amiable composition, when used, was usually inserted in contracts of long duration. Presumably, this is due to the complexity of such agreements, the uncertainty as to applicable principles or precedent as well as the important economic interests involved. Amiable composition may provide a more flexible and equitable solution to an existing dispute, conducive to continued business interaction.

As previously stated, the *UNCITRAL Arbitration Rules* and the *UNCITRAL Model Law* on International Commercial Arbitration both contain references to the concept of amiable compositeur. The *Model Law*, which provides for the concept of amiable composition, allows for an arbitrator to be named or appointed as amiable compositeur if two conditions are met. Firstly, the arbitration convention must specify that the disputes arising between the parties will be dealt with by an amiable compositeur. Secondly, for amiable composition to be possible, the laws of the governing countries must permit this type of dispute resolution.[18] This should be examined by

---

[16] *International Commercial Arbitration Rules*: ICC (1984).

[17] *Supra*, note 5, pp. 145-154.

[18] The *UNCITRAL Arbitration Rules*, Article 33. Also see the earlier discussion with respect to the reticence of a number of countries to allow amiable composition.

the parties on a case by case basis[19] and should be an important consideration in the choice of the place of arbitration.

Although the amiable composition offers to parties a relatively simple process and adaptable awards, the fact that the rule of law might be discarded presents certain risks, as the predictability of an outcome is, at best, difficult.

Whether parties would ever be wise to dispense with the application of the rule of law is doubtful. If an arbitrator's sense of fairness proves capricious or wrong-headed, little can be done about it if he is not obliged to follow any law (substantive or procedural); an arbitrator might well feel uncomfortable about undertaking to adjudicate by anything so vague as his own subjective insight. However, there does not appear to be any public interest which will be injured if parties should agree to dispense with law altogether:

> . . . governments of developing countries, involved in such contracts directly or through State enterprises, are often reluctant to agree on amiable composition if it means rejection of their own national law. They often feel that as a matter of principle their law should govern contracts essential to their economic development. This has occasionally led to combining a contractual choice of a national law with conferring the powers of amiable compositeur on the arbitrator. This practice is accepted by arbitrators and results in giving a single national law foundation to the contract, while still permitting the arbitrators to make an equitable application of national norms to the contract.[20]

Under the ICC Rules, the validity of amiable composition, and a decision made thereunder, is not dependent upon the procedural law of the place of arbitration. Thus, the decision to give such extensive powers to a third party rests entirely with the parties to the international agreement without regard to conflicts between divergent procedural law.

There are two schools of thought with respect to the powers of the amiable compositeur. The first is a more restrictive interpretation of the powers and duties of the amiable compositeur, i.e., he or she may use equitable principles to interpret the contract and resolve the dispute but cannot actually rewrite or modify the existing agreement. The second, to which I am more inclined, envisages the role of the third party, not only as a decision-maker but as a person who may be called upon in pre-determined circumstances to suspend, modify, vary or amend the agreement in accordance with the "spirit" of the original commercial document. In other words,

---

[19] Beguin, J., *L'arbitrage commercial international* (1987), p. 182.

[20] Craig et al., *supra*, note 16, p. 96.

the parties nominate an amiable compositeur with express powers to resolve disputes and actually modify the agreement between the parties in the future.

In the practice of international contract negotiations and international arbitration, the adaptation of contracts is one of the major subjects calling for attention in our time. In an article, published in the *Canadian Arbitration Journal*,[21] I set out a potential clause which may provide a mechanism for the third party to "fill any gaps":

1.    (1) If either party hereto contends that any of the circumstances set out in clause 3 herein may have occurred, it shall serve on the other party Written Notice (hereinafter called the "Notice") specifying the alleged circumstances and what modifications, variations, alterations or additions should be made to this Agreement in those circumstances. In default of agreement between the parties within 30 days, then any difference shall be referred to the determination of an arbitrator who shall be appointed in accordance with the provisions hereof.

(2) Such Notice shall call upon the other party within 28 days of receipt of the Notice, to concur in the appointment of an individual, having no personal interest in the operation or performance of the Agreement, to act as Arbitrator and whose name and address shall be set out in the Notice, and who shall have previously signified his willingness to act as such.

2.    The Arbitrator may make such modifications, variations, alteration or additions to this Agreement as he or she in his or her absolute discretion shall think fit and fair and appropriate having regard to all the circumstances of the case, and without prejudice to the generality thereof, such determinations may:

(a)    alter, add to or cancel the obligations and powers of the parties to the Agreement or any of them;

(b)    alter the financial obligations of either party;

(c)    suspend the agreement or any provision thereof, or extend the term of the Agreement or any of the provisions thereof;

(d)    take into account any additional or lesser burden which either party has had to bear as from the date of such change of circumstances;

(e)    be of general effect, or be for such limited period as the Arbitrator shall decide;

(f)    come into effect from such date as the Arbitrator shall decide which

---

[21]    (1986) 11 *Can. Arb. J.* 2.

may in the Arbitrator's discretion be a date prior to the date of his determination of the reference;

(g)    be subject to such conditions as the Arbitrator may decide in all the circumstances.

PROVIDED THAT the Arbitrator shall have no power to award the payment of any sum of money to one party to this Agreement by the other party by way of damages or costs.

3.    The circumstances referred to in clause 1 hereof shall be any of the following which occur during the term of the Agreement . . .

I would now seriously consider adding a clause expressly authorizing the arbitrator(s) to act as an amiable compositeur. As to the type of powers provided in the above provision, Craig, Park and Paulson comment that:

Modifying the contract may be *particularly vital* to the success of long-term projects, with respect to which the evolution of the product market, rates of currency exchange, technological developments, politics, relative competitive advantages, and the like, may make it highly desirable to provide for an arbitral adjustment of the contract. Otherwise, the sole alternative to a negotiated solution would be the termination of the contract with a possible award of interest, and both parties may agree at the time of negotiating the contract that such an end to their association would be in the interest of neither.[22] [emphasis added]

It is important to remember that the power of the amiable compositeur is limited by his or her jurisdiction or function as established in the contract, e.g., the agreement could provide that the amiable compositeur is dismissed on the consent of both parties. Such a clause may prove important should the amiable compositeur "run amok".

## 3. CONCILIATION OR MEDIATION AND ARBITRATION

The practice of the Foreign Trade Arbitration Commission as well as the Maritime Arbitration Commission is to combine arbitration, be it as discussed above or otherwise, with the process of conciliation or mediation. It is their view that arbitration and conciliation are interrelated, each complementing the other.

---

[22] See Craig et al., *supra*, note 16, pp. 72-73.

B.V. Orsini provides a typical clause which parties have included in their contract as an agreement for the submission of disputes to a third party:

> Any disputes arising from the execution of or in connection with this contract shall be settled amicably through friendly negotiation. In case no settlement can be reached through negotiation, the case shall then be submitted to the Foreign Trade Arbitration Commission (or the Maritime Arbitration Commission) of the China Council for the promotion of international trade, Peking, for arbitration in accordance with its provisional rules of procedure. The arbitral award is final and binding upon both parties.[23]

Should resort to negotiations fail, resort to amiable composition may provide the solution. Orsini notes that similar clauses are used extensively in some countries, such as Japan and China, particularly with regard to joint ventures. Redfern and Hunter, however, caution us that:

> Conciliation and mediation have their uses as a method of resolving international commercial disputes, but they are facilities which are little used in a current practice. A dispassionate and disinterested third party may be able to make the parties see the strengths and weaknesses of each other's arguments and so bring them, no doubt reluctantly, to some form of compromise agreement. In truth, however, by the time a dispute is referred to an independent outsider, the parties may well have already exhausted the prospects of arriving at a negotiated settlement. By resorting to arbitration, the claimant shows that he means business. The time for further negotiation may come when the arbitration itself is in progress.[24]

## 4. THE COMBINATION OF CONCILIATION AND AMIABLE COMPOSITION

By combining the above two processes within an international commercial agreement, the parties provide for a process which is entirely voluntary, carrying no risk, by which a neutral and jointly appointed third person helps the parties negotiate their own settlement. Failing this, amiable composition provides a binding means of settlement yet does not limit the arbitrator to strict principles of law, instead allowing the third party to

---

[23] "Joint Ventures — Conciliation and Arbitration Clauses and Some Items to Consider", Canada and International, 1982.
[24] *Supra*, note 6, p. 21.

consider other important sources of dispute resolution, i.e., trade usage, equitable principles, reshaping the contract, etc.

Redfern and Hunter[25] point out that an arbitrator acting as an amiable compositeur has greater scope to adapt a contract to the circumstances in practice because of his or her mandate to "find an equitable solution to a dispute, not based on a strict interpretation of the contract, and because of the difficulty of appealing against the award of amiable compositeur, so long as he or she has acted with procedural fairness."

Med-Arb (i.e., mediation-arbitration) means that the arbitrator may also act as a mediator. Section 3 of the *International Commercial Arbitration Act* permits this if the parties agree. Med-Arb has many advantages. If mediation fails there is no need to educate another neutral of the substance of the dispute. Also,

> Another advantage is that the parties will know that the neutral will decide the dispute if they cannot, so they will pay greater attention to her suggestions, including the rights standards she may advance . . .[26]

Med-Arb has several disadvantages. The key to a mediated settlement is that the parties reach the settlement themselves (through the help of the mediator) and hence are committed to it. Any party who believes that a solution is being imposed by a mediator (who also holds residual power as arbitrator) will be less committed to it. Also parties may withhold information that would be useful in reaching a mediated settlement but that would hurt them in arbitration. Finally, is it possible for the mediator to make an unbiased decision as an arbitrator, after the parties have bared their souls to the mediator and given confidential and potentially damaging information as a mediator?[27]

With the ever-increasing cost of litigation, the delays inherent to the court system and the trauma and uncertainty of trials, the growing emphasis in international commercial law on a need for alternative methods of resolving business disputes is a welcome change. The two methods of ADR, discussed above, be they combined or separate, will in my view, provide to both reduce formal dispute resolution of business conflict, and where said conflict requires a third party to render a "decision", resolve it more expeditiously and inexpensively.

---

[25] *Ibid.,* p. 23.

[26] Ury, W.L., Brett, J.M. and Goldberg, S.B., *Getting Disputes Resolved*, Cambridge: PON Books, 1993, p. 57.

[27] *Ibid.*

The joinder of a voluntary settlement process with a flexible, but binding, process of dispute resolution may provide the most satisfactory compromise. It will foster the continued commercial relationship of the parties where more traditional means of dispute resolution have, in many cases, irreparably damaged said relationship. Therefore, it is incumbent upon both the international business and legal communities to make use of the new means we have at our disposal. The provision for conciliation/ mediation and amiable composition should be seriously considered and negotiated as an invaluable part of the original commercial agreement. In this way, the parties provide a quick and equitable means of settlement of cross-cultural commercial disputes through negotiation and/or neutral interpretation and adaptation of the existing agreement.

# 13

## Mediation-Arbitration (Med-Arb): A New Dispute Resolution Tool

### 1. INTRODUCTION

Mediation-Arbitration (Med-Arb) is one of the most exciting new forms of ADR. It provides parties with the advantages of both mediation and arbitration in one proceeding; however, there are serious pitfalls in mediation-arbitration, as the most experienced practitioner will advise, and care must be taken in its use. Med-Arb is recommended, provided all parties, their lawyers, if any, and the mediator/arbitrator understand the basic principles and always ensure that these principles are followed.

Although we refer to this method of dispute resolution as new and innovative, it has in fact been in existence for a long time. Athenians in ancient Greece followed a procedure where the arbitrator was expected to first try to mediate between the disputing parties and only if this was not successful to continue with adjudication on the merits.[1]

### 2. DEFINITION

Med-Arb is a contraction for "mediation-arbitration" and refers to a hybrid form of dispute resolution process which combines mediation and arbitration. Typically, the parties involved in Med-Arb first attempt to reach a mutually acceptable solution to their problems through mediation, with

---

[1] Roebuck, D., *Ancient Greek Arbitration*, Holo Books - The Arbitration Press, Oxford, 2001, p. 207.

the help of an independent and neutral third party. If the parties are unable to reach a settlement during the mediation phase of the resolution, they progress to the arbitration phase. The arbitration ordinarily results in an award that is binding on the parties. This award reflects the agreements, if any, reached by the parties during the mediation phase and adds a final and binding decision by the arbitrator for those issues unresolved by mediation.

One of the multiple variations on the Med-Arb process is referred to as "Arb-Med" or as "armediation". The parties involved in Arb-Med start arbitration proceedings, but allow for mediation at some point during the arbitration. A new concept would be an interest-based arbitration where the parties would allow the arbitrator to render a decision based on their interests and not on their legal rights.

## 3. PROS OF MED-ARB

Med-Arb has many pros. With the high cost of litigation, the delays inherent to the court system and the strain and uncertainty associated with trials, there is a growing need for alternative methods of resolving disputes. Med-Arb is a process which could both reduce the disadvantages associated with formal dispute resolution and, where a conflict requires a third party to render a decision, resolve it more rapidly and inexpensively.[2]

Med-Arb is a single unified process. Consequently, it can be shorter in duration than the two separate processes of mediation and arbitration. As such, Med-Arb saves time, money and aggravation to the parties.[3]

Also, the Med-Arb process can be tailored to meet the specific needs of the parties. Consequently, the parties are allowed the opportunity to work out their issues in dispute while maintaining control of the situation. This enables them to walk away satisfied with the agreement, with the knowledge it was the best they could reach under the circumstances. Furthermore, the informality and the flexibility of Med-Arb allow the parties to feel as though they really are participants in the process.[4]

In situations where the parties have an ongoing relationship, Med-Arb can help them preserve this relationship by encouraging voluntary com-

---

[2] Nelson, R.M., *Effective Advocacy and the Use of* ADR, Ottawa: Gowlings, p. 149.

[3] Faber, L., "New Chapter Added to Manual: Med/Arb as an Appropriate Dispute Resolution Method" (March 1998) 15 ADR Forum 3 at 4 [hereinafter "ADR Forum"].

[4] *Ibid.*

munication and settlement, with arbitration only used to adjudicate the matters the parties cannot resolve during the mediation phase of the process.[5]

In addition, by combining mediation with arbitration, Med-Arb provides the parties with the assurance that if a mediated settlement is not possible, the matter will be finally decided at the arbitration, thus putting an end to the dispute. The arbitrator generally has the authority to make a final decision in Med-Arb, which is not an option in the mediation process alone.[6] If there is no agreement in mediation, the parties have no way of reaching a resolution of their dispute. The arbitration phase provides a clear end point, usually within an acceptable time-frame.[7] Arbitration does provide a binding decision.

Med-Arb constitutes a strong incentive for the parties to settle their dispute amicably. If the mediation phase of the process fails, the parties are aware that the arbitrator will issue a final decision, which may not correspond with the parties' objectives or interests.[8]

In situations where the same neutral third party acts as mediator and arbitrator, the costs will be reduced significantly. Indeed, the time it takes to educate a new neutral at the arbitration phase will be eliminated. Furthermore, the arbitration evidence process will be diminished considerably since the arbitrator will be familiar with the substance of the dispute and there will be less need for testimony and fact finding.[9]

Moreover, where the facilitator acts in both phases of the Med-Arb process, the parties are aware that he or she will make the final decision if they cannot settle their dispute through mediation. Consequently, the parties will pay greater attention to the suggestions or opinions which the facilitator may advance during the mediation process.[10] Furthermore, during the mediation phase, the presence of a neutral who will subsequently have decision-making authority may help the parties avoid the use of bargaining tactics

---

[5] Ohio Bar, "Alternate Dispute Resolution", online: http://www.ohiobar.org, Issue 04, Summer 2000, at 3.

[6] ADR Forum, *supra*, note 3, at 4; see also Casey, J.B., *International and Domestic Commercial Arbitration*, Toronto: Carswell, 1997, p. 1-14 [hereinafter "Casey"].

[7] Elliot, D.C., "Med/Arb: Fraught with Danger or Ripe with Opportunity?" (1995) 1 *Alberta Law Review* 163 at 164 [hereinafter "Elliot"].

[8] ADR Forum, *supra*, note 3, at 4.

[9] McLaren, R.H. and Sanderson, J.P., *Innovative Dispute Resolution — The Alternative*, Toronto: Carswell, p. 195 [hereinafter "McLaren"].

[10] Ury, W.L., Brett J.M. and Goldberg, S.B., *Getting Disputes Resolved — Designing Systems to Cut the Costs of Conflict*, Cambridge, Massachusetts: PON Books, 1993, p. 57 [hereinafter "Ury"].

such as posturing, overreaching and overreaction.[11] Finally, in the event the dispute reaches the arbitration phase, if the disputants trust the facilitator, they will often feel that he or she is the best person to make a final decision on the dispute.[12]

## 4. CONS OF MED-ARB

Med-Arb has certain disadvantages. The parties may have the tendency to work less hard to settle the case in an amicable manner knowing that an adjudicator will resolve the difficult issues for them.[13] Similarly, some neutrals might be tempted to turn prematurely to the arbitration phase whenever there is an apparent stalemate in the mediation.[14]

While it can be beneficial to compel parties to seek a negotiated settlement before arbitration, one of the problems with making mediation or conciliation a pre-condition to arbitration is that a party may seek to delay the process under the guise of attempting to settle the dispute.

In mediation, the disputants generally reveal their interests openly to the mediator so that the latter can assist in their communications and in the development of solutions that will meet their respective goals. In Med-Arb, a person performing both the functions of mediator and arbitrator is precluded from using the confidential information obtained during mediation in arriving at the arbitration decision. However, the question is whether the mediator can successfully wear two hats and maintain the integrity of each dispute resolution process by excluding from his or her mind the confidential information received from the parties during the mediation. Indeed, there is a possibility that the neutral's award be influenced by the knowledge gained during the mediation phase rather than that admitted by the parties in the arbitration phase under the rules of evidence. Armed with that apprehension, the parties could lack confidence and decrease their openness in the mediation process for fear that the facilitator will be unable, during the arbitration phase, to discount the unfavourable information. The parties may conse-

---

[11] Elliot, *supra*, note 7, at 164.
[12] ADR Forum, *supra*, note 3, at 4.
[13] National ADR Institute for Federal Judges, *Judges Deskbook on Court ADR*, New York: CPR Institute for Dispute Resolution, 1993, p. 28.
[14] Newman, P., *Alternative Dispute Resolution*, CLT Professional Publishing Ltd., p. 74 [hereinafter "Newman"].

quently fail to reveal information critical to the mediator's ability to help settle their differences because of their apprehension of bias.[15]

Similarly, the idea that the facilitator may caucus with each side independently during the mediation phase of the Med-Arb process may give rise to natural justice concerns. Indeed, our notion of justice includes the right to know and to be in a position to respond to an opponent's argument. However, when a party argues its case in a private meeting with the facilitator, its opponent has no way of knowing what was said and how it influenced the facilitator's opinion with respect to the dispute. If erroneous or dishonest statements are made during the caucus session without the other party being aware that such arguments were made, the situation could become inequitable. Some authors suggest that this problem can be rectified by avoiding the use of caucusing in the Med-Arb process,[16] or by warning the parties that, if caucusing is used, any information received in caucus that may influence the decision of the neutral turned arbitrator will be revealed to the other side.[17]

Another concern with the facilitator being both mediator and arbitrator is that he or she may have too much influence on the parties. Indeed, since the neutral has the power to make the final binding decision upon the parties, he may be in a position to coerce them into a settlement during the mediation phase by putting pressure on the reluctant parties and by insinuating that if they do not come to a settlement an award will be imposed. In such an event, there is less chance that the parties will implement and adhere to the settlement in a voluntary fashion, as they will feel it was forced upon them. Thus, the advantages usually associated with a mutually agreeable solution reached through mediation will not be present in such a situation.[18]

The skills required to be a mediator are different from those of an arbitrator. A good mediator needs to have good listening and conceptualizing skills. The mediator must be able to summarize concepts, ideas and positions. He or she needs to inspire confidence, respect and trust as well as be persuasive, patient, understanding and fair. On the other hand, a good

---

[15] Adams, G.W. and Bussin, N.L., "Alternative Dispute Resolution and Canadian Courts: A Time for Change" (Cornell Lectures, Cornell University, July 11 1994) [unpublished], at 7-8; Singer, L.R., *Settling Disputes — Conflict Resolution in Business, Families, and the Legal System,* 2nd ed., Boulder: Westview Press, 1990, p. 27; Newman, *supra,* note 14, p. 74.

[16] Koch, C. and Schafer, E., "Can it be Sinful for an Arbitrator Actively to Promote Settlement?" *The Arbitration and Dispute Resolution Law Journal* 153 at 180 [hereinafter "Koch"].

[17] ADR Forum, *supra,* note 3, at 5.

[18] McLaren, *supra,* note 9, p. 196.

arbitrator must be highly knowledgeable in the relevant area of law, be able to hear evidence, make findings of fact, undertake legal analysis and apply the law. Arbitrators must be judgment oriented, impartial and credible. Indeed, playing the role of mediator is quite different from that of arbitrator. Consequently, it might be difficult to find a facilitator that has the ability of being a mediator and an arbitrator, as well as possess sufficient knowledge and expertise in the subject-matter of the dispute.[19] In the event such a neutral cannot be found, the efficiency of the process could be substantially diminished.

Furthermore, if the same facilitator is used as mediator and as arbitrator in the Med-Arb process, there may be uncertainty in the parties' minds as to when the mediation phase has ended and when the arbitration phase has commenced. Moreover, confusion can be created as to the facilitator's role at certain points during the process.[20]

## 5. USING TWO DIFFERENT FACILITATORS INSTEAD OF ONE (A CO-MED-ARB)

Many of the above-mentioned disadvantages inherent to Med-Arb are caused by the fact that a single facilitator is often used in both phases of the process. Consequently, in order to address some of these concerns, the Harvard Negotiation Project has suggested a variation of the Med-Arb process called Co-Med-Arb.[21]

In the Co-Med-Arb process, there are two different neutrals. One acts as mediator and the other acts as arbitrator. The process is divided into two parts — one where no confidential information is divulged and one where confidential information is divulged. The two neutrals are both present during the non-confidential sessions, but only the mediator can attend the confidential sessions at which the parties try to reach an amicable settlement.[22] If the parties agree to settle during one of the confidential sessions, the arbitrator is called in to give the decision based upon the agreement reached by the parties. If the mediation fails or if the parties only reach a partial settlement, the unresolved issues are submitted to the arbitrator who

---

[19] *Ibid.*
[20] Casey, *supra*, note 6, p. 1-14.
[21] Elliot, *supra*, note 7, p. 178.
[22] *Ibid.*

gives a binding decision based on the arguments made by the parties during the non-confidential sessions.[23]

Some authors have criticized the Co-Med-Arb technique. They argue that it adds time and cost to the dispute resolution process because two different neutrals are involved in the process. They also believe that it may cause the joint sessions to be conducted in a more adversarial manner simply because the parties will wish to impress the arbitrator in case the dispute reaches the arbitration phase.[24]

However, it seems that the advantages of Co-Med-Arb outweigh its disadvantages. Indeed, the main advantage of choosing two different neutrals to act as mediator and arbitrator is the assurance that the decision-making process during the arbitration phase is not influenced by information obtained in the mediation phase. By using a separate mediator and arbitrator, both parties can be certain that the binding decision is being made by a completely neutral facilitator who is not influenced by what has occurred or been said during the mediation process.[25]

Furthermore, this variation of the Med-Arb process may eliminate some of the pressure the neutral may otherwise impose on the parties during the mediation phase in order to have them settle their dispute.[26] Finally, by having two different neutrals perform the duties of mediator and arbitrator, the parties will be in a position to retain the services of people who are experts specializing in each of these two fields. This will likely improve the course of the process.

## 6. THE RULES OF ARBITRATION AND MED-ARB

The parties in a dispute generally agree on the framework within which the arbitrator may exercise his or her powers. However, where the parties have not, in their agreement, determined if the arbitrator can involve himself in the reaching of a settlement between the parties, the arbitrator will have to act within the confines set by the different arbitration rules that govern his actions. Needless to say, all of these rules may influence the power of the arbitrator to engage in settlement discussions with the parties.[27]

---

[23] ADR Forum, *supra*, note 3, at 6.
[24] Newman, *supra*, note 14, p. 75.
[25] McLaren, *supra*, note 9, p. 193.
[26] ADR Forum, *supra*, note 3, at 6.
[27] Koch, *supra*, note 16, p.161.

The following are examples of how arbitration rules deal with the issue of mediations in the context of arbitrations:

## (a) International Chamber of Commerce Rules

26. If the parties reach a settlement after the file has been transmitted to the Arbitral Tribunal in accordance with Article 13, the settlement shall be recorded in the form of an Award made by consent of the parties if so requested by the parties and if the Arbitral Tribunal agrees to do so.

## (b) UNCITRAL Arbitration Rules

33. (2) The arbitral tribunal shall decide as *amiable compositeur* or *ex aequo et bono* only if the parties have expressly authorized the arbitral tribunal to do so and if the law applicable to the arbitral procedure permits such arbitration.

. . .

34. (1) If, before the award is made, the parties agree on a settlement of the dispute, the arbitral tribunal shall either issue an order for the termination of the arbitral proceedings or, if requested by both parties and accepted by the tribunal, record the settlement in the form of an arbitral award on agreed terms. The arbitral tribunal is not obliged to give reasons for such an award.

## (c) Rules of the International Commercial Arbitration Court at the Chamber of Commerce and Industry of the Russian Federation ("Moscow Rules")

43. (1) If, during arbitral proceedings, the parties settle their dispute, the proceedings shall be terminated. At the parties' request the arbitral tribunal may record the settlement in the form of an arbitral award on agreed terms.

## (d) Russian Federation Federal Law on Private Arbitration Tribunals in the Russian Federation ("Russian Domestic Statute")

32. (3) Solicited by the parties, an award for an amicable settlement is made by the Private Arbitration Tribunal, unless such amicable settlement contradicts the law or other rules or legislative acts. The content of the amicable settlement shall be set forth in a Private Arbitration Award.

It is interesting to note that none of the above-mentioned rules contains any prohibition against active participation of arbitrators in the settlement process between the parties engaged in a dispute. However, although the rules provide that settlement agreements can be recorded in the form of awards, most of them do not define what the arbitral tribunal's role could be in such a settlement. Indeed, most provisions deal with the form that a settlement may take, but they do not specify how the tribunals and the parties can reach such a settlement.[28] The only exception is section 33(2) of the *UNCITRAL Arbitration Rules*, which may potentially assist the use of Med-Arb by arbitral tribunals by providing that the arbitral tribunal may act as amiable compositeur if the parties authorize this type of action.

Although the above-mentioned rules do not specify how arbitral tribunals should get involved in encouraging the disputants to reach amicable settlements, it must be noted that more and more arbitral rules do include provisions that deal with the issue. Examples of such provisions can be found at sections 16 and 17 of the *Singapore International Arbitration Act 1994*, sections 2A, 2B and 2C of the *Hong Kong Arbitration Ordinance of 1989* and section 13 of the *WIPO Mediation Rules*.[29]

## 7. MED-ARB OR ARB-MED?

Is it best to mediate first and subsequently move to arbitration if the mediation fails? Or, is it best to initiate the arbitration first and pursue mediation at the proper moment in the arbitration proceedings?

Experts seem to have conflicting views on this subject. Some argue that it is often more appropriate to mediate before arbitrating the dispute. The reasons they put forward to support their opinion are the following:[30]

- If the mediation works, the parties will never be required to get into evidence and legal argument.

- The mediation process is generally very informal because the parties concentrate on finding solutions to the issues rather than on arguing what their rights are.

- Mediation gives more freedom to the mediator (i.e., to have private meetings with each party, if necessary).

---

[28] *Ibid.*, p. 162.
[29] Newman, *supra*, note 14, pp. 84-89.
[30] Elliot, *supra*, note 7, p. 178.

- Mediation can be limited in advance to a fixed period of time, and failing settlement within the agreed time-frame, the arbitration process starts.

- By mediating first, there is less intervention by a third person in the parties' dispute. Consequently, the parties keep more control over the resolution of their conflict.

- Mediation often has the effect of improving the parties' relationship rather than damaging it, as is often the case in arbitration.

- By mediating first, the parties are likely to save more money and time than if they arbitrated first.

Other experts believe that parties should start the arbitration procedures and then turn to mediation when they feel that a settlement can reasonably be contemplated. These experts argue that parties often discover they could reach an amicable settlement with the other party only after having been through the first steps of the arbitration process.

> In any event, it would hardly be promising to suggest negotiations before the parties have exchanged at least one round of written pleadings and have been able to evaluate their case in the face of the opponent's arguments. Obviously, as the case unfolds parties are in a better position to evaluate the relative strengths of their positions. It is precisely the possibility of being able to test the case in an adversarial setting before engaging in settlement discussions which renders this combination of conciliation within the adjudicatory process so effective . . .[31]

In Med-Arb, the mediation takes place before the arbitration begins. Accordingly, the parties have not yet been subjected to the adversarial process and the facilitator is probably not yet familiar with the full legal and factual arguments the parties may rely on during arbitration. In Arb-Med, the parties are aware of their opponent's arguments before they mediate. They therefore have a better capacity to evaluate the merits of their case and adjust their position accordingly. Consequently, they may be more willing to reach an amicable solution than if the mediation had taken place before the arbitration process had begun.[32]

---

[31] Koch, *supra*, note 16, p. 176.
[32] *Ibid.*

## 8. PRACTICAL CONSIDERATIONS WITH RESPECT TO MED-ARB[33]

An arbitrator who involves himself in settlement attempts made by disputants should always act in accordance with the parties' best interests and expectations, as well as in accordance with the precepts of natural justice.

Furthermore, the primary duty of the arbitrator is to adjudicate the dispute between the parties. Consequently, the arbitrator should not attempt to become an agent of conciliation with respect to the matter in dispute if the parties do not wish him or her to act in such a way. Forcing the parties to settle against their will may not only cast certain doubts about the regularity of the arbitration process, it could also imperil the validity of the award rendered subsequently. The question as to how far an arbitrator can go in acting as a catalyst between the parties in a dispute raises much controversy between the experts. However, all seem to agree on one principle: if an arbitrator chooses to propose the initiation of a settlement process, the proposal should be made in such a way that neither of the disputants has the impression that he or she must absolutely agree to the conciliation. In other words, the arbitrator should not act as a conciliator without first making sure that neither of the parties objects to it.

An agreement, whether it be formal or tacit, must therefore exist between the parties and the arbitrator before the latter undertakes any effort with respect to the conciliation of the dispute. This agreement, often referred to as an "armediation agreement", should not only allow the arbitrator and the parties to shift from an adjudicative to a conciliatory mode of dispute resolution, it should also establish certain rules with respect to the settlement process and how it is to be included into the arbitration process.

- **Define the arbitrator's role in the mediation process.** The agreement should leave no surprises to the parties as to what the arbitrator's role will be in the mediation process. Therefore, it should determine how the arbitrator will be expected to act during the mediation process: will the arbitrator be involved in the mediation or will a second neutral be chosen by the parties to act as mediator? In the latter case, how will the mediator be chosen? If the parties decide that the arbitrator will also

---

[33] *Ibid.*, pp. 170-173; Tashiro, K., "Conciliation or Mediation During the Arbitral Process — a Japanese View" (1995) Vol. 12, No. 2, *Journal of International Arbitration* 119 at 129; Elliot, *supra*, note 7, p. 175.

act as mediator, will he or she be expected to involve himself or herself actively in the settlement discussions or will he or she simply act as a negotiation co-ordinator?

- **Establish some ground rules for the mediation process.** The parties should agree on the ground rules that will govern the mediation process. They should, for example:
  - determine if the neutral is allowed to meet the parties individually in caucus sessions;
  - decide if the parties are allowed to terminate the mediation phase and institute or continue arbitration proceedings;
  - establish which mediation techniques the facilitator will be allowed to use in order to assist the parties in reaching a settlement, as well as which tactics the parties will be forbidden from using;
  - specify that the discussions held during the mediation are off the record; and
  - state that the mediation is conducted without prejudice to the arbitral procedure.

- **Set time-frames and objectives.** The agreement should include an understanding with respect to the objectives the parties wish to reach with the mediation. Although the parties usually aim for a full settlement of the dispute, they should not dismiss the possibility that they will reach only a partial agreement concerning certain issues. Similarly, the parties should decide if the mediation process should be limited by time.

- **Establish some rules with respect to evidence divulged during the mediation process.** In the event that the parties decide the arbitrator will also act as mediator, they should be aware that during the mediation process, he or she will likely come into possession of information which he or she would not have obtained in the arbitration process. Consequently, it is important to guarantee that the arbitrator's involvement in the mediation process will not prevent him or her from subsequently deciding the case, in the event the mediation fails. The parties should therefore, in the agreement, waive any objection against the arbitrator based on his or her participation in the settlement negotiations. Such understanding is crucial to protect the arbitrator's final award from any challenge by the losing disputant for bias or misconduct from the tribunal.

Apart from the considerations specifically addressed in the agreement, other factors should be taken into account while conducting the Med-Arb process. For example, there must be a clear separation between the mediation phase and the arbitration phase. Indeed, mediation and arbitration are two very different dispute resolution techniques and require that the parties involved take a different approach with respect to the dispute. Whereas in the mediation phase the parties must adopt a co-operative frame of mind, in the arbitration phase, they must conduct themselves in an adversarial manner. It is consequently very important to clearly separate the two procedures so that the parties and the facilitator always know which attitude they must take during the process and, more importantly, which rules apply to the situation.

## 9. CONCLUSION

Mediation is a process that allows the parties in a dispute to seek an amicable settlement which would fulfill their respective interests, regardless of their strict legal rights. As for arbitration, it is an adjudicative process through which the arbitrator gives an award based on the parties' respective rights, notwithstanding what their underlying interests may be. These two dispute resolution techniques seem highly incompatible. However, despite their apparent contradictions, they have been combined in Med-Arb with surprisingly good results. Indeed, Med-Arb provides both the flexibility of mediation and the certainty of a final resolution through the arbitration phase of the process, should mediation fail. With appropriate management, Med-Arb could become a suitable alternative to legal proceedings, which can often prove to be costly, time consuming and distressing for the parties involved.

# 14

# Epilogue — The Next 20 Years

The Dispute Resolution Revolution has been unleashed. Within 20 years, the principles and processes described in this book will be common throughout the world. It is not a revolution of the Right (even the large corporations have signed corporate pledges to use ADR) nor a revolution of the Left (even though mandatory mediation programmes empower the poor), but a dynamic shift in the way human beings will resolve disputes, either personally or through corporations. Institutions from the World Bank in Washington to the Superior Court of Ontario to the Chamber of Commerce and Industry in Tirana, Albania have embraced the need for effective dispute resolution in addition to trials. This shift will not eliminate litigation but litigation processes will be commonly seen as entry points to negotiated or mediated settlements. People will increasingly resort to interest based processes before litigation or the raw use of power.

Watch for the following trends.

## 1. ADR AROUND THE WORLD: DEVELOPING COUNTRIES

Develping countries are beginning to embrace ADR concepts and principles. Initially this adoption may be simply a response to demands by institutions such as the World Bank, and foreign investors that developing countries provide effective and uncorrupted methods of resolving disputes. Nevertheless, ADR has the capacity to effect long lasting legal reform in a country's entire legal fabric. The core components and values of ADR transcend culture. ADR will affect legal reform for the following reasons:

• **The laws of the country must recognize and enforce mediated agree-**

**ments as well as decisions of arbitrators.** The country's laws must recognize and enforce mediated agreements and arbitrated decisions. There must be a basic Arbitration Act which governs arbitrators. One comment coming out of a study of Sri Lanka's Commercial Arbitration system was that in order for arbitration to be successful it was necessary to:

> . . . ensure that the legal framework of laws and rules for arbitration is adequate to support efficient arbitration, and that parties may have confidence that courts will respect the finality of arbitral awards.[1]

- **Arbitrators and mediators must be fair and balanced and not corrupt.** Existing codes of ethics "universally condemn the idea of mediating in cases where the mediator has a pecuniary or any other kind of self interest in a particular settlement outcome".[2] The mediator is supposed to be "impartial in his or her views and neutral in his or her relationship to the parties".[3]

- **It is basic that mediators are to facilitate, not coerce, settlement; arbitrators are to treat parties fairly and render decisions based on the evidence.** There must be an "underlying commitment to an ideal of neutrality"[4] in ADR. "Self-determination and mediator impartiality and neutrality"[5] are the "central values which undergrid the codes of conduct"[6] of ADR.

- **Parties must understand that in mediation they cannot be forced to settle.** The crucial aspects of mediation are that it is a voluntary

---

[1] Chris Cervenak, "Exploring Sri Lanka's Commercial Arbitration System", Consortium on Negotiation and Conflict Resolution, Atlanta, Georgia, March 30-31, 2001, p. 7.

[2] Catherine Morris, "The Trusted Mediator: Ethics and Interaction in Mediation" in J. Macfarlance (ed.), *Rethinking Disputes: The Mediation Alternative*, Toronto: Emond Montgomery, 1997, p. 321. Morris is quoted by Wellington at para 52, see note 4 below.

[3] Moore, C., *The Mediation Process: Practical Strategies for Resolving Conflict*, San Francisco: Jossey-Bass, 1986. Moore is quoted by Wellington at para 55, see note 4 below.

[4] Alex Wellington, "Taking Codes of Ethics Seriously: Alternative Dispute Resolution and Reconstitutive Liberalism" (1999) 12 *Can. J. L. & Juris.* 297, at para 44.

[5] *Ibid.*, at para 51.

[6] *Ibid.*

process, a consensual process, and a non-binding process. The parties must all agree to participate in mediation, and be willing to "jointly explore and reconcile their differences". The mediator has "no authority to impose a settlement", and hence has no coercive power. The mediator does, however, have persuasive power, which may be influential in assisting the parties to resolve their differences.[7]

Included in the definition of mediation by an American organization, the Institute for Environmental Mediation indicates that the "dispute is settled when the parties themselves reach what they consider to be a workable solution".

• **ADR systems must not be used as fresh instruments of coercion and tyranny.** If they are allowed to be tainted with the brush of corruption, the ADR system is little better than the existing institutions which it was trying to improve.

• **The society must respect the people acting as mediators so that mediators are legally immune from either criminal or civil action.** The State legislation must ensure the confidentiality and privilege of the mediator sessions and protect mediators from subpoenas and other legal mechanisms.

• **Parties to a mediation or arbitration must have access to independent legal advice and the ADR process must not preclude the right to counsel.** Access to counsel and the availability of independent legal advice gives the process credibility and allows the parties to feel that they are not being short changed and are getting a good deal.

• **Unbiased independent and uncorrupt courts must exist to enforce mediated solutions and arbitrated decisions.** Even in societies in which there is comprehensive legislation governing ADR, uncorrupt and unbiased courts are needed in order to enforce mediated settlements and arbitrated decisions. Corrupt courts may not enforce these decisions. One Russian lawyer commented that:

> The law is not what is on the paper, it is what the bureaucrat says.[8]

---

[7] *Ibid.*, at para 12.
[8] *Ibid.*, at para 21.

Another said:

> You need to get honest, informed judges out into the regions ... We
> have well written laws, but we cannot enforce them. To do that, you
> must go to court. But our courts are very corrupt. To win a case, you
> need political or family influence, or a bribe.[9]

## 2. COLLABORATIVE LAW

The spirit of positive problem-solving embodied by mandatory mediation programmes has been further advanced in recent years. The concept
of collaborative law embodies this spirit and its evolution. This relatively
recent dispute resolution process requires total commitment from clients
and counsel to a non-litigious method of settling conflicts. Developed by
family lawyers in the U.S. in the early 1990s, the use of collaborative law
is beginning to expand beyond the family law field, into the commercial
and employment fields.[10]

Collaborative law focuses on problem-solving without recourse to the
threat of litigation. Counsel for both sides sign a written commitment pledg-
ing not to sue or threaten to sue. In order to galvanize this promise and the
commitment to settlement, both counsel agree to withdraw from the case if
continuing would be contrary to the spirit of cooperation; an impasse making
resort to the court process necessarily requires counsel and their respective
firms to withdraw from the matter. Both lawyers and clients are committed
to cooperating in good faith on all efforts to resolve the dispute. Such efforts
include interest-based negotiation in which clients play an active role, and
full and voluntary disclosure of all relevant information. In order for the
process to be effective, both counsel must be familiar with the collaborative
process. Such familiarity is gained by completing a training course in collaborative law.

Many lawyers are already familiar with the mediation process. Similar
skills are employed in the collaborative process, yet the collaborative process may be more "intuitive to lawyers than the Mediation process."[11]
Lawyers in the collaborative process must employ analytical thinking and

---

[9] *Ibid.*
[10] Pritchard, J. and Kronack, B.T., "The Collaborative Process" *The Saskatchewan
Advocate* 3:4 (December 2001), online: The Saskatchewan Trial Lawyers Association <http://www.stla.sk.ca/1201toc.shtml> (date accessed: 3 July 2002).
[11] *Ibid.*

creative problem-solving skills. There being at least four individuals involved in the process, the potential for creative solutions is greatly increased.[12] Furthermore,

> Collaboration seems to work much more effectively and quickly in remedying power imbalances in client relationships. Clients often are more comfortable with their lawyer at their side through the entire Collaborative process. This is not typical in the Mediation process.[13]

Such differences in the two processes necessitate further training in collaborative law for the lawyer already familiar with mediation.

The collaborative process provides certain advantages to clients: "they keep control, they get independent legal advice, they can avoid court and they can save money."[14] Furthermore, the clients participate in the settlement process, leaving them with a significant amount of control over the direction their dispute will take. The end result is clients who do not feel they have had a decision imposed upon them by a third party (i.e., the courts).

The advantages for counsel include more clients paying bills, faster turnover of files, less stress, and a better public image for the legal profession in general.[15] The collaborative process "addresses the public's longstanding need for a saner, less costly, and more interest based approach to dispute resolution. This leads to better-served, more satisfied clients . . ., happier lawyers, and . . . the possibility for increased respect for the role of the lawyer in general."[16]

## 3.  USE OF ADR IN INTELLECTUAL PROPERTY DISPUTES

The use of ADR in intellectual property disputes is on an impressive climb. Initially thought of as a process perhaps unsuitable for resolving adversarial issues involving trade marks, patents and the like, it is now more positively embraced by the intellectual property community. This may be predominately due to corporate demands and fiscal restraints demanding a

---

[12] *Ibid.*
[13] *Ibid.*
[14] Carter, T., "Collaborative Family Law" *Canadian Lawyer* 25:2 (February 2001) 10 at 12.
[15] *Ibid.*, at 12
[16] *Supra*, note 10.

less expensive and far more expedient resolution process, and one that provides parties the necessary control over timeliness of the decision and confidentiality of sensitive matters raised.

Global awareness of the ADR process and increased training for specialized mediators/arbitrators within the intellectual property field will catapult this option into the forefront. Multinational corporations are now demanding that their intellectual property counsel have in place ADR alternatives to seriously consider prior to initiating costly litigation. ADR has arrived in resolving intellectual property disputes internationally and its future is encouraging.[17]

## 4. CULTURAL SHIFT IN THE LITIGATION BAR

Mandatory Mediation processes will erode the "kill or be killed" style of advocacy.

## 5. GLOBALIZATION OF COMMERCE

Global transactions will demand that disputes be resolved through international standards, particularly the UNCITRAL Model Arbitration and Conciliation Rules (i.e., mediation).

Finally, may I end with a quote from the Book of Isaiah:

[6] The wolf will live with the lamb, the leopard will lie down with the goat, the calf and the lion and the yearling together; and a little child will lead them.

[7] The cow will feed with the bear, their young will lie down together, and the lion will eat straw like the ox.

[8] The infant will play near the hole of the cobra, and the young child put his hand into the viper's nest.

[9] They will neither harm nor destroy on all my holy mountain, for the earth will be full of the knowledge of the Lord as the waters cover the sea.[18]

---

[17] Nelson, R. and Bailey, M., "Intellectual Property in the 21st Century: The ADR Option", presented to the Canadian Bar Association Symposium on Intellectual Property and Alternative Dispute Resolution, Ottawa, November 22, 2002.

[18] Book of Isaiah 11:6-9.

# Appendix

## (Supplement to Chapter 2)

# Worldwide Developments

## 1. AUSTRALIA

It has not been until the 1990s that Australia became a serious player in the dispute resolution circles. In 1991, the government of Australia introduced the *Court (Mediation and Arbitration) Act* that allowed the Family Court and the Federal Court of Australia to offer litigants the options of mediation and arbitration in addition to the methods of ADR which were already offered.[1] Australia is keen on expanding and innovating its ADR practise, and dispute resolution courses are increasingly offered in universities as part of legal education, as well as in other disciplines.[2] The Australian ADR specialists, practitioners and professors have stressed the importance of establishing an Australian model of dispute resolution, which will not blindly follow the American or British model. Currently, Australia is aiming to develop itself as a dispute resolution centre within the Asia/Pacific region.[3]

Arbitration has been used in Australia since the 17th century when it was introduced by the first white settlers and the English *Arbitration Act 1697*.[4] However, there has been a massive resurgence of interest in ADR in Australia in the last few decades and Australian Federal Attorney-General has stated that the government firmly believes that mediation and alternative dispute resolution should be the norm rather than the exception. In 1975, the Institute of Arbitrators of Australia was established which provided a

---

[1] Astor, H., *Dispute Resolution in Australia*, Australia: Butterworths, 1992, p. 1.
[2] *Ibid.*, p. 5.
[3] *Ibid.*, p. xxvii.
[4] *Ibid.*, p. 6.

centre for professional training of arbitrators; in 1982, an Australian Commercial Dispute Centre was created; in 1985, the Australian Centre for International Commercial Arbitration was opened in Melbourne; and by 1990, all of the Australian states had adopted uniform Commercial Arbitration Acts.[5] Another important institution, the National Alternative Dispute Resolution Advisory Council ("NADRAC"), was established in 1995, and it currently acts as an advisory body to the federal Attorney-General on issues relating to the regulation and evaluation of ADR processes and procedures.[6] Australia also has professional ADR organisations such as Lawyers Engaged in Alternative Dispute Resolution, the Australian Dispute Resolution Association and the Institute of Arbitrators and Mediators Australia.

Arbitration is used by a wide spectrum of Australian courts and tribunals and it is often conducted by appointed lawyers or experts on the matters in dispute. The formal model of arbitration is governed by the Commercial Arbitration Acts of each state or territory and once the award is made it can be registered with a court and enforced as a court judgment.[7]

A research article by J. Fiztgerald, entitled "Grievances, Disputes and Outcomes: A Comparison of Australia and the United States", discovered that "even within a Western society, where litigation is the dominant method of dispute resolution, lawyers and court play only a marginal role in resolving disputes and only a small percentage of disputes is ever brought into court."[8] For example, dispute resolution in Australia seems to be particularly strong in the area of Family Law where it is called "Primary Dispute Resolution" instead "Alternative Dispute Resolution" since 95% of the matters are disposed by means other than litigation.[9]

In Australia, it is mostly the Federal Court and tribunals that have developed and utilized ADR processes and their emphasis has been largely on mediation and conciliation rather than on other techniques such as evaluation or arbitration.[10] In 1987, the Federal Court established an Assisted Dispute Resolution program based on mediation of disputes by registrars

---

[5] *Ibid.*, p. 10.

[6] The Australian Law Reform Commission, *Alternative or Assisted Dispute Resolution*, at 8, online: <http://www.austlii.edu.au/au/other/alrc/publications/issues/25/ch1.html> (date accessed: 28 January 2000).

[7] *Ibid.*

[8] *Supra*, note 1, p. 29.

[9] *Supra*, note 6, at 3.

[10] *Ibid.*, at 1.

of the Court and by 1997, more than 1300 cases have proceeded through this program.[11]

Although mediation is supposed to be a consensual method of solving disputes, the 1997 law and *Justice Legislation Amendment Act* provided the Federal Court with the authority to refer matters to mediation with or without the consent of the parties.[12] On the other hand, arbitration currently requires the consent of both parties and the appeals from arbitration in the Federal Court are limited to questions of law.[13]

There are different mediation models used by the various states within Australia. For example, mediation within the National Native Title Tribunal ("NNTT") is comprised of a process of principled negotiation whereby the negotiators focus on interests and not on positions, generate a range of options to an outcome, and insist that the result be based on some objective standard. NNTT is a Commonwealth tribunal. It was established in 1994 and it facilitates the making of agreements among indigenous people, governments, industry and others whose rights or interests may co-exist with native title rights and interests.[14] In a situation where those parties cannot achieve an agreement through mediation or negotiation, NNTT is empowered to proceed to arbitration. First of all, however, all native claims are directed to mediation. Mandatory mediation scheme under NNTT was considered a very positive process by Justice French who has been quoted saying that "all the money in Australia would be insufficient to pay the bill if all native claims were litigated in the courts."[15]

More than ever before, the aboriginal peoples of Australia are claiming formal recognition of their law and culture and way of living. Between 1994 and 1997, NNTT had received a total of 1210 applications, most of which were complex, multiparty claims. For example, the Ngurludharra/Waljan claim extended over 123,731.5 square kilometres in the Eastern Godfields and Northern Great Victoria Desert areas of Western Australia, and represented 262 parties, including multiple claimant groups with overlapping claims, local state governments, pastoral lessees and mining interests.[16] Like any formal dispute resolution tribunal, NNTT must act in fair, just and prompt manner. However, since it deals with native disputes it must be sensitive to aboriginal culture and customs, and therefore the proceedings

---

[11] *Ibid.*, at 3.

[12] *Ibid.*

[13] *Ibid.*, at 4.

[14] *Ibid.*, at 1.

[15] Dodson, M., "Power and Cultural Differences in Native Title Mediation" (1996) 3 (84) *Aboriginal Law Bulletin* 8.

[16] *Supra,* note 6, at 4.

at NNTT are informal and not bound by technicalities, legal forms or rules of evidence.

Another popular method of dispute resolution in Australia is conciliation, which is widely applied in human rights claims, and it is most frequently used for resolving industrial disputes and termination of employment claims.

Since the 1990s, various Australian industries have set up dispute resolution schemes. These schemes are mostly funded by a particular industry in question and they include the Telecommunications Industry Ombudsman, the Life Insurance Complaints Service, the General Insurance Enquiries and Complains Scheme, and the Australian Banking Industry Ombudsman. There is also the Internet dispute resolution, which provides mediation under the National Centre for Automated Information research aimed at solving problems related to the use of Internet. Another Internet helper is the Virtual Magistrate project, which deals with Internet complaints about messages, postings and files allegedly involving copyright or trademark infringement, misappropriation of trade secrets, defamation, fraud, deceptive trade practises, inappropriate (obscene, lewd, etc.) materials, invasion of privacy and others.[17]

Furthermore, there is the Australian Conciliation and Arbitration Commission, which is established under the auspices of the federal government and deals with industrial disputes in the private sector. The Commission was established in 1956 together with the Industrial Court of Australia (renamed Industrial Division of the Federal Court of Australia, in 1976). The Commission has the function of determining awards, whereas the Industrial Division has a judicial function, which covers such matters as interpretation and enforcement of awards.[18] There are various panels within the Commission that specialise in the area in which the arbitration is to take place. The Commission deals with very few strikes and rather handles mostly mundane settlement of paper disputes involving the making or renegotiating of awards.[19] The creation of the Commission has lead to the prosperity of the trade unions, which means that "Australia was, and continues to be, one of the most unionised countries in the world."[20] There are

---

[17] *Ibid.*, at 4-5.
[18] Hanami, T. and Blanpain, R., *Industrial Conflict Resolution in Market Economics: a study of Australia, the Federal Republic of Germany, Italy, Japan and the USA*, Deventer: Kluwer Law and Taxation, 1984, at 27, online: <http://wwww.niwl.se/WAIS/31304/31304280> (date accessed: 11 February 2000).
[19] *Ibid.*, at 27.
[20] *Ibid.*, at 32.

also some large statutory authorities such as the Australia Post and Telecom Australia that deal with industrial disputes.

With the multitude of ADR processes and institutions available in Australia, it is surprising to note that there is no accepted definition of conciliation and arbitration, and the only mention is made in section 51 of the Australian Constitution, which gives the Parliament the power to enact laws with respect to "conciliation and arbitration for the prevention and settlement of industrial disputes extending beyond the limits of any one State".

## 2. BRAZIL

Under the old arbitration regime, Brazil was considered by the foreigners to be an unattractive site to resolve a dispute, particularly an international one. Due to this sentiment, Brazil has followed in the footsteps of many other countries, like the United Kingdom, which have recently updated their dispute resolution laws. The new *Arbitration Act 1996*, in force in Brazil since November 23, 1996, provides a basis for the enforceability of agreements to arbitrate future disputes and extends the scope of recognition and enforcement of foreign arbitral awards.[21]

Brazil was hostile to arbitration awards until 1996, as agreements to arbitrate future disputes were unenforceable in Brazil before the passing of the *Arbitration Act 1996*. Enforcement and recognition of awards was impossible under old law for parties from outside of the Americas, as Brazil was only a member of the *1975 Panama Convention on Inter-American Commercial Arbitration* but not a party to the *1958 New York Convention on the Enforcement of Arbitral Awards*. The *Arbitration Act 1996* makes provisions for enforcement of arbitral awards from around the world.

The *UNCITRAL Model Law on International Commercial Arbitration* inspired the Brazilian *Arbitration Act*; however, it had to be modified in order to be sensitive to the Brazilian culture. The following points show the differences between the *Model Law* and the *Arbitration Act*:

- The Act applies to both domestic and international disputes relating to property rights at the parties' disposal.

---

[21] Mears, R.R., "Brazil Adopts New Commercial Arbitration Law", *Americas Practise Group*, at 1, on-line: <http://www.hayboo.com/leading/braziladopt.html> (date accessed: 20 January, 2000).

- There is no equivalent of Article 6 of the *Model Law* where a specific court is designated to carry out the supportive and supervisory functions.

- Since the Act retains the requirement of a submission to arbitrate, it defines the minimum obligatory contents of such document in Article 10, and suggests a few optional provisions in Article 11.

- The Act seems to allow only the arbitral tribunal to appeal to the courts to obtain coercive or injunctive orders, but future jurisprudence might extend such rights to the parties themselves.

- The Act requires that the arbitral tribunal consist of an odd number of arbitrators.

- It appears that a court decision appointing an arbitrator is appealable, contrary to the rule in the *Model Law*.

- Regarding the time limit to raise a challenge, the Act refers to "the first opportunity for the party to manifest itself", without fixing the 15-day time limit of the *Model Law*. If the arbitral tribunal denies the challenge, the *Model Law* provides for recourse to the court within 30 days, while the Act orders that this be left to the moment of a possible action for setting aside.

- Besides the rule of fair and equal treatment of both parties (Article 18 *Model Law*), the Brazilian Act adds a reference to the principles of impartiality and freedom of decision of the arbitrators.

- The Act differs from the *Model Law* regarding the place of arbitration since the former indicates that such place has to be named by the parties in the submission, prior to the formal constitution of the arbitral tribunal. If the parties have not done so, the court will determine it.

- Under the Act, arbitration commences when all the members of the arbitral tribunal accept their mission.

- The only provision contained in the Act regarding language concerns the sworn translation of a foreign award for enforcement proceedings.

- The parties are free to choose the applicable law, provided that this choice is not in violation of good morals and public order of Brazil. Parties may also agree on the application of general principles of law, international rules or trade usage.

- The Act allows a dissenting arbitrator to attach a dissenting opinion to the award. If a majority cannot be formed, the President of the arbitral tribunal has the deciding vote.

- The award must be reasoned, even if it is based on agreed terms. Other formal requirements for the award include a description of the facts, the decision and an indication of the time limit granted for the fulfilment of the award by the party.

- The Act allows for corrections of the award as well as an additional award or interpretation of the award, but sets shorter time limits for the request than the *Model Law*. The correction, additional award, or interpretation must be requested within five days of receipt of the award, and the arbitral tribunal is allowed ten days to comply with the request.

- The Brazilian Act provides fewer grounds for setting aside awards than the *Model Law*. The main grounds are nullity of the submission, incapacity of an arbitrator, non-observance of the formal requirements for the award, and the award being *extra* or *infra petita*.

- The Act contains a chapter on the enforcement of foreign awards, thus putting an end to the old "double homologation" system, which was extremely troublesome. The enforcement of domestic and international awards is dealt with in separate chapters. The grounds for refusal of enforcement of a foreign award are set out in Article 38 of the Act and are similar to those foreseen in Article 36 of the *Model Law*.[22]

## 3. CHINA

Since the beginning of 1980s, the People's Republic of China ("PRC") has been opening up to the outside business world by conducting economic

---

[22] Nehring, C., "Recent Developments in Arbitration Law and Practise in Brazil", at 1-2, on line: <http://www.lawinternational.com/articles/develop__ brazil.html> (date accessed: 6 February, 2000).

structural reforms, perfecting its legal system and strengthening dispute resolution methods such as mediation, conciliation, arbitration and litigation. China has a long cultural tradition of mediation, which survived the Cultural Revolution. In 1986 there were 950,000 mediation committees with 6,000,000 mediators that settled 7,300,000 disputes (in that year alone) involving marriage, inheritance, support, alimony, debts, houses and house sites, production and management, tortious damages, economic disputes and some minor criminal cases.[23] Mediation and conciliation are important steps even for the arbitration committees who always try to meditate or conciliate before arbitrating. In the three years from 1984 to 1986, the economic contract arbitration committees all over PRC solved by conciliation a total of 58,052 disputes, which amounts to 88% of all economic contract disputes resolved in that period.[24]

Chinese mediation, as translated from the Chinese word *tiaojie*, is not necessarily what one would define as "mediation" in the West. There is ample evidence that mediators in PRC often pressure or even coerce parties to accept a suggested settlement. Nonetheless, it is a very popular process and it is estimated that for every civil dispute that goes to court, the People's Mediation Committees resolve five to ten disputes.[25] Only court-mediated agreements in China are legally binding whereas mediations under other institutions have no binding legal effect.[26] Therefore, even though China has made a considerable effort in promoting and establishing mediation and conciliation across the country, these venues are not widely used by foreign parties. Hence, foreign parties usually choose arbitration out of the dispute resolution processes, since arbitral awards are legally binding.

People's Mediation Committees have been compared to western Small Claims Courts, the latter not existing in China, and the Committees' coercive measures are explained by the need of the mediators to act in a sense as Small Claims Court's adjudicators. Another reason for the coercive mediation in PRC is that mediation has become highly institutionalised, it has become part of the Chinese government which is not all that comfortable in letting individuals make their own deals.[27]

---

[23] Jianxin, R., "Mediation, Conciliation, Arbitration and Litigation in the People's Republic of China" in T.V. Lee (ed.), *Contract, Guanxi, and Dispute Resolution in China*, New York: Garland Publishing, Inc., 1997, p. 363 at 395.

[24] *Ibid.*, p. 396.

[25] Clarke, D.C., "Dispute Resolution in China" in Lee, *supra*, note 23, p. 369 at 394.

[26] *Ibid.*, p. 413.

[27] *Ibid.*, p. 419.

There are three types of arbitration in China: domestic arbitration for economic contracts, foreign economic and trade arbitration, and maritime arbitration. Domestic arbitration deals with disputes between Chinese legal persons or between a Chinese legal person and a Chinese natural person.

Maritime arbitration is governed by the Maritime Arbitration Commission, which was established in 1959 and it takes cognizance mainly of:

* disputes regarding remuneration for salvage service rendered by sea-going vessels to each other or by sea-going vessel to a river craft and vice versa;

* disputes arising from collisions between sea-going vessels or between sea-going vessels and river craft, or from damages caused by sea-going vessels and river craft, or from damages caused by sea-going vessels to harbour structures or installations;

* disputes arising from chartering sea-going vessels agency services rendered to sea-going vessels, carriage by sea in virtue of contracts of affreightment, bills of lading or other shipping documents as well as disputes arising from maritime insurance;

* cases involving damage caused by sea pollution; and

* other maritime cases agreed upon between the parties for submission to arbitration.[28]

The China Chamber of International Commerce decides the foreign economic and trade disputes. The Chamber was established in 1956 under the name of Foreign Trade Economic and Trade Arbitration Commission, and it has just recently revised and adopted the current China International Economic and Trade Arbitration Commission ("CIETAC" or "Commission") Arbitration Rules, which came into force on May 10, 1998.

In the beginning, the Commission was under a strong supervision by the Chinese government. However, at this point, the Commission has become more western and it has transformed itself into a major international arbitration institution, with most of its procedures complying with international arbitration practises.[29] In 1999, 123 out of the total of 428 CIETAC

---

[28] *Ibid.*, p. 365.
[29] "Alternative Dispute resolution: A route to reconciliation?" *Asia Information Associates Limited* (No. 2 February 1999) at 10, on line: <http://www.aial.com/

commissioners were from 26 foreign countries, which include members from USA, Italy, the Netherlands, Singapore, Germany, Switzerland, the United Kingdom, France, Canada, Spain, Belgium, Australia, Sweden, Republic of Korea, Russia, Thailand, Austria, Nigeria, and Japan.[30]

Since CIETAC is not an arbitration court but a Commission, it does not have judges or arbitrators *per se* but one chairman, several vice-chairmen and a number of Commission people. CIETAC appears to be one of the busiest arbitration tribunals in the world, hearing an estimated 800 disputes in a year.[31]

CIETAC handles disputes arising out of contractual and non-contractual commercial legal relations. These legal relations cover a wide scope of areas and were defined thus by the Supreme People's Court:

> . . . economic rights and obligations arising out of contract, tort or relevant provisions of law, including disputes concerning the sale and purchase of goods, lease of property, contracting for project work, processing arrangements, technology transfer, equity joint ventures, co-operative joint ventures, exploration and exploitation of natural resources, insurance, financing, labour, agency, consultancy services and transportation by sea, air, railway or roads, as well as product liability, environmental pollution, accidents at sea and ownership, but not including disputes between foreign investors and government bodies.[32]

Under Article 2 of CIETAC Arbitration Rules, the Commission would look into international and foreign-related disputes, where one or both parties are foreigners, the parties are stateless persons or foreign legal persons, the object of the civil legal relationship is located in a foreign territory; or the legal facts which give rise to, modify or terminate the civil legal relationship occur outside the territory of the PRC.[33] Other disputes considered by the Commission would be those that related to Hong Kong Special

---

prccc2.html> (date accessed: 25 January, 2000).

[30] Tang and Wang, "National Report: The People's Republic of China", *ICCA: International Arbitration Handbook*, 1997.

[31] Moser, M.J. and Yulin, Z., "Summary of CIETAC Arbitration Rules" in Barin, B. (ed.), *Carswell's Handbook of International Dispute Resolution Rules*, Toronto: Carswell, 1999, p. 428.

[32] *Notice of the Supreme People's Court of People's Republic of China on the Implementation of the Convention on the Recognition and Enforcement of Foreign Arbitral Awards*, issued on April 10, 1987.

[33] Interpretation of international or foreign-related disputes taken from *Supreme People's Court's opinion on Several Questions Concerning the Implementation of the PRC General Principles of Civil Law*, December 5, 1990, Article 207.

Administrative Region, Macao or Taiwan Region, as well as those which have been authorised by specific laws and regulations of the China, such as all securities disputes arising out of an arbitration agreement.

CIETAC will adjudicate a dispute between the parties based on their arbitration agreement, which could be concluded by the parties before or after the dispute. An arbitration agreement is to contain:

- a declaration of the intention to apply for arbitration,
- the matters to be decided by arbitration, and
- the name of the designated arbitration commission.[34]

CIETAC has recommended the following arbitration clause:

> Any dispute arising from or in connection with this Contract shall be submitted to China International Economic and Trade Arbitration Commission for arbitration which shall be conducted in accordance with the Commission's Arbitration Rules in effect at the time of applying for arbitration. The arbitral award is final and binding upon the parties.

Once the claimant has satisfied CIETAC that there was an arbitration agreement between the parties, that the application meets the formal requirements of the Arbitration Rules and that an advance payment of the arbitration fee has been paid, CIETAC sends the claimant a list of CIETAC arbitrators to choose from. The claimant and the respondent each choose one arbitrator and they mutually pick a third one. In a case where the parties cannot agree on the third arbitrator, this decision is left to the discretion of the Chairman of the Commission. Under Article 24 of CIETAC Arbitration Rules, the third arbitrator will act as the presiding arbitrator. This procedure will only be followed if the amount of the claim is not more than RMB 500,000 yuan, in which case it would be directed to the "fast track" and governed by summary procedure rules.[35]

When the parties challenge the validity of the arbitration agreement between them, and one of them requests CIETAC to make a ruling and the other applies to the People's Court, the Court's ruling shall prevail.[36]

Article 34 of CIETAC Arbitration Rules stipulates that the arbitration hearing will be done orally; however, the case may be examined on the basis of documents only, if the parties and the Commission consent to it. In

---

[34] *Arbitration Law of the People's Republic of China*, implemented on September 1, 1995, Article 16.

[35] CIETAC Arbitration Rules, Articles 64-74.

[36] *Ibid.*, Article 4.

Article 35 it is interesting to note that although the arbitration will *prima facie* take place in Beijing, with consent of the parties and the Commission, it may be conducted in another city in China or even outside of China.

A challenging aspect of doing business and resolving disputes in PRC is the fact that there are often unannounced changes in policy. A foreign investor might find himself or herself in a position where the previously approved legal terms of the contract become illegal and the Chinese partner then turns around and breaches the contract, legally. As well, the enforcement of awards in PRC is a difficult task and even though China is a signatory to the *1958 New York Convention on the Enforcement of Arbitral Awards*, in practise, the Chinese court will not always be very co-operative in enforcing such an award.

Another challenge in working and bringing disputes in PRC is posed by the Hong Kong question. Since July 1, 1997, the sovereignty over Hong Kong was transferred from United Kingdom to China, which resulted in two systems and one country. The arbitration regime in Hong Kong has been greatly influenced by UNCITRAL Rules and Common Law while the regime in China was structured on the prevailing practises of the 1950s, leaving a foreign investor exposed to two different systems within one country.

Disputes that are deemed "international" in Hong Kong are governed by the *UNCITRAL Model Law* (which was adopted by Hong Kong in 1990), unless parties agree otherwise. The Hong Kong International Centre, founded in 1985, is designated as the place of arbitration. Domestic arbitration is governed by the *Arbitration Ordinance,* which was based on English Arbitration Acts of 1950-1979.[37] The *Arbitration Ordinance* has undergone some revisions over the years but its fundamental principles have remained the same. The drafters of the Ordinance tried to "avoid the worst excesses of common law litigation whilst at the same time giving the Arbitrator as much power as possible in order to achieve the stated aim of arbitration, namely to direct the proceedings if the parties cannot agree on procedure or will not co-operate."[38]

Despite the rigid ideology in PRC, the Chinese lawmakers have actually allowed the contracting parties (where at least one of them is a foreign entity) to choose a foreign law governing their agreement and to choose place for potential arbitration outside of China. The only exception to this

---

[37] Ashman, V.M., "New York Convention and China's 'One Country, Two Systems'" *New York Law Journal* (July 2, 1998) 1 at 3.

[38] Kaplan, N., "Domestic Arbitration Rules of the Hong Kong International Arbitration Centre" in Barin, *supra*, note 31, p. 405.

freedom of choice are joint venture contracts and contracts for the co-operative exploration and development of natural resources.[39]

It is well established that before a claim proceeds to arbitration, the parties may try to resolve the dispute by series of negotiations. Negotiations in PRC have a very specific cultural connotation. "Keeping face" is a very important factor to most Chinese and thus they will negotiate in a way as not to admit to any mistake or shortcoming. "The Chinese party will fight to use informal methods to resolve the dispute, as undertaking more formal methods would effectively be an admission of failure. And if you embarrass your Chinese business partner during the course of trying to resolve a conflict you can wave goodbye to any further co-operation or compromise on their part."[40] Many commentators believe that if a dispute reaches the stage where the parties are forced into taking formal arbitration or legal action, then it is likely that the business relationship is beyond saving. The big cultural differences between the Western and Chinese cultures create an atmosphere more prone to misunderstandings, which creates more con-flicts and disputes between Western and Chinese businesspeople.

As Chinese favour negotiations, most of the contracts with a Chinese counterpart will contain a clause that conflicts should first be tried to be resolved through "friendly negotiations". The term "friendly negotiations" means that a considerable amount of time and effort will be spent on trying to come to an agreement with the Chinese associate. Trying to negotiate is considered to be the proper business etiquette and only as a last recourse the party should opt for mediation or conciliation of a claim, whereas outright litigation has always been considered a course of action to be avoided in China.

The reason for avoiding litigation in PRC could be summarised as follows: first of all, it is believed that the Chinese courts are biased in favour of a Chinese party; secondly, judges are generally deemed to lack expertise as, after the Cultural Revolution, they were appointed not from legal pro-fession but from amongst the retired military and bureaucratic personnel;[41]

---

[39] *Supra*, note 29, at 6.

[40] *Ibid.*

[41] The Cultural Revolution spanned the period of 1966-1976 and marked a time of chaos for China. Based on Mao's proposition that the state should "depend on the rule of man, not the rule of law", there was a complete destruction of the formal law enforcement apparatus in favour of a 'proletarian' legal order. There was very little legal education in the 1960s and 1970s and Ren Jianxin, President of the Supreme People's Court, estimated that by 1991, 40% of China's Judges were lacking college education. (*Ren Jianxin Stresses Need to Educate and Train Court Personnel*, in SWB/FE, August 28, 1990, at B2/1.)

thirdly, the concept of an independent judiciary remains unknown in PRC since the courts are viewed as organs that are to ensure the realisation of China's political objectives.[42] Furthermore, the *Civil Procedure Law* of the PRC does not allow foreign lawyers to appear in court, or even Chinese lawyers who work for a foreign law firm. Thus, a foreign party is forced to use local lawyers. As well, the monetary awards under Chinese court rulings are also generally much lower than what would be customary in the Western court.[43] Therefore, if a dispute cannot be resolved through "friendly nego-tiations", it usually proceeds to mediation, conciliation or arbitration, rather than litigation.

## 4. FRANCE

With the challenges associated with the phenomena of global economy and greater democratisation, there is an increasing need in France, as in other countries, for talented lawyers capable of managing complex issues through deal-making and dispute resolution in a rapid and effective manner. Mediation and negotiation are two skill-based methods, which have been used in France to solve disputes.

Traditionally, French negotiators have had the tendency to impose their views on their counterparts by taking very strong positions, thinking that their answers were, *a priori*, the right ones. This attitude limited their ability to reach mutually acceptable agreements and prevented them from finding solutions, which in turn often led to recurring conflicts. However, it seems that the French negotiators are becoming more and more aware of the fact that the parties they deal with are hesitant to accept non-negotiated outcomes. These negotiators are consequently replacing their one-way modes of decision making with two-way exchanges based on co-operation and reciprocal working alliances.[44] They also resort increasingly to neutral facilitators in order to resolve difficult issues or conflicts, rather than util-ising litigation as a usual method of dealing with problems. In the same spirit, the French government is taking action to increase the use of nego-tiation and mediation in internal matters. For example, the current govern-ment has declared that it would create 15,000 "agents of mediation" to assist

---

[42] *Supra*, note 29, at 7.

[43] *Ibid.*, at 8.

[44] Lempereur, A., "Negotiation and Mediation in France: The Challenge of Skill-Based Learning and Interdisciplinary Research in Legal Education" (1998) 3 *Harv. Negotiation L. Rev.* 151 at 4.

in the war against violence. In a further effort, the National School of Administration, which trains all high state employees, is currently implementing negotiation workshops for its students.[45]

However, despite increasing efforts on the part of government and institutions, it seems that for the time being, negotiation and mediation are methods that remain somewhat unknown and frowned upon in France. Indeed, the current context in France gives rise to several factors, which may limit the effectiveness of mediators. Firstly, it seems that when mediators intercede in a problematic situation, it is hardly ever by choice of the disputants, but rather by government appointment. Secondly, mediators often lack proper training in mediation. Thirdly, French mediators rarely perceive themselves as being strictly facilitators of negotiation and they have the tendency of acting as technical experts, imposing the solutions they prefer upon the parties.[46]

There also seems to be a certain amount of cultural resistance to the concepts of negotiation and mediation. Historically in France, the legal system grants the legislature the power to change or reform society. Indeed, the French constitution fosters a tradition of central legislative dominance and does not acknowledge a judiciary power alongside the legislative and executive power. Law has always originated from a political centre, which uses disinterested judges to support the authoritative character of legislation. In other words, courts and judges are attributed a confined role and are considered to be mere "mouthpieces of the law" (*bouches de la loi*).[47] Furthermore, the courts have always been considered as being out of the people's reach, because they rarely take actions that conflict with existing legislation or depart from the view of political powers. Consequently, most French citizens are not familiar with being active players in the dispute resolution process. This could be an obstacle to the development of ADR.[48]

Another obstacle to the development of ADR in France is the fact that the law is perceived as the product of confrontation, verbal opposition and struggle between ideologies where there needs to be a winner and a loser. These attitudes are contrary to the values underlying fruitful negotiations and mediations, and will need to be modified in order to allow parties to engage in creative legal problem solving.

The education system in France also contributes, to a certain extent, to the cultural resistance against ADR. Indeed, legal education in this country

---

[45] *Ibid.*, at 9.
[46] *Ibid.*, at 10.
[47] *Ibid.*, at 11.
[48] *Ibid.*, at 12.

focuses primarily on legislation and codification, which are considered the ultimate sources of legal authority. The study of factual situations focussed on human experiences is perceived as superfluous in legal teaching. Professors lecture *ex cathedra*, leaving little space for interaction with the students. Furthermore, law classes often contain hundreds of students, which make discussions almost impossible to hold. Due to all these factors, it is doubtful that skill-based ADR courses could be given in the present educational environment. Indeed, a good ADR course generally includes discussions as to what would lead to a good settlement or what would make the ADR process a success in the parties' eyes, and the present format of law classes does not allow for such discussions. Finally, the use of role playing and debriefing, commonly used to teach ADR, is not compatible, *a priori*, with the French teaching tradition, where there is a tendency to believe that case studies are not serious enough.[49]

Despite all the obstacles which tend to slow down the development of ADR in France, there is a greater understanding on the part of practitioners and on the part of the public in general with respect to the need for trained negotiators and mediators. This greater understanding will be significantly increased by providing adequate education on ADR to professionals and to students through skill-based learning, which could be incorporated at all levels, from high school to continuing education programs. Efforts are already being made in France to educate on ADR through the organisation of workshops attended by a wide range of participants. France is also using electronic communications to improve the development of its population's negotiation skills with the assistance of professionals from around the world. For example, in spring of 1997, future managers and lawyers from ESSEC Graduate School of Management took part in electronic negotiation simulations with colleagues from Harvard and Kellog. The French are also experimenting with innovative techniques for teaching negotiation skills. For example they started using video conferencing as a method of learning about international negotiations.[50]

Evidence shows that France is having more and more contacts with the ADR movement and that it is progressing rapidly by improving its systems of negotiation research and education. This will lead, ultimately, to an effective use of ADR in a wide range of situations.

In the past century, international commercial arbitration has been used increasingly to resolve international commercial disputes. In response to this growing trend, the International Chamber of Commerce, based in Paris,

---

[49] *Ibid.*, at 15.
[50] *Ibid.*, at 21.

established in 1923 the International Court of Arbitration. Since its beginnings, this court has administered over 10,000 international arbitration cases. Every year, parties and arbitrators from over one hundred countries and from diversified backgrounds (whether they would be legal, economic, cultural or linguistic) are involved with the ICC International Court of Arbitration.[51]

After a consultation involving many countries, the ICC Rules of Arbitration, which had been in effect for 20 years, were modified on January 1, 1998. These modifications aim at decreasing delays and reducing many uncertainties in order to keep up with the changes that occurred in the arbitration practice.[52]

Arbitral tribunals are responsible for conducting the ICC arbitration. They analyse the validity of each case and give a final award. Arbitrators from over 60 nations hold arbitrations in over 40 countries. The ICC International Court of Arbitration, which meets three or four times a month, monitors these tribunals. The role of the ICC is to oversee arbitration held under the ICC Rules of Arbitration.[53]

Parties who wish to include in their contract a desire to abide by the ICC Arbitration Rules in case of dispute are encouraged to use the following clause:

> All disputes arising out of or in connection with the present contract shall be finally settled under the Rules of Arbitration of the International Chamber of Commerce by one or more arbitrators appointed in accordance with the said Rules.[54]

It is recommended that parties also include in their agreement a clause as to the law that should be applied, the number of arbitrators, as well the country and language in which the arbitration should take place.[55]

---

[51] *Rules of Arbitration of the International Chamber of Commerce*, in Barin, *supra*, note 31, p. 2.

[52] *Ibid.*

[53] *Ibid.*

[54] *Ibid.*, p. 3.

[55] *Ibid.*

## 5. GERMANY

Germany, despite its economic strength, stability and modern infra-structure, is still an unpopular arbitration venue. Recently, new arbitration laws were passed in Germany in an attempt to change this situation. There is an expressed hope that a modernised and easily accessible arbitration framework will attract more arbitration parties to Germany. Here, the em-phasis is especially on the German-speaking East Europeans as a group.[56]

The main source of written arbitration law in Germany is the German Code of Civil Procedure (CCP),[57] which consists of ten books. The tenth book of the CCP contains provisions on German Private Arbitration Law that have been in force in Germany since 1877. The German reformers regarded these 19th century provisions, mainly unchanged since their in-ception, as incomplete and too difficult for foreigners to access. As a result, in 1991, the Federal Ministry of Justice initiated a law reform, which com-pletely revised the tenth book of the CCP.

Germany is now considered as a "Model Law" country. The new arbitration law, as contained in the tenth book of the CCP and in force since January 1, 1998, incorporates, almost word for word, most of the provisions of the *UNCITRAL Model Law*. The *Model Law*, according to the expert commission set up by the German Federal Ministry of Justice, was regarded as the most suitable archetype for international commercial arbitration. The new German Arbitration Law is a carefully prepared arbitral regime that provides for an extensive party autonomy and at the same time a minimal court intervention and mandatory provisions. The new law also allows for easy access by foreigners.[58]

The Arbitration Law from the tenth book of the German CCP is divided into ten chapters. The first eight chapters adopt almost literally the eight chapters from the *Model Law*. The ninth chapter of the CCP contains pro-visions regarding arbitral court proceedings. Section 1062 CCP contains provisions on the competence of courts for certain functions of arbitration assistance and supervision, for example, the challenging of arbitrator's jurisdiction, the determination of the admissibility or inadmissibility of

---

[56] Schaefer, J.K., "New Solutions for Interim Measures of Protection in Interna-tional Commercial Arbitration: English, German and Hong Kong Law Com-pared", Vol. 2.2 *Electronic Journal of Comparative Law* (August 1998), at 16, on-line: <http://law.kub.nl/ejcl/22/art22-2.html> (date accessed: 25 January, 2000).

[57] In German: *Zivilprozessordnung (ZPO)*.

[58] *Supra*, note 56.

arbitration, the enforcement of interim measures of protection by the arbitral tribunal or the declaration of enforceability of the award. Generally, the Higher Regional Court (Oberlandesgericht) as designated in the arbitral clause, or failing such designation, the Higher Regional Court in whose district the place of dispute is situated is competent to rule on the issues mentioned above (section 1062(1)). On the other hand, the taking of evidence and other judicial acts (section 1050) fall under the jurisdiction of the Local Court (Amtsgericht) where such judicial act is to be carried out. The courts issue their decisions by means of an order, which might be done without an oral hearing (section 1063). Usually, there is no remedy against the decision of the court.[59]

The Arbitration Law also contains a unique section 1066, which states that the provisions of the tenth book of the CCP apply *mutatis mutandis* to the arbitral tribunals which were established lawfully under the last will and testament or under other dispositions not based on an agreement. This provision is of no great interest to the international business arbitration; however, it is of great importance for many domestic fields of dispute resolution in Germany, especially in the area of consumer arbitration.

Today, there are more than 300 arbitration or conciliation boards (Schlichtungsstellen) for a variety of disputes in Germany.[60] Most of the conciliation boards deal with consumer matters such as banking, medical malpractice, insurance, construction and labour law matters. In most cases, conciliation procedures in the past have not been legally binding and based on voluntary participation. However, since January 1, 2000, a new law has established that in cases regarding relatively small monetary claims (up to 1,500 German Marks), neighbour-related[61] and libel law matters, a court shall reject to proceed with a legal action unless the plaintiff proves that an out-of-court settlement by a conciliation board has been tried.[62] In summary, one can say that the tenants of the *Model Law* are now applicable in almost all forms of alternative dispute resolution in Germany.

---

[59] See exceptions in Section 1065 CCP.

[60] Taupitz, J., "Out-of-court Conciliation for the Protection of the Consumer" (Seoul, 1996) *Journal of the Korean-German Society for Jurisprudence*, Vol. 12, at 421.

[61] Disputes between neighbours are very prevalent in Germany and there are lawyers who specialise in *Neighbour Law*.

[62] *Gesetz zur Foerderung der aussergerichtlichen Streitbeilegung*, December 15, 1999, BGBl. I 1999, 2400.

## 6. UNITED KINGDOM

England is a leader in both domestic and international dispute resolution venues. The London Court of International Arbitration ("LCIA") is well recognised and in the same league as the International Chamber of Commerce in Paris and the American Arbitration Association in the United States. The LCIA is the oldest arbitral body, having been established in 1892. It provides a comprehensive international dispute resolution service, both under its own Rules and under the UNCITRAL Rules, for operation under any system of law in any venue throughout the world.

ADR has been popular in England since the 1980s but it remained entirely outside the formal legal system until 1993, at which time the judges of the Commercial Court (a sub-division of the High Court, Chancery Division or Queen's Bench Division) issued a statement officially encouraging parties to use ADR. This process was further fostered in 1996 when the Commercial Court was given authority to adjourn proceedings for a specified period of time to encourage and enable the parties to proceed with ADR. This authority was quickly changed from mere encouragement to giving orders requiring the disputing parties to try dispute resolution outside the courts. In 1997, out of 67 disputes, 24%, were directed by court to be resolved using ADR and in 1998, out of 44 disputes, 19%, followed suit.[63] The Commercial Court is boasting that the court enforced ADR cases have an estimated 87% rate of success, with most of the cases being resolved by means of mediation.[64]

The test used by the Commercial Court to determine whether an order for ADR should be made involves comparing the size of the claim with the cost of pursuing it through regular court system. If the latter outweighs the former, ADR will be ordered. Partly due to the court ordered ADR, dispute resolution has grown steadily in England. An ADR group, which mediates disputes, reported an increase in the caseload from 23 in 1990, to 96 in 1996, and 158 in 1998; whereas the Centre for Dispute Resolution's caseload increased from 192 disputes in 1997, to 257 disputes in 1999.[65]

Mediation in the United Kingdom has been used extensively in trying to resolve the disputes arising out of parades in Northern Ireland. In the past years there has been a high degree of disruption and violence during parades

---

[63] Hales, M., *Court Enforced ADR: the English Approach* (August 23, 1999), at 2 [unpublished].

[64] *Ibid.*, at 3.

[65] *Ibid.*

in Northern Ireland[66] and mediation has been seen as perhaps one of the only ways to resolve the controversial disputes that arose after the parades. The disputes have been so emotional and irrational that they resulted in demonstrations against having them mediated. The demonstrators claimed that mediation was pointless as it was used in inappropriate situations, where for example, parties were not interested in a solution of the problem but created the dispute for the sake of the dispute itself.[67]

The mediation process used in resolving Irish parade disputes is not a structured model but rather a very fluid one, where the role of the mediator is mainly to facilitate a dialogue between the parties. Many of the mediators who have worked on the parade disputes are not skilled mediators but people who possess some less tangible qualities that proved beneficial to the process, such as inherent trust and respect in the community faced with the dispute. Of course there are also professional mediators from Mediation Network Northern Ireland, established in 1991, who have been working on these disputes.[68] Another group who has had a prominent involvement in the mediation in Northern Ireland is the Quaker House group, established in Belfast in 1982. Although, the Quaker House has kept a very low profile, it has been involved in many private political mediations in Northern Ireland.[69] The group has been quite successful, particularly due to the fact that it considers itself Quaker first and Protestant second and thus is perceived as impartial to the dispute. Other people that became involved as mediators in the parade disputes have included ministers, priests, and members from the business community, political officials and police officers.

Since the passage of the *UNCITRAL Model Law on International Commercial Arbitration* in 1985, more than 30 countries all around the globe have reshaped their arbitration laws, including United Kingdom. The new *British Arbitration Act 1996* came into force in 1997.[70] Under the *Arbitration Act*, the interim relief has shifted to the realm of arbitration and the British arbitrators are less at risk that their award will be set aside or not

---

[66] According to the *RUC Chief Constables Annual Report*, there were 3,161 parades in Northern Ireland in 1996, but there are no statistics stating how many of them ended up in violence.

[67] Kelly, G. and Nan, S.A., "Mediation and Related Processes in the Context of Parades Disputes", *Mediation in Practise in Northern Ireland,* at 1, on-line: <http://www.incore.ulst.ac.uk/publications/research/mediation/processes. html> (date accessed: 8 February, 2000).

[68] *Ibid.*, "Mediatory Roles in Marching Disputes: Selected Examples", at 1, on-line:  <http://www.incore.ulst.ac.uk/publications/research/mediation/sample. html> (date accessed: 8 February, 2000).

[69] *Ibid.*, at 2.

[70] *Supra*, note 56, at 1.

be enforced on the ground that the "arbitral procedure . . . was not in accordance with the law of the country where the arbitration took place."[71] The *Arbitration Act 1996* applies to both domestic and international arbitration.

The underlying principle of this recent *Arbitration Act* is to designate the court as the last resort venue and to grant interim relief in the first place to the arbitrator, except for Ex Parte Minerva injunction or an Anton Pillar order.[72] Under the *Arbitration Act*, the arbitration tribunal functions as a court subsidiary with an aim of reducing and limiting the court interference.

Another recent ADR-related reform came into force on April 26, 1999, and was based on suggestions made by Lord Woolfe. The Woolfe Reform made the courts more responsible for case management so that delay is to be kept to a minimum and there is more emphasis on ADR in order to free up some court time. The court is now able to stay the proceedings whilst dispute resolution takes place. Furthermore, when assessing costs, the court will consider the efforts made by the parties to try to resolve the dispute. Thus, a party can be penalised in costs for refusing to go through ADR where such refusal was unreasonable.[73]

## 7.  UNITED STATES OF AMERICA

Some commentators have complained that ADR in United States has been taken over by the legal profession:

> . . . ADR was just another stop in the 'litigation game', which provides an opportunity for the manipulation of rules, time and information and ultimately, money. ADR has become just another battleground for adversarial fighting rather than multi-dimensional problem solving.[74]

However, the American Arbitration Association ("AAA") maintains that dispute resolution is not another battleground for lawyers but a faster and cheaper way to deal with claims. The AAA deals with International

---

[71] Article V of the *New York Convention on the Enforcement of Arbitral Awards*, New York, 1958.

[72] *Supra*, note 56, at 16.

[73] *Supra*, note 63, at 5.

[74] Menkel-Meadow, C. "Pursuing settlement in an adversary culture: A tale of innovation co-opted or 'The Law of ADR'" (1991) 19 *Florida State University Law Review* 1 at 17.

Commercial disputes and uses its own International Arbitration Rules, which were amended on April 1, 1997. The AAA is a public service, not-for-profit organisation with its headquarters in New York City, and with many more offices located in major cities throughout United States. Hearings may be heard at locations that are convenient to the parties and are not limited to cities where the AAA has its offices.[75]

The standard arbitration clause of the AAA reads:

> Any controversy or claim arising out of or relating to this contract shall be determined by arbitration in accordance with the International Arbitration Rules of the American Arbitration Association.

Although the AAA is predominantly focused on arbitrating a dispute, upon the request of the parties to the dispute, the AAA is prepared to arrange for mediation or conciliation of such a dispute. Out of 80,000 cases each year that are dealt with by the AAA, about 800 of them have an international commercial aspect. The AAA encompasses an array of rules dealing with domestic and international disputes as well as rules narrowing on a specific industry. The AAA International Arbitration Rules were derived in 1991 from the UNCITRAL Arbitration Rules. However, they have expanded over time to cover areas which were not previously covered and are thus significantly different from the UNCITRAL Rules.

Under the AAA, there will usually be one arbitrator presiding over the dispute, unless it is considered that a tripartite panel would be more appropriate.[76] In an international dispute setting, all three arbitrators, regardless of who selected them, have to be impartial and independent. However, it is interesting to note that when there is a tripartite panel dealing with domestic US arbitration, the party appointed arbitrators are allowed, within some limits, to act as partisan advocates for the respective parties.[77]

Under Article 2(3) of the AAA International Arbitration Rules, a party can start the arbitration process by issuing a "statement of claim" and under Article 3(1) the opposing party has to file a "statement of defence" within 30 days, making this process very much similar to the court system. The arbitration tribunal enjoys wide powers to act as it sees fit and much like the court it is able to choose the way it wants to conduct the dispute (Article

---

[75] *American Arbitration Association Mini-Trial Procedures*, at 1, on-line: <http://www.adr.org/rules/commercial/mini-trial__procedures.html> (date accessed: 2 January 2000).

[76] AAA International Rules, Article 5.

[77] Carter, J., "International Arbitration Rules of the American Arbitration Association," in Barin, *supra*, note 31, p. 99.

16). As long as it is fair, the AAA can take interim measures, including injunctive relief, can order security for costs of such measures, and can apportion costs associated with applications for interim relief (Article 21). It can also order production of documents (Article 19), apply laws or rules it deems fit (Article 28), and it has discretion to award pre-award and post-award interest.

The AAA has also developed a mini-trial dispute resolution scheme in response to business needs. The idea behind mini-trial is to put the responsibility for resolving business disputes back into the hands of business people, whereupon the senior executives of the parties involved in legal disputes meet in the presence of a neutral advisor and, after listening to both parties, attempt to formulate a voluntary settlement.[78] The AAA has developed a 16-point procedure that is supposed to facilitate the resolving of the disputes by the senior executives, each one of these points being open to amendment by the parties.

The AAA also offers grievance mediation procedures whereupon several grievances coming from parties under a collective bargaining agreement can be mediated upon at the same time.[79]

In the United States, dispute resolution processes have become well known even to the average citizen and some call it "the wonder drug" that could cure the US legal system.[80] More than half of the American states now encourage or mandate arbitration and mediation to reduce backlogs, and to speed up case resolutions.

The main concern that the general public has in regards to the traditional method of litigation is cost. "In a 1999 survey by the National Centre for the State Courts, 68% of Americans said bringing a case in court was not affordable",[81] and it has become difficult in the United States to find a lawyer that would undertake to proceed with a claim worth less than $20,000. In comparison ADR appears to be quite a cost saver. For example, an average employment arbitration amounts to a total of $3,000, which is the same as what a lawyer would charge for an average retainer to undertake such a claim.[82]

---

[78] *Supra*, note 75.

[79] *American Arbitration Association Grievance Mediation Procedures*, at 1, on-line: <http://www.adr.org/rules/commercial/grievance__mediation__procedures. html> (date accessed: 2 January 2000).

[80] Brown, C., General Counsel for the National Arbitration Forum, headquartered in Minneapolis, Minnesota, *The Results are in: ADR has Something for Everyone*, at 1 [unpublished].

[81] *Ibid.*, at 2.

[82] *Ibid.*, at 3.

Another reason why ADR has blossomed in the United States is the speed with which the decisions are made. Up to 80% of the American public believes that the disputes brought into courts are not resolved in a timely manner, reinforcing the motto that justice delayed is justice denied. "The average civil case takes $2\frac{1}{2}$ years to resolve. Meanwhile, the average arbitration case is resolved in 8.6 months, about one-third the time of litigation."[83]

The American Bar Association has reported that an estimated 100 million Americans would not have been able to litigate their claims if it was not for arbitration, due to high costs, delay and complexity of the regular justice system.[84] It has also been suggested that since the disputants have to pay an administrative fee up front to commence arbitration, as well as graduated arbitration filing fees are sometimes required, there is less likelihood of frivolous claims being brought before an arbitrator.

---

[83] *Supra*, note 80, at 4.
[84] *Ibid.*

# Index

CO-MED-ARB
alternative to med-arb, as, 276-277

CO-MEDIATION
defined, 118
guidelines for, 118
use of seating arrangement to
maximize success, 118-120

*COMMERCIAL ARBITRATION ACT*
(CANADA), 219

CONFIDENTIALITY IN ADR, *See also*
PRIVILEGE IN ADR
arbitration, in, 145
exceptions to
generally, 42
malpractice by mediator/lawyer,
43
statutory provisions, 43
*Uniform Mediation Act* (U.S.A.),
relevant provisions, 44-45
fundamental element in ADR, as,
30-32
international arbitration, in, 227
mediation, in, 79-80
reasons for, 25, 30-32
sources of confidentiality, *See*
PRIVILEGE IN ADR, sources

CONFLICT
"Circle of Conflict"
diagnostic tool, as, 109
dual purpose, 106
mediation tool generally, as,
106-110
refocusing on bottom part of
circle, 110
six wedges
data, 108
generally, 106-107
interests of participants, 109
moods, 108
relationships, 107

structure/environment, 108
values, 107
strategic tool, as, 109-110
cost of poorly managed conflict,
48-49
defined, 47
dispute, distinguished from, 47-48
dynamics of, 86-87
responses to
accommodating, 111, 113
avoiding, 111, 113
collaborating, 111-112, 114
competing, 111, 112-113
compromising, 112, 114
diagram of responses, 112

CONSTITUTIONAL ISSUES
exemption from mandatory
mediation, 117
rendering mediation inappropriate,
77, 117
unsuitable for arbitration, 143

COSTS
arbitration agreement, set out in, 164

COUNSEL
arbitrators, acting as, 178-179
collaborative law, skills required,
288-289
mandatory mediation
challenge to traditional role, 134
early mediation, concerns,
137-138
role in mediation process, 81-82
need to understand human
psychology, 82
psychology of mediation, and, 92

COURT
arbitration
role during, 140, 149, 152-153,
156-157, 196-197

INTERNATIONAL ADR —
*continued*
United Kingdom, 310-312
United States, 312-315

INTERNATIONAL ARBITRATION,
*See also* INTERNATIONAL
ABITRATION AGREEMENT;
INTERNATIONAL CHAMBER OF
COMMERCE RULES;
*INTERNATIONAL COMMERCIAL
ARBITRATION ACT* (ONT.);
*UNCITRAL MODEL LAW*
ad hoc or institutional arbitration,
choice of, 228
advantages over other methods
confidentiality, 227
economy, 227
equal footing of parties, 227
final, binding decisions, 226
international recognition of
awards, 226
specialized competence of
arbitrator, 227
speed, 227
arbitral tribunal
composition, 241-242
jurisdiction, 242-243
basic features of international
disputes, 223-224
bias of arbitrator, 256-257
civil and common law jurisdictions,
tensions between, 220-221
*Commercial Arbitration Act*
(Canada), 219
considerations relevant to, 223-226
defined by *Model Law*, 248
discovery of documents, 146
drafting provisions of international
agreement, 224-226
foreign arbitral awards
Canadian enforcement generally,
218-223

enforcement, *See*
ENFORCEMENT, arbitral
awards
*Foreign Arbitral Awards Act*
(Ont.), 220
*International Commercial
Arbitration Act* (Ont.), 220,
221-222
refusal to recognize, grounds,
255-256
setting aside, 255
ICC arbitration, distinctive features
designation of arbitrators, 229
ICC International Court of
Justice, 228-229
monitoring of arbitral process,
230
remuneration of arbitrator fixed,
230-231
scrutinizing of arbitral awards,
231
secretariat of ICC court, 229
interim measures of protection,
240-241
interim orders, 238-239
international business disputes
generally, 217
International Chamber of Commerce
Rules, 145
international dispute, defined, 224
Kompetenz-Kompetenz power of
tribunal, 141
"New York Convention"
purpose, 218-219
ratification by Canada, 219
*UNCITRAL*, distinguished from,
219
place of arbitration specified, 144
power to rule on own jurisdiction,
141
purpose, 218
*UNCITRAL Model Law*, 219-223,
*See also UNCITRAL MODEL
LAW*

MEDIATION-ARBITRATION
(MED-ARB) — *continued*
"Russian Domestic Statute",
278-279
UNCITRAL Arbitration Rules,
278
use in ancient Greece, 271

MEDIATION BRIEF
advocacy opportunity, as, 92
contents, 96
cost considerations, 96
documentation to be attached, 97
drafting, 93-94
effective and ineffective briefs, 98
extensive brief, example of situation,
95
format, 94, 95
function of, 93
generally, 92-94, 95-98
relevant *Rules of Civil Procedure*
(Ont.), 94-95
simple brief, example of situation, 95
tone of, 97

MEDIATOR, *See also* MEDIATION;
MEDIATION AGREEMENT
activities of mediator
distraction, 64
empathy, 64
invention, 64
investigation, 63-64
persuasion, 64
attributes, 66-67, 87-88, 89
authority to settle, 71
choosing, 68-69
distinguished from arbitrator or
judge, 58
humour, use of, 89-91
initial meeting with parties, 69-70
knowledge, 66-67
parties, preparation of, 70-71
role of
client, 69

lawyer, 69
mediator, 57
skills, 66-67
tasks
analyzing information, 65
communicating information to
others, 65
documenting information, 66
facilitating agreement, 66
facilitating communication, 65
gathering information, 65
generally, 64-66, 88
managing cases, 66
therapist, role distinguished from,
82-83
training, key considerations, 68

MODEL CLAUSES, *See*
ARBITRATION AGREEMENT

*MODEL LAW, See UNCITRAL MODEL
LAW*

NEGOTIATION, *See also* POSITIONAL
NEGOTIATION; PRINCIPLED
NEGOTIATION
assumptions underlying theories, 22
creating value in negotiation
generally, 20-22
meaning, 21
effective techniques, parent-child
example, 9-13
fundamental facts underlying, 13
good faith, no obligation to negotiate
in, 23
growing sophistication of techniques,
2
mediation, distinguished from, 57
most common method of conflict
resolution, 9
positional negotiation, compared to
principled negotiation, 13
successful negotiation, useful
techniques